You Are Oprah

Igniting the Fires of Greatness

by Howard Glasser, M.A.
Creator of the Nurtured Heart Approach
with Melissa Lynn Block, M.Ed.

You Are Oprah – Igniting the Fires of Greatness

The Nurtured Heart Approach is a trademark of the Children's Success Foundation.

For information contact: Nurtured Heart Publications
                             4165 West Ironwood Hill Drive
                             Tucson, Arizona 85745
                             E-mail: adhddoc@theriver.com

For information about bulk purchasing discounts of this book or other Nurtured Heart Approach books, videos, CDs or DVDs, please contact Fulfillment Services at 800-311-3132.

For orders within the book industry, please contact Brigham Distributing at 435-723-6611.

Cover Art by Alice Glasser
Book design by Michael Kichler
Copy editing by Chris Howell
Printed by Vaughan Printing, Nashville, TN

Library of Congress Card Catalogue Number: Pending

ISBN 0-9822552-4-1

Printed in the United States

First Printing: January 2009

*This book is dedicated
to the inherent greatness
of every person.*

Contents

Foreword

Written by Puran and Susanna Bair

This is a very important book. It fills a missing link in the process of becoming a fulfilled and complete human being. Furthermore, this book is an important contribution to the emerging 'culture of the heart' whereby we appreciate and apply in our daily lives the great wisdom and power of our hearts.

What we know of ourselves through our intellect is limited, even trivial, compared to the vision of the cosmic being we can see from the inside out with the eyes of our hearts. Awakening out of the culture of the mind, we discover ourselves to be entirely different and more wonderful than we had imagined.

As you read this book, your mind may deliver the warning it always gives: *no one is great, certainly not you, and any attempt to ascribe greatness to others will only inflate their egos.* These thoughts come from a place of scarcity and fear, which in turn comes from a mental faculty that is unaware of the limitless wonder of every human being. The latter is a vision only the heart can see.

We find that people do indeed have a problem with ego – one's sense of self-esteem and place in the universe. The problem is not that they think too much of themselves, but that they think too little of themselves. The worst braggarts are typically the most starved of real self-confidence. Those who are most unlikely to admire the greatness of others are most unaware of the glory of their own being.

We are, each one of us, embodiments of the universe – an integral part of creation. In knowing this, we can come to know our true selves. This knowing is accomplished through turning our senses inside. Howard's book is about how to inwardly reflect and know one's true self: a self that is as great as all of creation.

We also need the feedback of others to see ourselves rightly. This is the best function of a community, and it's a function that only a community can provide: to recognize for each member of the community what is their greatness. Even when we sense we have an inherent greatness, the influence of culture can cause us to incorrectly see or attribute that greatness. One may think his power to make money is his greatness because that's what the culture tells him, but his family and friends might admire a very different aspect of him: his skill in parenting lovingly, for example. Or one may think her greatness is her harmonious effect on others, while those who know her appreciate most her passionate idealism. With the tools provided in this book, readers will learn not only how to reflect upon their own greatness, but how to reflect others' greatness as well – and how to hear input from others from a place of seeing that greatness is a given.

When the true qualities of one's greatness are recognized and admired, a door opens to the realization of one's real self. This is the greatest gift one can give another. I hope this book will inspire you to give generously of this gift of insight from your heart that sees to the heart of another that you see in all its glory.

"And since you know you cannot see yourself so well as by reflection,
I, your glass, will modestly discover to yourself that
of yourself which you yet know not of."
– **William Shakespeare**, Julius Cæsar, Act I, Scene II.

Puran and Susanna Bair
Authors of *Energize Your Heart,* a book on Heart Rhythm Meditation, and co-founders of The Institute for Applied Meditation (www.IAMheart.org)

Preface

Written by Susan McLeod

Howard Glasser once said to me "'Why' is overrated. It's unimportant. A waste of time. I just really don't care about why."

Earth-rocking words, coming from a therapist.

I had previously held the notion that unearthing 'why' is the reason therapists exist. But not so for Howie. With his simple formula, you don't have to dredge up or trudge through the sludge of the past to be your greatness. You don't have to hit the couch or the mountaintop to get yourself fixed. You don't even have to fix others or the circumstances of your life to be great. No kidding.

Having been a devotee of 'why' for decades, I am exquisitely conversant in the ideas presented in most of the best-selling self-help books. In them I have found inspiration, comfort and hope – but no lasting change in me. Before my exposure to the ideas in this book, I lived with constant awareness of a checklist of my shortcomings that needed to change and an understanding of each that was nothing short of poetic. Life wasn't about greatness; it was about doing the best that I could despite all of my 'whys.'

All the while, I lived with a nagging suspicion that I was *great*…a knowledge, in my heart of hearts, that I wasn't nearly so flawed as I'd made myself out to be. How to release that greatness into action, into my daily life? The stick of religion didn't prod me to my greatness; the carrot of enlightenment didn't entice me to my greatness. But birthing a challenging child did, because it created a crisis in my life that led me to Howard Glasser.

My happy family bubble popped when my firstborn son turned out to be an intensely challenging child. It was hard to accept that I – who studied early childhood education, who holds a master's in communication, who taught children's church for a decade, who knows the power of thought, the impact of words, has faith to move mountains, has the spirit of GOD – yes, that I was being overtaken by negativity and a punitive parenting cycle as fast as blue sky retreats from thick black storm clouds.

The conventional solution was Ritalin for my son and Zoloft for me. Pills to make it all go away – to make it all better. That's the best wisdom the world offered. Thank GOD I had the wherewithal to say "No thank you." I didn't want to thwart what seemed like the butterfly's struggle to escape the cocoon – a necessary fight for life, freedom and transformation.

Thus began the search that led me to Howard Glasser and the Nurtured Heart Approach – the approach that Howard developed to transform difficult children into their greatness. I read the book, implemented it in my home, and it indeed worked like a magic pill! It revolutionized my relationship with my challenging child immediately and permanently. It gave me skills to pull him and our family from negativity into positivity and success.

But there was more. My emotions roiled while I read *Transforming the Difficult Child: The Nurtured Heart Approach*. I cried over not having had the approach to help my son the first four years of his life. But mostly, truth be told, I cried for myself, wondering what I would have been like if I had been raised with his approach.

At the next 'girls' night out,' I related the approach to my two closest girlfriends. Neither of them have children. Their immediate reaction was: "Everybody needs that! Let's do that with each other. Let's use the approach on ourselves." So the adventure began. I started to take the simple principles and techniques from the parenting approach and applied them to myself. I began to re-parent myself for greatness.

Did it muzzle my inner critic? Finally kill her off once and for all? Oh, no, a much finer fate was in store for her: *With Howard's approach, I transformed my inner critic to an inner greatness coach.*

My experience is far from the first time Howie's approach has transformed an adult. For the past 12 years, every time a parent coach, an educator, a therapist or a social worker finds his approach, light bulbs start popping about the myriad of ways to apply it. When Howie teaches adults the approach, as he has to thousands, they get pretty excited about using it to help others transform. But they are in utter awe of what it does for them personally. Just being immersed in the energizing greatness environment that Howie's work creates is deeply transformative.

And his protégés are using the approach in so many ways. Substance abuse addicts, couples in crisis, foster parents, social agencies – all have been helped immeasurably by this work, which boils down to letting go of those 'whys' and stepping into one's inborn greatness. As for me, this is the most freeing thing that's ever happened in my life. I let go of *why* and stepped into the power of how to fan my own embers of greatness into a roaring fire that fuels my passion.

I don't recall my shortcomings. I don't care about my whys or your whys. Thanks to Howard, I now know HOW to see my greatness, be my greatness, live my greatness. Now. Anybody can. There's a reason Howard Glasser isn't into why. The gift of his own intensity to the world is found in his name: he brings us a simple no-fail formula for HOW.

And guess what? It's not about changing. It's about choosing. That's one power we all have, and Howard Glasser shows us how to use our choices to transform ourselves.

Susan McLeod
Publisher, www.energyparenting.com

About the Authors

Howard Glasser, M.A.

Howard Glasser is the founder of Children's Success Foundation and designer of the Nurtured Heart Approach. He and Jennifer Easley are the co-authors of *Transforming the Difficult Child: The Nurtured Heart Approach* (1999, 2008), currently the top-selling book on the topic of ADHD. They also collaborated on *Transforming the Difficult Child: True Stories of Triumph* (2008). He is also the author of *All Children Flourishing – Igniting the Greatness of Our Children* (2008); *The Inner Wealth Initiative* (2007) with Tom Grove; *Transforming the Difficult Child Workbook* (2008) with Joann Bowdidge and Lisa Bravo; and *101 Reasons to Avoid Ritalin Including One Great Reason Why It's Almost ALWAYS Unnecessary* (2005).

Howard has been a featured guest on *CNN* and a consultant for *48 Hours*. He lectures in the U.S. and internationally, teaching therapists, educators and parents about the Nurtured Heart Approach, which is now being used in hundreds of thousands of homes and classrooms around the world. Howard is former director and clinical supervisor of the Center for the Difficult Child in Tucson, AZ. He has been a consultant for numerous psychiatric, judicial and educational programs. Although he has done extensive doctoral work in the fields of Clinical Psychology and Educational Leadership, he feels his own years as a difficult child contributed the most to his understanding of the needs of challenging children and to the success of his approach.

He is proudest of the fact that he is responsible for keeping more children off of psychiatric medications than any other person. He and his amazing daughter Alice live in Tucson, Arizona.

Melissa Lynn Block, M.Ed.

Melissa Lynn Block is a writer and editor who specializes in helping others put their ideas, methods and stories down on the printed page clearly, elegantly and accessibly. She has clients from many disciplines, including physicians, therapists and educators. She has written, ghostwritten and co-authored more than a dozen books and frequently crafts articles, newsletters and Web content under her own name or as a ghostwriter for others. She lives with her husband, two children and various critters in Santa Barbara, California. She can be contacted at ideokinesis@verizon.net.

Acknowledgments

This book is a manifestation of an ongoing experiment that I began 10 years ago and that has profoundly and irreversibly impacted my life and now the lives of many. Looking back, I am in awe of the courage, willingness and tenacity of so many people in relentlessly applying the Nurtured Heart Approach, originally developed for the challenging children with whom I have worked, so I want to start by expressing my acknowledgment and appreciation to all of them.

I am forever indebted to those intense and difficult children who first inspired the clear and powerful nature of this approach as it came into existence, as well as to the many parents, educators and colleagues who ceaselessly demonstrate the viability of this work in homes, schools and treatment centers all over the world and who contribute to evolving it into ever-greater levels. Prominent in this group are Tom Grove, Lisa Bravo and Gabrielli LaChiara, who assist me and lead the way at our Advanced Trainings; and Susan McLeod, Jennifer Easley and Jan Hunter, who among the many great therapists and educators certified in this work are major contributors to bringing the Nurtured Heart Approach to the world.

I am indebted to Puran and Susanna Bair for their brilliant Heart Rhythm Meditation work and for the synergy they have created in our shared interest in igniting the greatness of others.

I am particularly indebted once again to Melissa Block for her amazing ability to translate my, at times, loosely formed notes, conversations and thoughts into a wonderful literary style. What an amazing talent to be able to mold ideas into a complete, coherent, flowing volume, utterly faithful to the author's voice and notions; and to make each and every piece come to life beyond anything I could have accomplished on my own. I am so appreciative of her great skills and attitude. What a gift she is to my life.

I am also greatly indebted to two other people who have made this book come to life. Chris Howell has made a huge contribution to the flow, impact, correctness and readability of this book by way of her great and encompassing skills as an editor. Michael Kichler has, once again, magically put all the components into beautiful book form by way of his wonderful talents and skills as a graphic artist.

Last but not least, I want to thank my wonderful daughter Alice for contributing her magnificent and inspiring art for this cover. I am so appreciative of the love and support this amazing child brings to my life.

Howard Glasser

I will always be grateful for the presence of Howard Glasser in my life. Howard is a true original, a practical mystic, and a mover and shaker who has made an immeasurable difference in the lives of so many families and individuals, mine and me included. I'm constantly awed by his brilliance and by his gift for making everyone around him feel just as brilliant! His work came into my life just as I became a parent, and it has been a major support for me as I've raised my own children. Over our years of collaboration, he has become a dearly loved friend. Thanks also to Tom Grove, Susan MacLeod and all the other Nurtured Heart practitioners who contributed to this project. This is truly a remarkable group of people and I feel privileged to collaborate with them all! Thanks, Howard, for making me a part of it.

I would also like to thank my husband and partner, Patrick; editor *extraordinaire* Chris Howell; my wonderful friends Amanda, Nicola, Sabine and Sumati; and my beautiful, nurturing children and step-children, Sarah, Noah, Julian and Tristan. With your love, intelligent feedback and support, I'm standing stronger in my own greatness than ever before.

Melissa Lynn Block

How to Use This Book

My recommendation is that you read this entire book, cover to cover. Then, keep it handy and open it to a random page whenever you feel the need for guidance or a 'greatness boost.'

And now, if you want to stick with me and keep reading, set your intention. If your intention is to create greatness, who does that hurt? There's nothing anyone can do to stop you once you set this intention. Your intention wins.

A Note about Use of the Word 'God'

As some readers may be put off by the use of the word 'God,' I'd like to take a moment to explain that we refer not to the God of any particular religion or tradition, but to the creative force and indefinable spirit to which greatness is so often attributed.

Throughout history, cultures have used multiple names to describe and honor this 'great mystery.' Some of these names translate to phrases such as God is Grace, God is Beauty, God is Love, God is Wisdom, God is Power and God is Compassion. These various names, many of which are still used today, allow us to consider and honor the *qualities* of divine 'greatness.' What almost every faith seems to agree upon, whether it reveres one name for God or many, is that God is great.

You've heard of 'Movies on Demand.' We ask that you consider 'Greatness on Demand' – a bottomless cache of greatness that you can call up as desired and as needed. This is way more interesting than any film you'd rent, because it's *your* movie. You are director and producer.

When you acknowledge and name individual qualities of greatness in all their magnificent splendor, your appreciation for and understanding of greatness can expand as far as you are willing to take them. You can become the beneficiary of the greatness of your own making. This book offers you ways to begin on that path. If traditional concepts of God don't ring true for you, consider each reference to God in this book as a reference to this concept of 'Greatness on Demand.'

Enjoy the journey, and namaste.*

---

* Namaste (nam-a-stay) is a Sanskrit word meaning "I see the God within you" or "I honor the Spirit in you, which is also in me."

Prologue

When faced with a radical crisis, when the old way of being in the
world, of interacting with each other and with the realm of nature
doesn't work anymore, when survival is threatened by seemingly
insurmountable problems, an individual life-form – or a species –
will either die or become extinct or rise above the limitations of its
condition through an evolutionary leap.
– Eckhart Tolle, *A New Earth: Awakening to Your Life's
Purpose* (Plume Books, New York, NY: 2005)

I know for sure that what we dwell on is who we become.
– **Oprah Winfrey**

The Nurtured Heart Approach was developed to help intense, hard-
to-handle children shift into a thriving, flourishing state of success.
As a therapist who often treated children with behaviors that made
them difficult or impossible in school and at home, I knew that therapeutic failure would lead many of these kids into a lifetime of taking
powerful psychiatric medications.

The more I learned about these medications – stimulant drugs
like Ritalin and Adderall, antidepressants like Prozac and Paxil, and
atypical antipsychotics like Risperdal – the more I knew that there
had to be some other, less dangerous way to help these children. As
news story after news story emerged about the dangers of pediatric
use of some of these drugs and the ineffectiveness of others, I became
more and more motivated and dedicated to finding a non-drug
approach that made a difference. Fortunately, a combination of intuition, experimentation, collaboration and divine guidance supported
me in creating the Nurtured Heart Approach.

This approach has enabled me and many others to transform
'problem' children into flourishing children who are no longer candi-
dates for medication and who can fully and joyously participate in
life, both at school and at home. Their intensity is *transmuted* – redi-
rected from creating havoc into positive pursuits. The approach is a
set of tools that adults use to irresistibly draw an intense child into

using that beautiful intensity to propel success rather than to create mischief. It has turned out to be an effective tool for transforming children and teenagers – and even adults – whom the world might otherwise have given up on.

In previous generations, these intense children were often directed into sports or scouting or other activities that would help channel their over-the-top life force. The Nurtured Heart Approach is about parents and teachers learning ways to channel that life force throughout each day. It is a direct method that allows adults to create, within each interaction, an avenue through which that child's intensity can propel him in only one direction – that of greatness.

As it turns out, as soon as children begin to experience feeling great, they begin to act out greatness wherever they go and in whatever they do. This is a much more acceptable and exciting manifestation of a child's life force than problematic behavior.

Since 1994, the Nurtured Heart Approach has been my full-time job, my life's work and my spiritual calling. The approach has changed a great deal since I first began to teach it in the late 1990s. It has evolved and expanded, due in no small part to the enthusiastic collaboration of many wonderful teachers, parents, school administrators and therapists. The approach has been implemented in countless homes, thousands of classrooms, hundreds of schools and even (at this writing) a couple of school systems.

In the first few chapters of this book, you will learn about the Nurtured Heart Approach: how it works, what its theoretical underpinnings are, and how it can be used creatively. **This book, however, is not about using this approach on children.** It's about using it with adults – yourself and the important others in your life. You may, as you hone your own version of this practice, even begin to use it with those with whom you have only incidental contact. When I refer to the application of the Nurtured Heart Approach on one's self in these pages, I'll usually call it *greatness practice* or *greatness work*.

And isn't greatness what almost everyone, knowingly or unknowingly, wants? Do you want to be less loving and compassionate tomorrow? Do you want to be less respectful and wise? And for that matter, do you want other people you encounter to embody less of any of these great qualities?

If asked, almost anyone would emphatically say that he or she wants to express and be witness to expression of more of these sorts of qualities, not less. But how often do the people in your life purposely fan the flames of these qualities – which are qualities of greatness – in you or in themselves? How would propelling these qualities of greatness impact our direct sense of accomplishment and fulfillment in our lives?

In my other books, I wrote at length about parents becoming their child's therapist. This book is about becoming your own therapist – about mounting a personal and spiritual intervention on your own behalf.

I have been exploring this aspect of my work for years and, while doing so, collaborating with many dazzling parents, counselors and teachers – including my dear friends and meditation teachers Puran and Susanna Bair, creators of a form of heart-centered contemplation. The practice they teach, called Heart Rhythm Meditation, will be highlighted in this book as a perfect complement to the self-created, propelling nature of the approach you are about to venture upon.

It's a wonderful and rewarding process to use the Nurtured Heart Approach to shine light on the greatness of a child; and it's truly magnificent to dive headlong into this larger adventure of igniting greatness within yourself and in your life.

If you are curious about the reference to Oprah Winfrey's name in the title of this book, rest assured that you will find out, in upcoming sections, just why I invoke Oprah so prominently in a book about the practice of igniting greatness.

Chapter 1

Nurturing Inner Wealth

The Nurtured Heart Approach is a set of notions and strategies that enables adults to energetically and vividly *recognize, appreciate and reflect to a child his or her positive choices.* This, in turn, creates what I call *inner wealth,* a deep and lasting kind of self-esteem that comes from actual experiences of being held in esteem, day after day, for all the ways in which the child is not just "being good" or even "being great" – but for the ways in which his very existence, along with his everyday choices, are *held up as qualities of the greatness he possesses.*

Self-esteem is generally believed to be an attribute you can just *have,* regardless of your experience. Everyone knows someone who seems to have remarkable self-esteem that doesn't appear to result from or be reflected in that person's actions or achievements. Conversely, everyone knows someone who achieves amazing things but who, tragically, seems to have little or no self-esteem in interacting with the world at large. Inner wealth is a truly *congruent* experience: the greatness one feels matches the manifestations of that greatness out in the world, and those accomplishments go hand-in-hand with the inner beliefs that support further adventures into greatness.

Without inner wealth, it is difficult to love and enjoy your own strengths and gifts to the world. You end up doubting your contribution, or even the very way in which you walk the planet. You wind up searching the faces of others to see what *they* want, instead of trusting what you want and the utter value of who you are. You make decisions from an uncentered, unaware place, simply trying to please others. There's nothing wrong with pleasing others, but it is far more satisfying when its basis is a strong center of self-value, meaning and inner wealth.

Inner wealth is the result of accruing a predominant and prevailing sense of successfulness. It entails acquiring a sort of 'portfolio' of successfulness by way of first-hand and irrefutable experiences and recognition of successes – large, small and in between – and tying that into the greatness, there for the taking, that resides within each of us. It's a more all-encompassing, richer, deeper, broader experience of one's own self-worth, capacity for happiness, ability to relate well with others, and capacity to do good in the world, all emanating from honest life experiences of successful thoughts, actions and choices.

Recognizing and cultivating inner wealth in a child is the foundation of the Nurtured Heart Approach. The child's inner wealth grows as a result of having all the evidence of his greatness witnessed and reflected back to him. It's putting the horse of self-esteem in front of the cart: Instead of saying "If she had more self-esteem, she wouldn't be having so much trouble in school!" we say "How can we show her the ways in which *she is already successful* – and make further success irresistible?" This builds inner wealth, a kind of self-esteem that is not subject to the vicissitudes of life.

What makes this approach work so well and so easily is the fact that the communication between adult and child is at the *soul level.* Most of us feel far more comfortable at the level of the mind, but there is so much interference here – particularly when we talk to children. Communication at this level of the heart slides directly into the child's heart, past any and all defenses.

As adults learn to powerfully wield this approach with the children in their lives, they experience the intense joy of helping those children thrive. They in essence become the child's therapist – a role that, in this context, simply means that the parent or teacher is the agent of change in the child's life.

Inner wealth isn't just for children; and if these tools can enable you to become a therapist to your child or student, they can also enable you to brilliantly bring about your own fulfillment. ❄

Chapter 2

Become Your Own Therapist

Think of the curiosity, adventurousness, fearlessness and capacity for unconditional love that characterize most children, especially very young children. A small child is totally comfortable with his greatness.

He's the center of the universe, ready to follow every whim and fully express every emotion. Unless you're one of the few lucky adults who has held onto your childish wonder, curiosity, profound belief in self, and capacity to love with your whole heart without reservation, interactions with people and circumstances in your life almost inevitably diminish these wonderful childlike qualities. Doubts and fears inevitably creep in along the way. You may have ended up in a place where worry, misery and doubt – 'WMDs' for short – are fairly familiar companions.

I know this first-hand. Around the time my first book came out, about a decade before I sat down to write this one, I noticed that despite the positivity I was espousing in my workshops and writings, despite my belief that I was a thoroughly positive person, I had a tendency – especially when under pressure – to be consumed with worry, doubt and fear. At the time, due to a funding snafu, I was facing the dissolution of the counseling center I had worked so hard to create. I became nearly overwhelmed with worry, fear and anger.

When I was able to step outside of my emotional firestorm to consider the big picture, I could see how my thoughts seemed to have default settings, just like my computer. My mind, left to its own devices, simply defaulted to negativity when it felt threatened in any significant way. This setting was most visible under pressure, but I soon saw with equal clarity how it also showed up in more subtle ways – even when things were going smoothly. I saw how these defaults were causing me to take a negative, defensive stance in my life that was enervating and troubling.

In a moment of clarity, I sensed that I could make a shift to an entirely different way of being – a different set of defaults – that would enable me to thrive even in tough circumstances. Once I experienced that initial revelation, the rest just came to me: I saw that I could use the Nurtured Heart Approach *on myself* to change that default setting. I could picture the possibility, almost as if I were choosing some advanced setting from a remote pull-down menu in the system preferences of my computer.

I could be my own therapist, just as I could be a child's therapist. I could use the tools of the approach to change the programming in my mind and heart, just as I can upgrade my computer with new downloads that will change its programming and improve its functioning. All I had to do was figure out which pop-up boxes, which windows, which menus were key and how to access and use them skillfully.

Once I saw in a fully detached way – not just theoretically or intellectually, but from the inside out – that my existing defaults tended toward WMDs, I absolutely knew that I could *change those defaults.* I knew I could reach a place in my consciousness where I would automatically revert to inner wealth, positivity and success. And I knew and trusted that this change would be enormously beneficial.

I somehow realized that I didn't have to analyze the old software to understand *why* it was there up until now. Neither did I need to know *why* it wasn't working. Rather, I could simply download the new software of positivity. It seemed evident that the greatly improved new software would not obliterate my history – instead, it would *overwrite the influence of the old software,* creating a new and uplifting influence. Along with these realizations came an instant sense of knowing that this adventure would inevitably impact the 'hardware' of my being in wonderful and great ways. However: What I did *not* know at the time is how this would come to inspire my own sense of greatness and that of others.

Rather than merely wishing I could be as great and powerful as Oprah Winfrey, or any other person who seems to possess tremendous inner wealth and is using their power in exciting and dynamic ways, I could actively cultivate my own greatness. I could, in essence, *be Oprah* – I could be in my own version of greatness so completely that I would truly "live my best life."

This book is the product of my exploration of this process. It is based on my own inner work and on workshops I have designed and conducted over the years. The response to this work has been stunning and gratifying, and I am excited to share my path to inner wealth with a larger portion of the world by putting it down in book form. ❄

Chapter 3

Qualities of Greatness: The Oprah Connection

Over the years, I've been struck by how often friends call me in the middle of the afternoon to exhort, "Hey, turn on Oprah, she's doing something really cool today." These calls typically don't happen when she's doing celebrity interviews or make-over shows, but rather when she is immersed in a powerful and inspiring project.

The regularity of this phenomenon got to be intriguing. It spurred me to consider: What is it that Oprah is offering up to the world, and what is within her that enables her to pour out so many wonderful, inspiring and magnanimous acts? As I pondered and marveled at this woman's aptitude for doing good, I began to profoundly appreciate the qualities – such as wisdom, compassion, power, intelligence and radiance – that brought me to see her as so amazing and so influential.

Most people are not fully aware of what they see in a woman like Oprah that makes her so compelling; they don't necessarily see it as 'greatness' per se. They do, however, see that it isn't Oprah's projects themselves that inspire such admiration; rather, it's something about the qualities she reflects and brings to the table that *ignite* these projects: Her persona, her identity, her way of talking to herself and to others – all seem to have such a remarkable effect on her world and on us. That certain something personified by Oprah is what I call greatness. Those qualities she embodies are *qualities of greatness.*

I eventually came to realize that our very own qualities of greatness are not only a *given*, i.e., already within us, but they are there for the taking – really, *there for the awakening.* It dawned on me that so many of us are trying, in our own ways, to bring forth our own positive qualities – variations of many of the very same qualities we see in someone like Oprah. Those of us who wish, hope and pray to be more like her or other people of greatness only need to tap into our own greatness to do so. It's not her projects that form her greatness, it's her greatness that manifests in her projects.

I saw how I could conspire with the universe to consciously culti-vate my own greatness. I asked myself: *Just how far can I barrel down the road in this adventure? How far up this mountain can I climb?* And this has been my journey and experiment since the year 2000, when I chose myself as the experimental guinea pig.

Oprah has become, for so many, an icon of greatness. How do we fan the flames in ourselves that already burn so brightly in her? The flame is not an accident. Making the blaze more and more magnifi-cent is not an accident either. Creating and building up the blaze of greatness is an intentional act.

I have come to believe that the approach described in these pages could bring about an enormous shift in the way people think and feel. Eckhart Tolle, who is quoted in the book's first epigraph, writes about a needed evolutionary shift that will bring about a new earth; in the second epigraph, Oprah speaks succinctly and powerfully of the way we can literally 'create' ourselves with our thoughts. I am convinced that my approach to fostering inner wealth and greatness is a way to effect such a shift in our own minds and hearts and to create our-selves in the image we choose. It is not the only way – but one way, and a potent way at that. This work is dear to my heart, and it's an honor to share it with you. ❈

Chapter 4

A New Psychiatry

Between 1994 and 2003, diagnoses of bipolar disorder in children rose 40-fold. In 1994, 20,000 children were being treated for bipolar disorder; by 2003, that number had climbed to 800,000. How is it possible that this disorder – which is most often treated with potent anticonvulsant and atypical antipsychotic drugs, even in toddlers – could truly be affecting so many more children in such a brief period?

One study from researchers at Brown University Medical School found that there is likely a significant over-diagnosis and misdiagnosis of this disorder in adults. They gathered 700 adults who had been diagnosed with bipolar disorder and gave them a standardized, comprehensive psychiatric diagnostic interview. *Fewer than half* of these adults turned out to meet the disorder's widely agreed-upon criteria, which are themselves a highly questionable barometer.

Why would psychiatry's criteria for diagnosing bipolar disorder constitute a "questionable barometer?" Because financial conflicts of interest are extremely common within the committees that decide what constitutes a treatable mental illness. A study published in a leading psychology journal in 2008 found that *one hundred percent* of committee members who created diagnostic criteria for mood disorders (a class that includes depression and bipolar disorder) and schizophrenia had conflicts of interest involving funding from pharmaceutical companies.* In this same study, conflicts of interest were almost as rampant for committees creating guidelines for anxiety disorders (81.3 percent had financial ties with drug companies), eating disorders (83.3 percent), and premenstrual dysphoric disorder (83.3 percent). This means, in the most basic terms, that *the fox is guarding the henhouse.* When a psychiatrist or psychologist determines that someone has a mental illness, he or she bases this on criteria created by a team of doctors that is almost certain to have a vested interest in more people being diagnosed and treated with medications.

About 350 people in the Brown University study were mistakenly diagnosed with a severe, permanent mental disorder and possibly prescribed powerful psychiatric medications to treat it. If not for this study, they might have gone on for the rest of their lives believing they had what is considered by the medical community to be an incurable mental illness. Brown University's Mark Zimmerman, the study's author, stated in an interview that "believing that one has bipolar disorder when one doesn't can have serious consequences...The drugs given to treat it can have harmful side effects, including damage to the kidneys, liver and immune or endocrine systems." Additionally, he says, some patients "are very much invested in their diagnosis and disorder and live a lifestyle that is consistent with that. They stigmatize

---

* Study reference: Cosgrove L, Krimsky S, Vijayaraghavan M, Schneider L, "Financial ties between DSM-IV panel members and the pharmaceutical industry," Psychother Psychosomatics 2006;75:154-160.

themselves. They view themselves as not being able to do certain things. Some patients are looking for a magic 'pill that will cure all ills' when they really need to do the hard work of psychotherapy." (In my opinion, standard psychotherapy has its merits, but it also has a few fatal flaws that you will learn more about later in this book.)

According to estimates from the National Institutes of Mental Health (NIMH), 26.2 percent of American adults (18 and up) have a diagnosable mental disorder in any given year. About half of these people can be said to have more than one such disorder at a time. Depression is the leading cause of disability for Americans aged 15 to 44.

The NIMH also tells us that 6.1 percent of American adults have generalized anxiety disorder; 6.8 percent exhibit social phobia. Diagnoses of certain disorders – especially bipolar disorder – have shot way up in recent years, an increase so dramatic that many wise minds in psychiatry and elsewhere are beginning to think that it's high time to put on the brakes.

Millions of people have resigned themselves to the idea that they are mentally ill or chemically imbalanced and need treatment for life. Many therapists and psychiatrists, myself included, maintain that a large proportion of these people are actually *not* ill. Surely there are real symptoms, but I contend that only a very small percentage of people who have symptoms of depression, anxiety or ADHD actually require treatment with medications. For the rest – even if their 'chemicals' (usually meaning brain neurotransmitters such as serotonin, norepinephrine and dopamine) are imbalanced – modern research is demonstrating that they can change that balance by changing the way they think and talk to themselves.

Case in point: According to award-winning journalist Robert Whitaker, a well-known expert on the risks of psychiatric drugs and author of the book *Mad In America*, psychiatric drugging of children began in earnest around 1987. Whitaker, in an interview with Michael Shaughnessy at Ednews.org, says that before this time in which stimulants and antidepressants became widely prescribed to children, "juvenile bipolar disorder was exceedingly rare. But if you take the quantified risk with these two drug [classes], in terms of their potential to stir mania and psychosis, and then you apply that risk to the number of kids so medicated with those drugs, then you could expect that there would be about 750,000 cases of drug-induced 'juvenile bipolar illness' today, and that about equals the number of kids so diagnosed."

What Whitaker is saying is that this so-called epidemic of mental illness in children appears to actually be an *iatrogenic,* or doctor-caused, phenomenon. Both stimulants and antidepressants disrupt neurotransmitter balance in ways that lead to side effects that include mania and depression, which then leads the child to be diagnosed with bipolar disorder.

The authorities don't, by and large, see it this way or give this message to the public. According to the Web site of the Depression and Bipolar Disorder Alliance, "some 20% of adolescents with major depression develop bipolar disorder within five years of the onset of depression," and "up to one-third of the 3.4 million children and adolescents with depression in the United States may actually be experiencing the early onset of bipolar disorder." It seems to be a given that the depression itself is a harbinger of a more serious disorder later on – there's no consideration, in these statistics, that the drugs given for depression might have something to do with the later bipolar diagnosis!

We can no longer afford to stifle or deaden life force with medications, except as an absolute last resort to protect people's safety. When the choice is made to use a psychotropic medication, I believe that we must acknowledge the price of doing so. There is always a great price to pay for tamping down life force with a pharmaceutical. Any person who is prescribed a drug to treat a mental health problem receives a meta-message that something is wrong with his or her life force – that the person and those around him or her cannot handle this life force, and so it needs to be medicated away. Even if one's intensity and life force are only modestly moderated by drugs, this has a dramatic impact on one's ability to live life passionately and to fulfill one's own visions and dreams.

Psychiatric drugging is, at its root, not about healing the patient – in fact, these drugs are not considered a cure at all, just a way to treat symptoms of a problem likely to be chronic – or about making a mentally ill person feel better. (Actually, once a person has been on these medications and then stops taking them, there are almost always withdrawal symptoms that may be severe enough to convince the person that he or she really *is* mentally ill.) It's about making him or her *easier to handle*. It's about him or her being forced to fit into schools and workplaces that aren't a good fit. At its most extreme level, psychiatric drugging is a sort of 'chemical lobotomy' that reduces one's life force and energy far enough to make one totally manageable. Success, in this realm, is about creating what Brian Doherty, a writer for the magazine *Reason,* calls "treatable zombies."

At this point, readers may find my credibility strained. You might be asking: *How about those who are frankly and dangerously mentally ill? Aren't there people who, without medications, will end up living much less satisfying lives where they can't work, go to school or have healthy relationships – and who will be a danger to themselves and others?*

Yes – there are such people in every society. For a very small proportion of people who merit a diagnosis of mental illness and who seem to benefit from careful use of medications, I would assert that the benefits of such medications outweigh their risks. Still, there is considerable evidence that there are non-drug alternatives that work as well or better than psychotropic medications – even with a mental illness as severe as schizophrenia.

Beginning in the mid-18th century, the Quakers created centers for people with mental illness that were distinctly un-hospital-like and involved no surgeries or abuses (other asylums, at the time, were treating the 'insane' with terrifying cruelty). These centers focused on "moral treatment," where patients were treated with kindness and kept in a pleasant environment where they got plenty of fresh air and natural light. They were expected to fulfill certain responsibilities and were kept busy with activities.

In the 1970s, psychiatrist Loren Mosher conducted an experiment based on the foundation of moral treatment. He created a care center called Soteria for people with schizophrenia, where newly diagnosed schizophrenics lived with a non-medical staff who had been trained to listen and offer caring support. In this two-year study, patients treated in Soteria had equal or better outcomes on eight individual measures when compared with people who were treated with medications in hospitals. The patients treated at Soteria were also far less likely to relapse.

Here's where I go with the meds question. What would people do if they realized how dangerous these medicines actually are? And I mean not only in a life-or-death way (and most antidepressants now have black-box warnings because of increased risk of suicidal behaviors and violence), but in many more subtle ways – the way they change your personality, cause myriad bothersome side effects (mania, anxiety, bad dreams, intense restlessness, insomnia, weight gain or loss), make you unable to go as deep as you need to go in order to heal, rob you of the feeling that you are in control of your own mind and your own life. Knowing all this, the general populace might indeed rally around people who are in crisis and encourage the person who's suffering from depression or whatever to transition to a better place where they can parent, work and love.

Soteria and moral treatment are wonderful foundations for caring for anyone suffering, whether it's to the extent of being disabling or not. We only think we "need" the drugs because that's what the psychiatric establishment – which is in a deep and unholy alliance with drug companies – is telling us.

I think we'd all be better off if we reserved medications as a last resort and found some other way that wouldn't drive a wedge between a person and the great personal energy and intensity that is needed for anyone to have a life of fulfillment and accomplishment. The Quakers knew how to do it. In their hospitals, they cared for people gently and tenderly, fed them good food and made sure they had fresh air and felt like valued parts of a community.

I believe that, for any of us to be truly fulfilled, we need to come to see the truth and beauty of our life force and greatness. This turns out to be a lot easier than even the simple act of taking a pill, and it's a lot less expensive than psychotherapy or a visit to the pharmacy. And the techniques are easy to learn. Teachers, parents and counselors who come to my workshops to study the Nurtured Heart Approach can learn as much as they need to know in only a single day. They can rapidly get up to speed so that they are able to work fluidly with this approach. The same goes for applying the approach to one's self. In fact, it's even quicker and simpler than learning it for use in an educational, parenting or counseling setting. ❄

Chapter 5

Positive Thinking, Greatness Thinking

For much of its history, psychology has seemed obsessed with human failings and pathology. The very idea of psychotherapy, first formalized by Freud, rests on a view of human beings as troubled creatures in need of repair. Freud himself was profoundly pessimistic about human nature, which he felt was governed by deep, dark drives that we could only tenuously control. The behaviorists who followed developed a model of human life that seemed to many mechanistic if not robotic: humans were passive beings mercilessly shaped by the stimuli and the contingent rewards and punishments that surrounded them....A watershed moment arrived in 1998, when University of Pennsylvania psychologist Martin Seligman, in his presidential address to the American Psychological Association, urged psychology to "turn toward understanding and building the human strengths to complement our emphasis on healing damage." That speech launched today's positive psychology movement.

– Craig Lambert, "The Science of Happiness,"
Harvard Review, August 2007

Positive psychology is about focusing on building strength rather than trying to mine out weaknesses. By putting our efforts and attention into understanding what makes a person successful rather than what makes a person fail, we can discover tools for living better lives and having better relationships. In the place of traditional psychology's (sometimes endless) exploration of shame, guilt, fear and anger, positive psychology puts its emphasis on how to best use our strengths and live in our happiest place – and how to be more resilient when things go wrong.

You can alter your neurochemistry with your thoughts, just as your body can affect the way you think. Giving a compliment to someone else causes his or her serotonin to rise; and it makes the compliment-giver's serotonin rise, too. This is a manifestation of a behind-the-scenes optimizing of neurotransmitter functioning – for that matter, brain functioning. Although I haven't done the biochemical research necessary to determine whether my work on cultivating greatness actually alters brain chemistry, I believe that it can.

Undeniably, the way I propose is much less risky than the biopsychiatric approach – the widespread and ready use of potent neurotransmitter-altering medications to kick depression, anxiety and other modes where we fail to live in our own greatness. By exposing ourselves to any of these medications, we in essence send ourselves the undermining message that we are not great, that we do not currently trust and believe in our life force. We send ourselves the antithetical message that we need something outside of ourselves to make our life force more livable and workable.

In the greatness practice, we don't eradicate, ignore or condemn frustration, sadness, grief, anger, anxiety or depression. This is not about pretending that these emotions and states of mind do not exist, or about denying ourselves the healthy experience of these emotions and states. But we do learn to hitch ourselves up out of the downward spiral these emotions and states can draw us into. We learn to *use the energy generated by problems, fears, doubts and pain to reset to iterations of greatness.* You will see more on this as we progress.

With the right intentions and the right strategies, the defaults to worry, misery and doubt (WMDs) can be changed. We can, as Puran Bair once said, "blast depression away with greatness." ❄

Chapter 6

Love in Action

We either make ourselves happy or miserable.
The amount of work is the same.
– **Carlos Castaneda**, Peruvian-born American author

We've all heard that, without some level of self-love, you cannot love another. This book is about how to actualize that very love – how to put it into motion in optimal and powerful ways. It will give you tools with which you can constantly see and remind yourself of the greatness that you've been given and the greatness that is unfolding in yourself and others. It will give you the ability to fan the flames of the magnificence within yourself.

This is not a kind of self-love that is arrogant, selfish or conceited; it is the kind of self-love that gives one the inner strength and forti-tude to do what is right and helpful in the world. An arrogant, selfish or conceited person continually pumps himself up because he is *lacking* this inner wealth and fortitude. When we come to rest comfort-ably in our own greatness, loving ourselves with a fullness of inner wealth, we don't need to suck the life out of others to fill ourselves. We can give abundantly without becoming depleted. Our whole being becomes one of abundance. Giving, then, becomes a choice that is as natural as breathing.

The reason for our suffering may be that in our collective past, we have brought worry, misery and doubt to the editing room we use to construe the 'Now.' Instead of lugging the excess baggage of WMDs with us into each consecutive Now, we can choose to fully embrace these very same moments in the light of greatness. In seeing and living in greatness, we bring into form the splendor we've been longing for.

You can let the 'Now' dictate itself to you, reactively pursuing its seeming demands as it unfolds; or you can be like the film editor who knowingly transforms the rough footage into a work of art.

You can realize that, even if you do not intentionally shape your Now, it is being shaped by your habitual ways of thinking and reacting to others. You may as well be intentional about it.

In *Prelude to a New Dream*, Miguel Ruiz wrote:

There are thousands of agreements you have made with yourself and with others...with your dream of life, with God, with society, with your parents, your spouse, and with your children. The most important agreements are the ones you've made with yourself. In those agreements you tell yourself who you are...what you feel, what you believe, and how to behave. The result is what you call your personality. In these agreements you say, "This is what I am, this is what I believe...I can do certain things and some things I cannot do...this is possible and that is impossible." One single agreement is not such a problem, but we have many agreements that make us suffer, that make us fail. If you want to live a life of joy and fulfillment, you have to find the courage to break those agreements that are fear-based and claim personal power. The agreements that come from fear require us to expend a lot of energy, but the agreements that come from love help us to conserve energy, and even to gain extra energy.

You are the producer and director of the movie that is YOU – that is your life. You can tilt the camera any way you choose to capture any next frame. You can construe each frame any way you wish, and you have the rights to the voice-over. A zillion different people are going to see the same unfolding Nows in a zillion different ways anyway, with endless nuances that are theirs alone. The interpretation of the Now is up to us. We might as well take this liberty in a way that is exciting and enhancing.

The funny thing is that *we all already do this subconsciously*. This is what Castaneda was talking about when he said that whether you decide to be happy or unhappy, your level of effort will be the same. You edit your every Now – you may as well do it in a way that enhances happiness, confidence and joy.

As soon as we are clearly awakened to how important this editing process is to our well-being and that of others, we can proceed in a knowing and conscious manner that changes our lives forever. ❄

Chapter 7

Beyond "Be Here Now"

Okay, dear readers, now is a good time for an important caveat that will help you decide whether you want to continue on with this book.

If you aren't interested in living in your own most powerful place, you might as well put this book down right now. If you don't think that your life could benefit from more joy, more positive energy, more compliments, better self-esteem, more compassion and love, or a more expansive sense of greatness, this book isn't for you. If you don't much feel like improving your relationships, your personal accomplishments, your sense of self and humanity, or your work-related achievements, you can shelve this volume and move along. If you are not prepared to be your greatest self, that's understandable, because being fully in your greatness is a great responsibility – one you may not choose to undertake at present.

But if you forge ahead, I appreciate the greatness you are demonstrating in making such an important decision. And I will also assume that you want to improve your life in a core and profound way but you haven't yet found the right, most powerful path to effecting the change you envision. The Nurtured Heart Approach is one path to making the shift you know you want to make – the change that you might sense is already there, awaiting you. It's simple and clear and will give you a confident and knowing sense of how to proceed. It doesn't require that you sit on a mountaintop in lotus pose for weeks awaiting enlightenment, and it is not about obtaining anything you don't already have.

This book outlines a rigorous practice of seeing things differently. It's a *greatness practice,* designed to be used in the context of real life – a set of tools you can begin to use right away in any moment to change for the better the way you talk to yourself and react and respond to others. As you apply these tools, you realize the greatness you already possess. As you put your attention on that greatness, it unfurls and expands…and *voilà* – you're living in your greatness.

One friend of mine once called me a "practical mystic," and this is reflected in the practice I will describe in these pages. This book is about practical methods that will enable you to create your own version of Now. It is an evolution beyond the classic Ram Dass exhortation to "be here now," which I've often found a difficult instruction to follow. Instead of being here *now,* be here *knowing.* Mine your own great intelligence and creativity to *create* your now, instead of simply being a bystander or a witness in each precious moment.

One reason we have suffered: in our collective past, we have brought worry, fear and doubt into the editing room of the Now. We can henceforth choose to do otherwise.

Ram Dass speaks of "luminous consciousness" – and this is a gorgeous thing all by itself – but the question I wish to raise is: What do you want to *do* with your luminous consciousness once you get there? Do you even need to wait to get to 'there' or is there a way to joyously move in the direction of luminous consciousness and to grow our luminosity with each tiny increment, enjoying its glow as we go?

Is there a way to set this luminosity in motion in each new Now, so that there is not so much a goal but a constantly growing awareness of and competence in our own greatness? Is there a way to put this kinetic luminosity to use in the world? I believe that the answer is yes.

Mullah Nasruddin was a 13th century Sufi philosopher and wise man. Tales about Nasruddin often relay important lessons through funny stories and anecdotes. According to one such story, he lost his ring in the basement of his house, where it was too dark to see anything so small. He went out on the street and began to look for the ring there. A passerby asked him, "What are you looking for, Mullah Nasruddin?"

"I lost my ring in the basement," the mystic answered.

Of course, the man was surprised, and asked, "Why don't you look for it in the basement where you have lost it?"

"Don't be silly, man!" Mullah Nasruddin is said to have replied. "How do you expect me to find anything in that darkness?"

Looking for reality through your senses is like the drunk losing his keys in the dark and only looking around the lamppost, because that's where he can see. When you think that reality is only what you see, hear and feel, you forget that the information that comes in through your senses is always being interpreted. That *interpretation* is your reality.

You can interpret sensory input according to your habitual defaults, or you can choose the way you interpret that input. This book is about choosing to interpret in the energy and the language of greatness rather than the language of WMDs. You will be amazed at how infusing this Now with greatness impacts the greatness of every subsequent Now. It's like setting a boulder in motion at the top of a mountain – seeing and exhibiting greatness in this moment tumbles you into next moments that are full manifestations of ever-expanding versions of that greatness.

An artist I know told me once that she finds it frustrating when people respond to her lifelike figure drawings and portraits by saying things like "Wow, I could NEVER draw something that looks realistic..." and sometimes adding that the best they can do is a smiley face with a stick figure attached. "People who think they can't draw aren't *seeing*," she pointed out. "There's a way to accurately interpret what you see into lines on the paper. But if you aren't willing to really see and to make the effort to put what you see on paper, you haven't begun to try to draw." The smiley face with the stick figure is comparable to the default thinking to WMDs. We default to putting a symbolic representation on the paper instead of seeing what is in front of us – its true shape, definition and feel. But we can make the choice to exercise our powers of observation in a more intense and detailed fashion, and we can begin to translate that into a reality that resonates and sings rather than protests and moans. ❄

Chapter 8
Just Say No...to the Pursuit of Happiness

Most folks are about as happy as they make up their minds to be.
– Abraham Lincoln

Be yourself; everyone else is taken.
– Oscar Wilde, noted playwright, poet and author

Before my realization that one could use the Nurtured Heart Approach on one's self to create new defaults to success, I was already the author of an acclaimed book on dealing with challenging children. This book has helped thousands of parents, teachers and therapists with a highly positive approach that focuses almost exclusively on recognition and gratitude. Given that I had not only developed that approach but for years practiced and taught it, I was espousing positivity left and right, naturally thinking of myself as an amazingly positive person. Then I discovered, with a shock, that I was living a lie.

My *energetic* reality was, in actuality, fanning the flames of adversity. I was giving lip service to positivity, but pouring the intensity of my own inner energy, the life force of my being, into worry, misery and doubt. At that point, I started to investigate ways to turn this high level of recognition and gratitude back onto myself in ways that were truly beneficial. I now call this "greatness work." This work is about tools for becoming and remaining present in greatness in the context of our busy brains and busy lives. It is not, however, about pursuing happiness.

Let me explain. The mere pursuit of happiness holds the same dangers as the pursuit of pain. Neither fully prepares you for happiness, joy or greatness in this moment. Both set you up for reverting to the past or future. Whenever you experience worry, misery or doubt, you are anywhere and everywhere but Now.

Why on Earth would anyone ever engage in the pursuit of pain, you ask? Any time you mine the past's painful moments and hope for a better, happier future, that is exactly what you are doing – if inadvertently. If you have ever been in therapy, you understand what I mean by the pursuit of pain.

Traditional therapy is almost always about delving into past issues, problems and painful moments in an attempt to process, reframe and move toward a future that differs from the present. Although no one would dream of pursuing pain intentionally, this is the end result when you direct your energy out of the Now and into what you believe you lack. As you focus on problems and issues, the meta-message of your life force is that this Now isn't good enough; and that problems are more compelling than the beauty of the moment. This is even the case if you are trying to create solutions. I propose a different tack entirely: finding a way to be in each next new moment, with clarity and purpose – like using the refresh button on your Web browser to take you to another delightful dimension of life.

Before I began this practice of cultivating greatness, I was pretty dedicated to "being here now," in the moment, and it was hit or miss. Sometimes it was joyful; sometimes not. Then I met a couple of gurus who seemed to be in joy *all the time*. I thought: *Some part of the instruction manual must be missing. Maybe I didn't listen carefully enough. How do I get to joyful all the time?* Not everyone wants this, but I sure did and still do.

Hold on there, you might be thinking, *didn't you just say that this work is* **not** *about the pursuit of happiness?* Yes, I did say that, but it is the *pursuit,* I believe, where we go wrong. As long as we are in pursuit of something, we establish the mindset that we do not have it in *this present moment.* And as we focus on pursuing something we do not have, or that we had before but do not have anymore, we are energetically expressing love of something we currently lack.

A key realization for me as I developed the Nurtured Heart Approach was that when we lecture, yell, punish or otherwise have a strong reaction to a child's poor choices, we are in essence sending the child the message that he is most loved and most cherished when he makes those poor choices. Children are most drawn to adults when they radiate the most animation. And if that is most vividly present when things are going wrong, the child sees that enhanced adult presence in response to wrongdoing as motivation. Even if the adult is reacting with anger or trying to create as negative an experience as possible for the misbehaving child, the child still becomes hooked on that hit of adult energy and continues to misbehave to get more of it. (More about this in chapters to come.) Similarly, when we put our energy into what we do not have, we are pouring that energy, accidentally, into celebrating what is lacking and what we are not happy about.

When we stop *pursuing* happiness, we stop pouring energetic devotion and love into the past and the future, neither of which actually exists in the present. Then, we can settle into a joyful, purposeful relationship with the everlasting Now.

(In some schools of thought, a distinction is made between the definitions of 'happiness' and 'joy,' with the latter described as a state of being that embraces all of creation – the spiritual dimension of happiness. Here, I'll use these two words interchangeably.)

It could be said that our cultural obsession with hunting for a spiritual reality has dissociated some of us from our naturally joyous state. Through variations on the theme of "you'll find enlightenment soon" (someday, if you do these 'good' things and don't do these 'bad' things, you will become enlightened), we fall into the trap of separation from the divine.

Yoga teacher and writer Mark Whitwell says "Looking for IT – looking for the Divine – is like looking for your wallet." In other words, it creates a psychology of not having, or of not being – a feeling that something essential is missing or lost. As we continually focus on what we do not have or what we want to have, we pour precious energy into that sense of lack. This is similar to the inadvertent messages constantly given to children, where we accidentally celebrate them – give them a lot more energy, a lot more of our being, emotion and relationship – when things are going wrong...when they are lacking or falling short of expectations.

You have exquisite control over your vision and interpretation of the world through which you move each day, each moment. Put 1,000 people in the exact same setting and expose them to the very same stimuli, and they'll each experience it through their own filters and choices of what to bring to the forefront for emphasis – and what to allow to drift unseen to the rear of the frame. This greatness practice is an exciting elaboration and magnification of the tired old 'glass-half-full' question.

As I have explored the inner work described in this book and taught it in workshop settings, I have seen how we can create the Now instead of allowing our default perceptions and reactions to take control. We can breathe life into the version of Now that we choose – not only through our senses, but through the conscious, intentional filters we apply to what we sense and experience.

Julie, a young mom, told me, "When I go around in my house, I often catch myself looking at the floor and other surfaces, just looking for dirt, clutter or grime. I literally scan for things out of place, for messes to clean up. My eyes go there as though magnetized. It's endless, of course, and so I get really cranky and overwhelmed really fast…unless I can get myself to just *look up* and see other, more beautiful aspects of the house – the art on the walls, the carefully chosen objects on the mantle, the family pictures, the kids enjoying their afternoon in their toy room."

We can choose to focus on the junk, the dirt or the mess. Of course, as soon as you dust, new dust arrives to take its place; as soon as you shampoo the carpet, in trounces the dog with his muddy paws! Or we can choose to focus on what's beautiful, seeing the mess as only a fraction of the total experience rather than pouring lots of energy into 'that place of things being wrong.' (This doesn't mean we need to ignore the mess and live in squalor, either!) What I told Julie was, "That's a great reset…but consider, too, that you can channel that energy of frustration right back into empowering greatness. You can catch yourself in that frustrated place of eyes magnetized to dirt and clutter, reset yourself, and move that energy into acknowledging the greatness already existing in you and in your home!"

My approach to cultivating greatness works because it has its roots at the deep level of the energy that drives our perceptions, thoughts and responses. It doesn't fundamentally change this energy; it simply transmutes it. At first, it might feel slightly uncomfortable or even wrong, just because it's so different from the usual experience of life. Imagine you've spent your whole life upside down; upon righting yourself, you're going to feel strange for a while! However, on a deeper level, you will feel absolutely right and better than ever – unless you happen to be a bat, an opossum or a three-toed sloth.

At its root, this book is about *being great*. It's about finding and awakening the greatness that is already YOU. Oprah's name is in the title because her greatness is impossible to miss. It's there for all to see. My assumption is that Oprah's greatness is not an accident. I assume that she has found her own ways to fan the flames of her existing greatness and to discern and evolve new and even more magnificent aspects of her greatness. And with a few new downloads and upgrades of the software for seeing and perceiving, you will find your own greatness equally impossible to miss – and you will develop, at the same time, a heightened perception of the greatness in others.

This book is about discerning what "great" means and learning at least one way – but preferably many more – to go about igniting the greatness that you are and the greatness of the people whose lives you touch.

If you find yourself arguing against the points that follow, relax and put the book aside. What I am about to share is simply my truth, not the Gospel. My intention is to simply share the experiences and processes that have made an enormous difference in my life. These experiences keep unfolding and deepening as I keep checking in to confirm that they are continuing to work. I also keep checking in to discern whether the greatness I invoke is serving myself and others well. I can only say that I would never be writing this book if, for a second, I thought it was not genuinely serving this purpose.

Warning: If you dive into this work, you will find that the unfolding of your greatness will take on a life of its own. It may begin to feel like you're going out on a limb into a whole new way of thinking and perceiving. Do you think you can handle it? Is there a way to go out on a limb…and then to dance on it? This is the heart of greatness practice, and it's never the same dance twice. It never will be. And if you commit to it, you'll get to the point where you're OK with this uncertainty – where, perhaps, you will even learn to love it.

You should only take on this adventure if you are intent upon the unfolding of your greatness. This is a transformation you have to want. It's not for everyone. It does require effort, clarity of intention and the desire to live a fulfilling and wonderful life. If you have an unfulfilled desire to believe in yourself, to live in positivity and to live in greatness, this is a path that I believe will take you there.

Not believing in yourself can be the greatest, most nagging curse. It can undermine every choice, every action. Conversely, deeply believing in yourself can be the greatest blessing, infusing each choice and action with strength and power. The approaches described in this book will help you awaken to the trust and belief in yourself that's literally there for the taking. ❄

Greatness exercise. In the early days of the human potential movement, Dawna Markova, Ph.D., coined the phrase "random acts of kindness." I'd like to introduce the notion of 'random acts of greatness,' where we tell others about their greatness at any opportune moment. Begin to acknowledge the successes and qualities of people around you – the things that you see in them that make them great. But keep in mind that successes and qualities don't have to be big or major to be reflective of greatness; acknowledge the common or seemingly mundane signs of greatness, too. As you celebrate the greatness of others, you will begin to see it in yourself more and more.

Chapter 9

On Greatness

Greatness lies not in being strong, but in the right using of strength.
– **Henry Ward Beecher,** prominent clergyman,
lecturer and social reformer

The greatest thing a man can do in this world is to make the
most possible out of the stuff that has been given him.
This is success, and there is no other.
– **Orison Swett Marden,** motivational writer

I've written several books pertaining to the Nurtured Heart Approach. But they all can be boiled down to something deeper and more essential: They are all about *manifesting greatness*. A Nurtured Heart moment is a moment of remembering who you really are by appreciating qualities that directly pertain to the heart: wisdom, kindness, joy, compassion, intelligence and other qualities of greatness.

Greatness is the splendor of living one's dreams, the bounty of living one's passion and the valor of bringing that greatness to the world. This practice begins with literally *accusing* ourselves of goodness any time we see even a glimmer of a quality we wish to uphold and enhance in ourselves. Then we can feed those qualities with our energy and recognition, growing them into greatness. We do the same with others.

We are always either choosing to live by our greatness (our soul's light of all we are and can be) or by our lesser selves (our doubts, fears and worries) or by many modern forms of subconscious oblivion. This Nurtured Heart/greatness practice is a set of tools for recognizing greatness in ourselves and in others and for doing so consistently enough to eventually replace – or at least become more powerful than – those fears, doubts and worries in our minds and hearts.

It's hard to live by your greatness…until it is tasted, sensed and experienced. Once this happens, however, it's hard to turn back! Once you commit fully to this warrior path of your own truth and that of others – greatness – then you are truly choosing the life your higher self desires and envisions. Then, before you know it, the universe starts to kick in its support. It provides so much evidence that living by greatness works.

Someone asked me recently what I do for work. Before I could think about it, I responded "I'm an arsonist!" Why would I say this? Because my work is about *igniting the fires of greatness*. Start out with the intention to live in your greatness, and then refuse to be swayed from that intention. From there, use techniques described in this book to turn that spark of goodness into a raging blaze of greatness.

This practice provides us with a preview of a part of us that is, potentially, ready to awaken and come forward; and another part that is ready to fall away if we choose to no longer give it power. The key is to literally *hijack yourself* into this experience through the use of the techniques described throughout this book.

Seeing yourself in the light of greatness is a great gift. Once you take this path, you may never want to turn back. Gratefulness = greatfulness = great fullness = full of greatness.

"God is great" is spoken in many languages by people of many faiths. The greatness of God, or the greatness of any version of the divine ascribed to by a particular faith, is so widely accepted; and yet, universally, it seems so hard for so many people of these many traditions to fully drink in their very own greatness.

Only star-like beings such as heroic performers in sports, high achievers in the arts or sciences or other such celebrities seem to merit this kind of recognition – and then only in general terms. We credit them with greatness, but we don't generally acknowledge the component aspects of that greatness – the actual qualities of which it consists.

Isn't growth in specific areas of greatness what we are trying to achieve in our lives? Do you want to wake up tomorrow less great as a compassionate person, as a creative or loving person, as a thoughtful or considerate person? When we really think about it this way – in specific terms of greatness – we all want to be as great or greater tomorrow than we are today.

In quite a few faiths, it is customary to connect with and praise deities in highly specific terms. Some ancient and modern faiths have 100 or more names or descriptors for the divine. God is often described in terms of wisdom, grace, compassion, mercy, beauty and creativity to name just a few of these qualities. God is also known in many faiths as the almighty, the grantor of redemption, the provider of security, the just and many more names.

These are, in essence, qualities of greatness, and all these characteristics are inherent in human beings as well. Indeed, they are the qualities that connect us to our own divinity. Why not have 100 names or more for our own reflections of these divine qualities? After all, we could not see these qualities in our deities if we did not possess at least a glimmer of them in ourselves.

The greatness practice can be opened up to people of all belief systems with this syllogism: If God is great, and I wish to invoke the spirit of God in my life, then in part my invocation is to greatness.

If my prayer is about energetically connecting me to the divine, I choose to praise or pray at times with these specific divine qualities in mind rather than a global concept. In this way, I use prayer as a vehicle to further aspire to greatness on this earth in the forms of me and you and to make these aspects of divine presence so much richer and real as a personal experience.

Nevertheless, as deftly as we can attribute greatness to the divine – or to the divine we see in the few notables and icons who stand tall in their great deeds and great qualities – the average person struggles to accept attributes of his or her own greatness.

Recognition of your own greatness happens as you become aware of the constant unfolding of greatness in the Now. Its presence is a given; there it sits, ripe fruit ready to pick. All you need to do is discern it and enjoy it. You do so by putting your energy and focus there.

This is not about being happy-go-lucky, skipping through life and ignoring everything that doesn't send you over the moon. It is not about refusing to acknowledge the existence of anger, grief, fear and pain. Even while experiencing difficulties and challenging emotions, you not only can experience greatness, you can also use the enormous energy of these experiences and emotions to provide trajectories of greatness above and beyond the ordinary. (More on this in chapters to come.)

Living in your own greatness is about creating your own voice-over to any frame you select in the movie that is your life. It's about reflecting greatness with determined power and commitment. This can be done in this moment – no matter what happened in your childhood, last year, 10 minutes or 10 seconds ago – and regardless of whatever you anticipate will happen in the moments to come.

As you nurture yourself with focused intention and unswayable purpose, you take responsibility for your choices in the moment, giving yourself credit for all you are doing right in the Now. You gain power over your life as you remain fully committed to de-energizing all the WMDs that, predictably, will float in. You can move past the old self that sees itself as trouble, as inadequate, as a failure, as unworthy of love – as anything but great; and you can cultivate a new self-image that is all about your own greatness. And you can move from current levels of positivity to greater greatness all the time. When you set this intention strongly for yourself, everybody wins.

If you can feel one single spark of greatness in yourself or another, nothing stands in the way of your fanning of that flame. Nothing stands in the way of creating a new and brighter flame of greatness that then begins to have a life of its own. You see, it is a *given*.

How do I know that? Here you are, reading an inspirational piece. You wouldn't be doing that unless you were determined to learn and grow. You would have no interest in such a thing unless you were already conscious enough to appreciate the beauty of being inspired and determined to take steps to improve your life. These are all already magnificent qualities. And they in turn show wisdom and spirit, still other qualities of greatness.

In my experience, I have seen again and again that purposely fanning those flames creates a series of further awakenings to the greatness that is already inside. As you tentatively begin to breathe life into this fire, you first find that, at least in some ways, you are indeed already '*being* greatness.' Encouraged, you keep the air moving and find yourself *standing* in greatness. The fire takes on a life of its own, and before you know it, you find you are *living* greatness in bigger and bigger ways. All you have to do is fan that spark until it catches, and keep on feeding it. The great news is that the oxygen of simply *breathing* into it fuels that fire, and before long, it becomes a bonfire of greatness that consumes everything in its path. Instead of the winds being a deterrent, they propel and fuel this fire of greatness. Rain cannot extinguish this kind of fire. It brightens every person and every situation and can be seen from miles around.

You may not know this yet, but *YOU are that bonfire of greatness*. It is already within you, and the universe will celebrate your fanning the flames. This is not a game of hide-and-seek; you already are everything you wish to be. Once that fire is going, enjoying it will be simple and captivating. You will no longer have to seek out happiness. It will just be part of the joy of living in this manner. As you enter a space of being your greatness, everything around you will manifest in relation to this aspect of your being. You will attract others who are also living their greatness. You will see this quality in others as plainly as you see it in yourself. Lesser parts will no longer interest you or surface in your life.

Greatness exercise. I believe you can manifest and magnify greatness any time you decide to. I'd like to prove it is there for you. Allow me to take you on a quick journey to the truth of your life, assisted by the wonders of modern technology. I call this exercise 'Googling Greatness.' It will work just wonderfully if you read it to yourself and pause now and then to feel it fully; it will be even more wonderful if you can have someone else read it to you out loud as you close your eyes, breathe deeply and visualize as you go along. (Reciprocate for the other person when you're done.)

Imagine that you sit down to log onto the Internet. Much to your delight, you find that your connection is perfect and immediate. The access to sites is instantaneous and breathtaking, revealing information to which you have never before had access. And so, in delighting in this, it dawns on you to go to a search engine to see what you can find. In an inspired moment, you decide to enter in your name along with a plus sign and the word GREATNESS.

Much to your surprise, you find that the search nets you much more than you could ever have imagined. You find hundreds and hundreds of results. You scroll down and click on the first one that intrigues you in some way.

When you open it, you are stunned. Your heart starts beating faster than it has in a long time. You can't believe what you have come up with. Every page is loaded with notes about your particular qualities of greatness. Each paragraph has descriptions of qualities that amaze and excite you, just seeing them in print.

For example: One paragraph tells you that you have the great quality of being loving. Another talks about your great quality of being collaborative. Yet another talks about your greatness in terms of your brilliance – your ability to see around corners with your amazing insightfulness. The pages of qualities go on and on and on.

The other quirky thing about this treasure you've found is that so many of the paragraphs have parts that are high-lighted in blue. Just for the heck of it, you move the cursor over one, and you find that it's a link. You double-click on it, and it instantly leads you to page after page devoted entirely to evidence and examples of that one single quality men-tioned in that highlighted paragraph.

For example: This first link you open up has to do with the greatness of your wisdom. The link contains many pages all about your wisdom, featuring a long list of bullet points that document, to the minute, times that you exercised this qual-ity. On the 7th of March, 2001, for example, you were standing in line at the supermarket at 4:11 in the afternoon. The person in front of you was getting irritated that the clerk was listen-ing too long to the person in front of him. You wisely found a way to bring a smile to his face by using your sense of humor.

This is only one of dozens upon dozens of bullet-pointed examples evidencing your wisdom. The list goes on and on, with even more links to other qualities of greatness. Those links lead you to more pages about your sense of humor and kindness. You see other examples of ways you exhibited humor and kindheartedness through tense situations, help-ing others to suffer less stress.

Following one more link, you find another page that, at first, makes no sense. It seems to document times when you've been told or felt things about yourself that contradicted your greatness...perhaps times and dates during which kids or adults called you names or said harsh things to or about you. Then you see that each and every instance shows irrefutable proof that, had these people known about *themselves* what you now know about yourself – that they, too, are really great – they never would have said anything that did not support your greatness. Indeed, they wanted to support your greatness all along but just didn't know how. They simply wanted to connect with you, but at that time, with what those people did not know about themselves, that connection could only come through in the hurtful way it did.

Reading this is making you feel more alive than you've ever felt before. You are stunned. You decide you need to take a break and close this down for a while.

There's a glitch, however. Every time you attempt to close the page, it springs right back at you like a jack-in-the-box. Along with it pops up a box that simply says, "You might want to read this." It then proceeds to let you know the catch: the terms and agreements of having access to these pages.

It says: "To close this page and go on to anything else, you need to agree that you cannot now, or ever again, dismiss what you have read. You also cannot turn your back on what you now know.

"Further: you must agree to purposefully fan the flames of these qualities of greatness. You must agree to go back again and again to these pages until you embrace these qualities in a core way.

"Additionally: you must choose to be purposeful in NOT giving energy to anything that distracts or contradicts this in you. Rather, as soon as you feel the pang of that energetic impulse toward distraction from your greatness, you must quickly experience it and then reset yourself to purposefully MAGNIFY GREATNESS – that of YOU and that of OTHERS."

And in a flash, you agree.

It's official. There's no turning back.

I exhort you to experience your greatness. Even if you've seen just a glimmer of a quality, you have that quality, and it's yours. Even if you're seeing it in another…or if seeing that quality in a movie stirred one hair on your head or one extra beat of your heart, then that quality is in you. It exists, and it can be propelled. ❄

Chapter 10

On Intention

The pleasantest things in the world are pleasant thoughts: and the
great art of life is to have as many of them as possible.
– **Michel de Montaigne,** Rennaisance scholar

This default setting to worry, misery and doubt can make using the Nurtured Heart Approach difficult. Doing it well requires a strongly held intention to fire up our focus on successes, 'come hell or high water.' It requires that we tell the complete truth to the child we are working with, but even more, to *see* a truth that is all about success. We can't reflect success to a child if we don't see it, and we can't see successes unless we really know what we are looking for.

This requires techniques that expand and breathe new life into the definition of success, and those techniques are in this book. But techniques alone aren't enough. It also requires a level of resolve and determination: an unswayable intention to do whatever is necessary to give that child experience after experience of success.

It follows that this greatness practice begins not with learning any set of techniques, but with setting your intention to live in your own greatness.

Intention is enormously powerful. It is about bucking habit and taking your life and your power seriously. Both of these shifts are challenging in our culture, which encourages us to stay stuck in old habits and to avoid taking ourselves seriously for fear of being seen as arrogant or egotistical. Each of us gets to set our intention in our own lives, but this is easier said than done. Many forces conspire to prevent us from stepping into our own power.

Let's say you have a corner in your home that tends to get cluttered with stuff that doesn't seem to have its own place. You can look at that clutter and it can bother you enough for you to dive in and deal with it. But when you go at it with intention, you are saying to yourself and the world, "I am taking responsibility for this corner. I am reclaiming this space in my life. Those are objects I can move. I can inflict my power on this part of the world." Intention is the opposite of reactivity. Instead of simply reacting to the mess, you set an intention to take control over that space.

Intention implies a shift of consciousness that gives rise to action and change. The healing and the change happen with the intention. Any technique is an afterthought – a useful afterthought, perhaps, but not the key to transformation.

During my days living in New York City, I had a somewhat successful woodworking business. A man named Keedon, who was from Ethiopia, hired me to help with the remodel of an old farmhouse he and his American wife, Angie, had bought upstate. We became friends. Keedon had a radiant beauty, the likes of which I had never seen. Growing up in Paris, he had danced with Balanchine, and when we met he was working as a top New York City model. He possessed a radiant intelligence and a positive attitude. His presence stopped people in their tracks.

This renovation involved an enormous amount of demolition of interior walls and old lathe and plaster wall coverings. It created endless debris. We called ourselves the 'Crowbar Brothers' and joined forces in room after room, creating knee-deep piles of debris everywhere. Once the old stuff was down, we'd look around with a sense of accomplishment, but for me, the triumph was tinged with dread because such a massive cleanup was ahead.

I could easily have become overwhelmed. For Keedon, however, the attitude was "No problem!" He would start in one corner or another with a shovel and wheelbarrow, pile it high with debris, and wheel it out with glee. And next (which at first I found incomprehensible) he would take a broom and *sweep the newly revealed square foot or two of floor.* Then he would tackle the next square foot or two and add another cleanly swept bit to the room.

Before meeting Keedon, my approach to this task would have been to randomly skim the debris down from the top to try to lower the overall depth of the pile. I would have worked and worked at it, not seeing any progress until it was all done. My style would have led to overwhelm and exhaustion, while his created energy and a growing sense of renewal. By revealing even a square foot of the finished product, he effectively created a vision and a growing unfolding of that vision. He created a luminosity that motivated energetic movement in the direction of completion. With each couple of square feet he cleared and polished, he created a sense of accomplishment that he could then relish as he moved forward to the next step. This was a beautiful example of intention in action.

In a similar way, we can set an intention to clean and polish one small corner of our inner selves. We can see and appreciate a glimmer of helpfulness, gracefulness, lovingness, kindness, courage, or any one of the other qualities of greatness, and we can feel and sense and relish even that small corner. And this will move and motivate us to keep expanding into the greatness we already possess. All that we need to start with is some recognition – some intention to renew, some elbow grease and a satisfied glance – to encourage energized continuation of the task at hand. ❄

Chapter 11
The Soul Level of "The Secret"

You might have read Australian TV producer Rhonda Byrne's book *The Secret*. Millions of people did, and it had a strong effect on many of them. If you haven't yet read it, the gist is that, with the power of positive thinking, you can manifest anything you desire in your life – and when you think negative thoughts, you attract negativity into your life. Byrne famously posits that we can even create inclement weather with our thoughts and that we can create abundant material wealth simply by understanding and applying the power of positive thinking.

Many people who read *The Secret* are most intrigued by the personal-gain aspect of the book. *Put your note on the wall, think rich, believe rich, imagine your life as a rich person, and the requisite funds will appear.* It's about the universe as a giant shopping mall, waiting to cater to those who catch wind of 'the secret.' The book also creates a dividing line between those who understand and apply this secret, and those who can't or won't. It encourages us to turn our backs on those who, for whatever reason, just don't get it. And when Byrne's techniques for manifesting our desires through positive thinking fail, it's never the fault of the techniques – it's the fault of the person who didn't use them correctly.

The "Publishers Weekly" review of this book stated that "supporters will hail this New Age self-help book on the law of attraction as a groundbreaking and life-changing work, finding validation in its thesis that one's positive thoughts are powerful magnets that attract wealth, health, happiness... and did we mention wealth? Detractors will be appalled by this as well as when the book argues that fleeting negative thoughts are powerful enough to create terminal illness, poverty and even widespread disasters."

One might think that the greatness practice is similar to the practices divulged in *The Secret*. They do have some similarities, and I believe that energetically, Byrne is on the right track. But I see the greatness practice as *the soul level of The Secret*.

To practice the Law of Attraction as described in *The Secret* – the idea that you can bring what you desire into your life by thinking vividly about it – you have to come up with very specific intention and vision. Byrne encourages readers to meticulously construct their visions, to the extent that they can actually *inhabit* them. The logic goes, then, that matter will fall into shape around that vision and intention, and your desires will manifest themselves in concrete reality.

With greatness work, your intention is simply to energize the core aspects of your greatness and the greatness of others. This precedes specific vision of or intention toward material wealth, physical health or other concrete ends. In the process, you become addicted not to your vision of having a billion dollars or living to be 100 while always looking like you're 40, but to *greatness itself.* As you love this life more and more, giving and receiving ever more love from the universe, visions will come to you without your having to construct them. Such visions are organic and congruent with your true nature – to what your soul really wanted in the first place. These visions are true to your divine inheritance. Prosperity on a soul level will then emerge in surprising and delightful forms. Some will directly or indirectly relate to money; but ultimately, a narrow view of wealth as something that's only about finances limits one's view of true prosperity. The prosperity that comes in alignment with greatness will always be congruent with what is in your heart.

With this intention, you awaken the remembrance of your inborn greatness – quite a different thing from invoking/evoking it from an outside source. You are giving your soul a voice, allowing it to say what it has always wanted to say and be what it has always wanted to be. Moving one's soul even one inch closer to actualizing its greatness brings a truckload of prosperity in every shape and form.

Puran Bair's take on the concepts of *The Secret* is that the universe is, indeed, a wish fulfillment system – with a delay. The purpose of the delay, he says, is to give us the time and space to ascertain that we really want what we are wishing for. When we wish for wealth or that perfect partner, the universe responds not to the wish itself, but to our underlying confusion about what we want. We might have held a clear vision of what we wanted for 10 minutes or 10 hours, but as soon as we begin to entertain doubt, we have undermined the integrity of that vision. Energetically, we have refined the vision to be one of doubt…and that is what is delivered. As you begin instead to focus your intention on seeing and being in greatness, ambivalence disappears. You become released from doubts about what it is you *really* want. In the resulting place of clarity, you live your way into your wishes. ❄

Chapter 12

New-Age Hell

Mark Whitwell, founder of the Heart of Yoga Foundation, talks about "new-age hell," where people are caught in endless seeking rather than understanding deeply that they are *already there*. They already have 'it.' They already are greatness. So many seekers get caught in the rat-cage of trying to know God as though they were not already living and breathing this fullness. At a workshop I attended with Whitwell, I remember him saying "If we take a shower every day, and we have a sense of knowing this feels good, it becomes a non-issue. We shower every day. We don't then have to take three and one-half showers on Sunday in order to have this feeling. We have direct intimacy with our own life."

If you are looking for happiness and enlightenment, you are, in effect, reinforcing unhappiness and un-enlightenment. Seeking the solution is what creates the problem. We all come here as perfect vehicles of love.

Buddha said "Life is suffering." J. Krishnamurti, a renowned writer and speaker on philosophical and spiritual subjects, said "The end of sorrow is the beginning of wisdom." I don't find these statements to oppose one another; the Buddha found that suffering could be overcome by being present and good in each Now. This is where sorrow ends and wisdom begins.

The soul sees beauty, grace and greatness. To be congruent with your soul is to see and say what your heart sees, feels and wishes to express. The heart is always truthful and crystal clear and always expresses the soul's desire. Just ask your heart and you will receive. It's always there for the taking. ❄

Greatness exercise. Do you ever find yourself wishing for the opposite of what you thought you had wanted? The heart and mind often wish for opposing things. If you place your attention precisely in the heart, your intention becomes clearer.

Bring yourself to a quiet moment and choose to give your heart a voice. Ask your heart what it wants. It will always tell you the truth. Give your heart's voice a hundred votes. Ask your heart what quality of greatness is wanting to come forward at this time in your life. Is it the greatness of generosity, of independent thinking, of intelligence, of bravery, of the ability to experience deep emotions? Is it the greatness of wisdom, compassion, thoughtfulness or power? Think not in terms of what you wish you had but think you don't; try to identify a quality that you already see a glimmer of in yourself.

Invoke this greatness in the simplest possible way for now: envision yourself standing tall in this quality. Imagine yourself feeling the excitement of being that quality and saying to yourself with pleasure "I am this greatness."

Chapter 13
Your Thoughts Can Change Your Brain

The idea that the brain can change its own structure and function through thought and activity is, I believe, the most important alteration in our view of the brain since we first sketched out its basic anatomy and the workings of its basic component, the neuron. Like all revolutions, this one will have profound effects. The neuroplastic revolution has implications for, among other things, our understanding of how love, sex, grief, relationships, learning, addictions, culture, technology, and psychotherapies change our brains.
– **Norman Doidge, M.D.**, *The Brain that Changes Itself*
(Penguin, 2007)

People with amputations often experience sensations in the limb that was amputated. Sometimes, these sensations have to do with actually moving the limb; in one experiment, a neuroscientist found that a person with an amputated arm could actually feel the arm reaching out to grab something on the table. Often there is a feeling of "fullness" of the amputated limb or a feeling like the limb is shorter than the limb on the other side.

More often, the phantom limb experiences pain. The person usually reports that the pain is much like what is experienced when a limb that has "fallen asleep" begins to get sensation again: pins and needles, burning, cramping or stabbing sensations.

Phantom limb pain is believed to be caused by damage to nerve endings that continue to send information to the brain. That information is translated within the brain as the existence of a phantom limb or as pain in that limb.

One researcher found a way to cure this pain by altering the brain's perceptions. He used a special mirror box that enabled the amputee to think that he was "moving" the amputated limb. The mirrors made the person's existing limb look like it was actually the amputated limb, and this perception of moving the amputated limb allowed the brain to change in response. This relieved phantom limb pain in this particular experiment. The patient's brain was altered by this treatment in a way that changed its translation of those signals from the vicinity of the amputated limb.

When a person loses his sight, the centers of the brain that process auditory information – the information that comes in through hearing – expand, and hearing becomes more sensitive. A person who has suffered a stroke and resulting paralysis can regain function with the right kind of therapy – therapy that trains an undamaged part of the brain to do the work the damaged part used to do.

When it comes to thought, memory and intelligence, an old dog *can* learn new tricks. New brain cells can form in response to the right kind of stimulation. When we learn from emotions and social interactions, our brains change.

Neuroplasticity describes the ability of the brain to change its physical structure in response to the environment. 'Neuro' refers to the cells that make up the nerves and brain; 'plastic' means changeable or modifiable. For most of the history of modern medicine, scientists and doctors have believed that brain structure is set for life by the time we reach adulthood; but in recent years, major discoveries have tossed that notion on its head. The brain changes physically with each activity and thought – not only at the level of the different lobes and structures of the brain, but also at the level of the genes that orchestrate the brain's function.

Depression affects specific circuits in the brain. This is being confirmed, at this writing, by research into the use of electrical stimulation of those circuits as a fix for severe depression that is not responsive to therapy or medications. Norman Doidge, the physician quoted in the epigraph for this chapter, traveled around talking to neuroscientists and patients as he wrote his book; about these travels, he writes in his blog: "I saw people rewire their brains with their thoughts, to cure previously incurable obsessions and traumas."

When it comes to shifting the brain out of depressive patterns, it turns out that behavioral interventions like those used in therapy have *more* specific effects on these neural circuits than antidepressant medications do. When psychiatrists prescribe medication after medication to try to cure a patient's depression, they are using what amounts to blunt instruments in comparison to the fine, delicate tools that can be wielded with the right psychotherapeutic interventions. These kinds of interventions, research shows, can affect neurochemical circuits very specifically.

In the brain, an area called the *prefrontal cortex* is strongly involved in the making of decisions. It is connected to another area, the *amygdala*, which picks up on threats to one's safety. Depressed people have greater activity in the amygdala than non-depressed people. In people who recover more quickly from stressful events, there is greater activation of the prefrontal cortex (PFC) than in those who don't bounce back as well; the PFC, it seems, overrides the amygdala's stressful messages...you know, those WMDs.

PFC activity also affects hormonal activity in the body. A study of teenagers who had strongly activated PFCs showed lower levels of *cortisol* – the so-called 'stress hormone' – in the evenings, when cortisol is supposed to drop low to allow for rejuvenating sleep. The conclusion that can be drawn is that higher PFC activity means a better response to stress and improved ability to rest and relax.

Here's the kicker: many experts believe that you can increase PFC activation with your thoughts. Stronger interconnectedness between PFC and amygdala, as well as other changes in brain anatomy, can be built with intentional activity...intentional activity such as the greatness practices described in this book.

Fear, worry and doubt have a similar effect on neurochemical balance in the brain and body. These emotions/thoughts trigger biochemical changes. Even a tiny morsel of WMD will create a wave of negative biochemical reactions in the mind and heart. The flip side is that even a small movement into seeing and being greatness will create positive biochemical reactions. There is no real division between thought and the body. They are inextricably intertwined. So why not learn to use this to our advantage?

This is a brand new frontier, but it's some of the most compelling information to come up in psychiatry in centuries. It may be the key to getting us out of the diagnose-and-medicate trap and into a new groove where transformational thinking is seen as far more precise a medicine than any pharmaceutical chemical.

Many professionals already view symptoms of depression, anxiety and other frustrating circumstances as indicative of an existential crisis that calls out for holistic healing, not the masking of symptoms with medications. I have found that healing in a core way comes from using the energy of the 'problems' to propel the shift to greatness. With this diversion of WMD energy, the very same intensity that has been stuck and gone awry becomes the source of further greatness. In medicating the intensity away, we risk giving the message that something is essentially wrong with the medicated person's life force. But if instead we redirect this intensity, the beauty of that person's life force is revealed. ❄

Chapter 14

Inhaling into Your Blueprint: An Introduction to Heart Rhythm Meditation

Most spiritual practices ask us to look at our true selves – at the self that is not the ego, nor the expectations of others, but that is our divine inheritance – the blueprint from which we are all made. This true and fundamental foundation is what each human being shares, but it is easy to forget in the complexity of modern life. In this greatness practice, we refer to this true self as greatness, and it comes from and resides in the heart.

An important aspect of living in your greatness is living from the heart. Ask your mind about your greatness and it may waffle, rationalize and cast doubt. Ask your heart, the seat of your soul and the soul of the universe, and you'll get nothing but clarity – emphatic, energized, uncompromised positivity. Your heart is, subconsciously, already opening doors. Even when we have amnesia about what the heart wants because of distractions, needs, drama or fears, the heart remembers.

Puran and Susanna Bair teach people how to live from the heart, and they do this through a practice called Heart Rhythm Meditation. Puran and Susanna happen to be great friends and colleagues of mine, and we have discovered that our heart-centered approaches can be used collaboratively to deepen and intensify one another. These meditation practices center you in your heart, which is where you can most easily make the leap to believing in your own greatness.

Heart Rhythm Meditation (HRM) is based on the teachings of two Sufi mystics, Pir-o-Murshid Hazrat Inayat Khan and Pir Vilayat Inayat Khan. In the Introduction to his first book, *Living From the Heart: Heart Rhythm Meditation for Energy, Clarity, Peace, Joy, and Inner Power* (Three Rivers Press, 1998), Puran writes that Heart Rhythm Meditation allows you "to become conscious of the beats of your heart and thereby get in touch with your most basic rhythm and your deeper feelings. You will gain the ability to tune your attitude, approach, and actions to express harmony and the other qualities of heart, especially love, creativity, and courage." (page 1)

The first step is to become aware of your heartbeat. It is easiest to feel the heartbeat throughout the body (not by taking your pulse, but experienced from the inside) while holding your breath, so try taking a big breath in and holding it as you feel your heart beating. Hold the breath for 20 to 30 seconds to get the full feeling of the heartbeat in every part of your body. Notice where its beat is especially pronounced.

The next exercise Puran suggests is to breathe more or less normally, but with an extra three seconds spent in exhalation. This is to expel stale air that is normally found in the lungs and to create more space for a fuller inhalation. At the bottom of each exhale, you will strongly feel your heartbeat. This practice is the foundation of Heart Rhythm Meditation; try staying with it for a few minutes, resetting your focus on the heartbeat any time your mind begins to wander.

In *Living From the Heart,* Puran writes that "the inhalation that follows a full exhalation is so powerful that it can make whatever change you envision. There are two requirements: having a vision and an exhalation." (page 153)

Continue feeling the heartbeat as you next do this: For eight beats of your heart, inhale; for the next eight counts, exhale. Keep your awareness fully in your heart (out of your mind); if it wanders, gently reset your attention back to your heartbeat. This is *breathbeat,* connecting lungs and heart.

Puran says that "using this method of conscious heartbeat linked to conscious breath enables conscious change." When we link HRM to the Nurtured Heart Approach used internally, we are attaching conscious heartbeat and breath to conscious purpose and vision. This is a way to choose change with a purpose, in a direction that can both create and fulfill your inner vision of yourself. "When you realize your light nature," Puran writes, "you will be happy to change anything that would allow you to be more luminous." This light nature is your greatness.

Let's assume that this light nature is already present in you, although it may be obscured by your personal history or current situation. If you choose to believe this, the next thing to do is reveal it. It's just like cleaning a room: one needs to start somewhere. No matter where you start, you can go from that place to eventually completing the task.

The equivalent of clearing a little space in that messy room is to consciously create a powerful exhalation and powerful inhalation. At the same time, pick a quality that you are drawn to, one that you would like to have more of within yourself. Say it to yourself as if you already possess it. You're creating successes and choosing how you see yourself.

I might only get a fleeting glimpse of that luminosity when I own any of the qualities of greatness listed in Chapter 19. But that luminosity can ignite and expand with continued recognition. Again: that light nature is your greatness. Its luminosity is increased through practice.

Think of the heart as a container with a reflective surface. This surface reflects any and all light into the heart center. Light beams from the bottom of the heart, plus the clarity of the rest of the heart, multiply and amplify it.

Being great is an act of love. Filling this heart container with the greatness you recognize in yourself and others creates a rate of refraction that is your luminosity. Once you find and fan the light of your greatness, you have started the stage of your life in which you are living it. Living it, breathing it and heart-beating it out to your world will create a luminosity that will provide a lot of light for a lot of people.

We'll revisit Heart Rhythm practices throughout the remainder of this book. ❄

Chapter 15

Composting 10,000 Dead Chickens

Puran Bair, meditation teacher and creator of Heart Rhythm Meditation, also happens to know a great deal about composting. He was inspired to learn how to make compost by a composting expert who helped a commercial chicken farmer, who had lost about 10,000 chickens to a virulent illness, turn all of those thousands of poultry corpses into compost.

Picture in your mind's eye how large a pile of meat, feathers, bones and viscera this composting expert was being asked to turn into dirt. If you compost vegetable wastes from your kitchen, you've probably been told not to put meat or bones into your compost. If you've done so by accident, you may have ended up with ruined compost and a noxious odor of rotting flesh emanating from your compost bin. How could anyone make compost out of exactly these ingredients?

As it turns out, there are techniques that will turn all those chicken carcasses into soil in the course of only a few weeks – without bad odors, putrefied groundwater or invasions of vermin.

The composting bin for achieving this end has to have a moisture-impermeable floor (concrete is best), a roof and three components: a nitrogen source (birds, manure, plant litter), a carbon source (pine shavings, peanut hulls, straw) and specific aerobic organisms – bacteria that make quick work of decomposing the animals. With all of these ingredients in place, the composting process creates so much heat that any disease-causing bacteria are killed off. This is a clean, efficient, environmentally sound way to dispose of 10,000 dead chickens. To do it, you just have to know how it's done.

One could think of the Nurtured Heart Approach as a similarly clean, efficient way of improving your life. Composting is a form of alchemy, and so is this approach: You take ingredients you already have possession of – worry, misery, doubt – that may be debilitating and even destructive in their current form and turn them into something else by taking advantage of their underlying intense energy. You use specific strategies to compost them into greatness – fertile soil in which you can root, grow and be nourished. ❄

Greatness exercise. Here you will be using the breath, synchronized with the heartbeat, as a rhythmic structure for a greatness meditation that will move negative energy – your very own personal 10,000 dead chickens – into appreciation of greatness: rich soil ready for planting.

Recall a recent instance when any personal worry, misery or doubt came rolling in uninvited. Purposely and consciously feel the angst of the emotion underlying whatever the issue was. Feel it deeply and intensely for a brief few moments.

Then, lock in to the idiosyncratic power of that negative emotion. Use the 'energy' of that feeling to propel a single thought pertaining to your greatness. Send that energy into an appreciation of a particular quality of your greatness: you being thoughtful, considerate, intuitive, wise or efficient; making a choice worthy of appreciation; or any other quality that comes to mind. It might just be a simple statement such as "I have the greatness of wisdom." Move your energy to support the choice to recognize and appreciate your greatness.

Then, introduce breath to this thought of greatness, synchronizing the breaths with your heartbeat. Aim to make the inhale and exhale equal in length, taking the same number of heartbeats. Send the thought of greatness deeply into your heart on the inhale, and deeply out to the world on the exhale. Keep this up for a few minutes, using the propulsion of the emotional energy.

Compare how it feels to 'breathe' this with your eyes closed and then again with your eyes open looking out into your life. Relish the thought. Enjoy the energy of greatness!

Chapter 16

Upside-Down Energy

When I teach parents, teachers and counselors how to use the Nurtured Heart Approach with children, I begin with a few concepts – concepts that are so simple that they sometimes, at first, evoke a touch of surprise from people who are used to things being complicated. I used to like complex ideas, theories and practices, too, but I became exceedingly simple when I realized that simple works better. Have you ever heard that old medical school axiom, *when you hear hoof beats, think horses, not zebras?* Starting with the most obvious, uncomplicated answer to a tough question just makes good sense.

For example: Just about every adult has, at some point, known a child who seemed *addicted* to pushing boundaries. Whether it's someone else's child or your own, when you look at him, you see a kid who seems to have a vendetta against adults, launching headlong into breaking rules and causing chaos. Many explanations have been offered to explain the behavior of the difficult child, including brain dysfunctions, early childhood wounding, unmet developmental needs, parental incompetence, family dysfunction, need for independence, physical illness, and need for a better diet. Psychologists and educators devote countless hours to ferreting out solutions for difficult children in hopes of solving the problem and giving the child motivation to straighten up and fly right. While all of these elements can play a role in a child's behaviors, none of them has yet been found to tell the whole story.

In my therapy practice, I specialized in working with exactly these types of children. (Having been a difficult child myself, I felt empathy for these children and sympathy for adults who were doing all they could to help the child turn things around.) And I tried all kinds of complex approaches to help them and their families achieve a more peaceful, successful way of being.

When I first started out, it seemed that every bit of advice I gave actually ended up making the situation worse instead of better. All the recommendations I was giving had been taken from classes I had attended or methods I had been taught or read about. Every bit of it – as intellectually appealing as it may have felt at the time – seemed to backfire. And when it did, I naturally tried harder and used the advised strategies in a more determined way. And still, things continued to fall apart. Somehow, I was contributing to the demise of these families.

Then, through a combination of intuition, divine guidance, and what felt like total molecular recall of my own challenging childhood, I developed the ability to feel, see and sense the energy between each family member during each interaction I witnessed. This led me to develop an approach that brought about so many rapid turnarounds that other child therapists began to send me their toughest cases.

In fact, I am most indebted to the toughest cases. It was those many and varied challenges that really 'cooked' the approach I began to experiment with. The really tough cases made it clearer and clearer that this approach could work with virtually any difficult child. (It soon became apparent that it could also help even the high-achieving, great-behaving kids flourish at even greater levels of inner wealth.)

In the first few years of its spinning into existence, this approach didn't have a name. Then one day, I remembered an event from 15 years earlier. I had been at a meditation retreat and suggested to a teacher that he name his method "The Nurtured Heart Approach." After a few moments of quiet and peaceful thinking with closed, contemplative eyes, he turned to me and said "No, that's the name for *your* approach." Mind you, at that time, I didn't even *have* an approach. I was taking a break from my work as a psychologist to pursue interests in art and spiritual practices. Fifteen years later, the approach had been born, and the name fit like a glove.

What was I doing that others weren't? I was boiling the seemingly complex problems of the difficult child into an issue of *upside-down energy;* in other words, that adults were often giving significant energy to the child's poor choices, but rarely to his or her good choices.

Imagine little Tommy throwing a punch at his friend Trevor during an argument. The parent in charge, if he is a responsible and good-hearted parent, is likely to spend a lot of time talking to Tommy about how we don't hit, it's not nice to hit, our friends don't feel safe around us when we hit, how it makes everyone feel bad and how Tommy is having *bad behavior* when he hits. Or, some parents might even preface this lecture by physically grabbing or spanking Tommy in a way that shows him that, while he isn't supposed to physically hurt someone else, adults can and do overpower those who are smaller than they are. No wonder children end up confused.

Whether the child gets a gentle lecture or a spanking, the end result is that the child gets all kinds of lively energy, connection and relationship in response to his poor choice. Even the parent who merely begins to warn Tommy not to hit as the argument escalates is giving energy to Tommy's decision to break the rule.

The meta-message to the child is, "Don't break the rules! And by the way, here's 100 bucks. Now quit breaking the rules already!" The more intense the child, the more he tunes into that energetic message, and the harder it is for him to resist the call of that 100 bucks (in the form of the parent's focus, attention, relationship and energy) for his negative behavior. Of course, no one would actually give a child even a cent for breaking a rule on purpose, but my point is that *energetically*, we inadvertently hand out the big bucks all the time. Children feel relatively invisible when they are not breaking the rules and perceive the juicy connection when they do.

Fast-forward to a few minutes later, as the boys play quietly with a building toy. They're sharing and cooperating. Do you think the average adult has anything to say about this? No; he or she is probably doing his or her best to get something else done before the wheels fall off again. If anything, the responses are energetically low-key, and Tommy begins – rightfully so – to feel invisible. And now, not only is Tommy drawn to getting energetically re-connected – to getting that next $100 bill from the adult in charge – but Trevor is being drawn to get a piece of this action, too. There are so many rules to be broken and there is so much connection to be had.

It's not at all diabolical. It's not a child out to ruin a parent's day. It's simply a child falling under the spell of a compelling force field. We all want close connection and intimacy; we all want to feel the life force of those who are meaningful to us. Children brilliantly and readily read how that is best available. (We all do, for that matter.)

Traditional approaches to discipline usually involve relatively neutral, un-energized feedback when things are going right...when the child is following the rules. Typically, the most the child gets is a lukewarm "good job!" or "thank you!" in return for her good behavior. But when she breaks rules and pushes boundaries, she is lavished with energy and relationship in the form of detailed, colorful lectures, warnings, threats, admonishments, reprimands, discussions, consequences and – usually – parents who get a lot more animated and interesting to be around when they're getting their buttons pushed.

Inevitably, during rounds of button-pushing, the adult is much more present and shows up in juicier ways, creating a relatively more intensely charged connection when things are going wrong. And the more things proceed on the wrong track, the harder the adults try, and the more energetic evidence they inadvertently deliver, belying their true goal of persuading the child not to break the rules.

The bottom line of the Nurtured Heart Approach is this: *The intense and difficult child is actually an energy-challenged child* who is drawn to the strongest possible texture of adult energy. He doesn't care how he gets it. He wants that million-dollar check but doesn't see that there's a negative sign in front of it.

The Nurtured Heart Approach takes advantage of the difficult child's overwhelming craving for adult energy and quality connection time by bringing forth detailed, colorful recognitions and appreciations *when the child is following the rules* or *when the child isn't breaking any rules*. It details several specific strategies for doing this. The techniques give adults tools for pouring their energy into acknowledging the child's successes. This immediately begins to provide the child with first-hand experiences of success, which grow the child's inner wealth.

As the upside-down energy of usual disciplinary approaches is turned right-side up, the child has an experience of what I call *time-in*. As the emphasis shifts to positives, rule-breaking and boundary pushing are *de*-energized. Energy is no longer given to negativity. Through trial and error and intense observation – not only my own, but that of many others who have worked this approach and helped me refine it – these techniques have been fine-tuned to the point where they work reliably and beautifully and can be applied with increased intensity to deal with even the most intense child.

One of the biggest challenges adults face in applying the techniques of the Nurtured Heart Approach to children in their lives is their own conditioning. Most adults were raised with traditional disciplinary approaches, and they are deeply conditioned to put far more energy toward what's going wrong than what's going right. Most adults do this to themselves, too, placing much more energy and emphasis into criticism and judgment than into seeing how they and others are successful. They don't see qualities of greatness, but instead see problem after problem that needs fixing in themselves and others. (If I'm wrong about you, great – you're way ahead of where I was when I started to do this work on myself.)

If you consider yourself to be a relatively positive person, consider right now the 'charge' or level of energy you give to WMDs. Is it qualitatively stronger than the energy you give to your own successes? Are you qualitatively more available and vivid, more emotionally demonstrative, when something's wrong than when things are going along smoothly?

If you are, don't worry – you're in the majority. Most of us are more present and 'alive' when we are faced with problematic thoughts or events than when we are pleased with something positive. In response to the good stuff, we are relatively low-key. We delve into problems with so much more tenacity than we typically display to energize gratitude and success.

In fact, we are generally far better at seeing problems in the first place than we are at seeing successes. Whether we believe in evolution or not, we have to admit that once upon a time, many generations ago, our ancestors had to avoid predators in order to survive. This was a matter of species preservation, and we wouldn't be here now if this did not exist in our ancestors. It wasn't prudent for them to wait until a predator was upon them to make the urgently important decision to flee or to fight; they needed to sense out any tiny increments of danger – any small hint that something was possibly headed their way.

Fast-forward a few million years. What parent can't walk into his child's room and automatically see – with great vividness – all that remains to be completed or that hasn't been started and needs to get done? Genetically, we are still wired to maintain that gift for seeing, microscopically, what's wrong with the picture. We still have remnants of that fear-based brain that gets called into action at the drop of a hat. And when it engages, we are so talented at waxing poetic over what we perceive as wrong. We can go on and on almost effortlessly, the momentum building, fortifying the arguments we make in favor of how the situation needs to be fixed. In comparison, how well do we launch the argument for what is already going right? How vivid are our positive comments? What recognitions do we make for what is done right aside from "thank you" and "good job"?

Do you shrink from the very idea of giving yourself a pat on the back for successes, thinking that this somehow makes you egotistical or arrogant? Do you silently wait and hope for others to acknowledge your successes? Would you like to know how to acknowledge them in a way that would propel not only their qualities of greatness but your qualities of greatness as well?

I have developed some simple techniques that can help you talk to yourself in a way that makes you your own greatest fan – and, at the same time, the greatest fan of others. (There's no shortage of greatness to go around; ultimately, your greatness enhances rather than diminishes mine. It's not a competition.) You can even cheer yourself or others on for your successes with the energy of an admiring audience at the concert of a famous rock star. Instead of being sidetracked, mind-blown, confused, blaming or depressed when things go wrong, you can go to greatness and give yourself or others a new chance at success in any next moment. As you read further, you'll find out how. ❄

Greatness exercise. Check in with your own thoughts periodically throughout the day. How do you talk to yourself? Do you talk to yourself at least as gently as you would talk to a cherished and revered loved one? Or do you criticize and talk down to yourself surprisingly often? How often do you heartfully, enthusiastically acknowledge yourself for things you've done right?

Adults learn early on to energize negativity and to avoid making a big deal over successes, and this pattern, whether in blatant or subtle ways, can so easily become a default setting. With this greatness work, we will turn this pattern around.

For now, just hold the knowledge that most of us could stand to be a good deal kinder to ourselves. Who would it hurt if we were? For that matter, who would it hurt for us to root ourselves on, just as we'd root for our favorite teams? Consider the possibility.

Chapter 17

Why Oprah?

This book is not really about Oprah Winfrey.

My point in bringing up this magnificent woman with whom most of the planet is on a first-name basis is to hold her up as an example of greatness. She exemplifies greatness.

She is admired by hundreds of millions of people around the world – myself included. She has positively impacted many, many lives. Aside from the schools in Africa and other human rights and charitable work, aside from the big giveaways, and aside from her book club that has renewed interest in great books to a culture that seemed to have forgotten them, what we see and sense in Oprah again and again is the level of greatness she has manifested. And what ultimately attracts us to her and to other people who are great, I believe, is our interest in manifesting *our own* greatness. I have come to believe that manifesting greatness is a choice – a choice that people can make in any and every moment of their lives. In my experience, people get excited about making that choice as soon as they sense it's there for them – and once they sense what's at stake if they do not go in that direction.

Oprah might well have more daily issues to face than the average person. Someone whose presence is so amplified and magnified is bound to have amplified and magnified challenges as well. However, I am also certain that her problems do not dictate her inner state; that, as for any mystic, it's the other way around – *her inner state dictates her view of the challenges.* My guess is that when she senses a problem on its way, she reads it as a sign that she needs to push herself to even greater heights. I seriously doubt she spends much time sitting around obsessing about potential future problems or about any mistakes she's made in the past.

Surely, great things are expected of Oprah by others and by herself, and these expectations themselves might play an enormous role in a person's ability to step up and manifest magnificence.

Jesus Christ was hailed as a savior and great teacher from birth; this must have affected his ability to step into and live in his own greatness in each moment...to feel and experience it deeply, to see it in others and to stand in greatness under any and all circumstances.

Maybe Jesus got to manifest his greatness so clearly *because* everyone saw his divinity from early on and treated him accordingly. Consequently, the 'portfolio' of who he was had only this stunning information. Wouldn't it have been the height of sadness if Jesus had not had the inner strength or resolve to handle the responsibility thrust upon him? Or if he had doubted his 'transmissions' from God because he did not have the inner wealth to believe in himself? Or if he became frightened by the daunting task of delivering his message against huge opposition? How many others have fallen short of their missions because they lacked the inner wealth to live their birthright of greatness? Every day, a great many people pass out of this life without ever having seen themselves reflected as people of greatness.

As far as I have seen in my own study of this subject, attaining the kind of greatness we see in Oprah requires that we hold a clear expectation and intention that each new progression of Nows will be a success and not a disaster. And it requires as well that we have a powerful and clear plan for when a problem actually does begin to emerge. We acquire that expectation through experiences of success whereby we can 'hijack' ourselves into a new and powerful portfolio of who we *really* are: persons of greatness, with many unique and exciting qualities of magnificence that make us the perfect complement to life on this great planet. ❄

Greatness exercise. Think of the person you most admire – your favorite, most respected human being. How is that person great? Make a list of the qualities you most admire in this person. Then, tuck the list away; we will return to it later.

Chapter 18

Shamu: Molecules into Miracles

How do you teach a multi-ton orca whale to leap over a rope strung high above its pool? That is the question faced by trainers who prepare Shamu, the orca whale, to do this famous stunt. The trick has been taught not to one single Shamu, but to his many namesakes over the years.

Do Shamu's trainers dangle a fish high in the air, hoping to get this amazing creature to jump for it over a rope? No. They actually start with the rope much lower than you might think. In fact, they start with the rope at *the very bottom of the tank.*

As soon as the whale first cruises over the rope, he gets recognition and affection from his trainers. Slowly, gradually, the rope is raised, and Shamu eventually makes the connection between swimming over this twisty thing in his tank and the energy of rewards and appreciation he receives. Eventually the rope comes out of the water and Shamu keeps going over it to get *the energy.*

When adults are introduced to using the Nurtured Heart Approach with children, they hear this story early on and are reminded of it often. The key point is that *we can practically guarantee success for Shamu if we start with the rope at the bottom of the tank.* It may be difficult to make this shift – from the high expectations we are accustomed to having of ourselves and others to a mindset of setting the bar *low* to absolutely *ensure* success. But the Nurtured Heart Approach eventually actualizes those very high expectations at far better levels than stringing that rope high above the pool, dangling a fish, and hoping, wishing and praying for the whale to catch on. There's truly an art to creating successes that wouldn't otherwise exist.

We can also guarantee success for a difficult child if we learn to find ways to see and colorfully acknowledge positives where we haven't seen them before; and you can put yourself into experiences of success and greatness by doing the same for yourself.

A difficult child often spends most of her days feeling like a failure, like a bad egg. She is constantly chided, scolded, lectured and warned. When I try to teach her parents this method, and I tell them the method involves noticing and acknowledging what their child is doing right, I am sometimes met with an incredulous look and maybe even something like: "Boy, it's going to be a long wait before she does something right!" Occasionally, I hear a reference to 'hell freezing over' before this challenging child does anything worthy of praise.

I know many adults who see themselves in this same way – as virtually incapable of doing things right. Self-deprecation and self-criticism can run rampant and are often considered far more acceptable in various adult circles than self-congratulation and celebration of even the smallest accomplishments, but my experience shows that, when adults begin to turn this around, their lives are quickly transformed for the better.

Here's the key: These parents can no longer wait for the child to leap over the bar in the form it has previously (and, usually, arbitrarily and inconsistently) been set; neither can the adult wait for himself to stumble into some great success. They have to *start seeing success where they never saw it before.* Like Shamu's trainers, they need to lower the bar in a way that makes failure to drift over it impossible. And they need to make a really big deal out of it when this happens, even if that minor success was totally unintentional – a much bigger deal than the one made over problems, doubts and fears. The beautiful result is that the parents are celebrating the child, or the adult is celebrating herself.

Most parents have heard the exhortation to "catch the child being good." This is on the right track, but in my experience – and in the experience of many parents with difficult, intense children – this way can fall short. It leaves you in the wings, waiting and waiting to "catch" success. When dealing with a highly challenging child, the adult who waits to catch that child doing good is in a disempowered position. When you wait for yourself or another to hit some arbitrary high-water mark of success, you might have to wait a long time before giving the recognition that you or that other person would find so beneficial.

In both the Nurtured Heart Approach and the greatness practice, you are, in essence, *hijacking* yourself or the other person into an experience of success. Although it might sound a bit dishonest to hold this intention of "creating" successes, the truth is that a river of greatness runs just beneath eye level all the time. Once you see this, it's a matter of simply adjusting your sights to witness and reflect upon that greatness more often.

For example: Right at this moment, you are reading about creating greatness. What does this, alone, say about your greatness? The truth is that you are a person who is determined to be your best. You care deeply about how you conduct yourself and how you impact others. If this were not true, you would already have abandoned this book. It follows that you have the greatness of caring, determination and wanting to be beneficial to others.

The Nurtured Heart Approach for parents helps them 'create' the child into success and then to show her how great a place that is to be: how fun, how energized, how loving. Then, over time, the child will actually raise the bar herself and will be all too happy to keep clearing it. She will know exactly what to expect when she does: loving, energized acknowledgement of her greatness. It will be a sense of joy, accomplishment and contribution. This energized sense of success will eventually be internalized.

This does not mean that the parents should lower their standards, make things up or lie to their child in any way. It means changing their definition of success to encompass behaviors reflecting rules NOT broken, positive values and the many, many facets of a child's creativity, adventurousness, emotional experience and ways of relating to others. The parents are stating the underlying truth of the success that's been there all the time.

For some children, the rope has to start lower: "Wow, Jordan, I am seeing that you aren't hitting your sister right now, although I can see how mad you're getting. That's great self-control, great handling of big feelings." Or, "Ethan, I can see that you are looking at the candles on the dining room table and that you have a piece of scrunched-up newspaper in your hand. I see that you might be considering setting that paper on fire. You're displaying excellent respect for the rules by not doing so. Thanks so much."

Praising a child for *not* hitting? For *not* starting a fire? Yes, that's what I mean by *starting the rope at the bottom of the pool*. In doing this, you are creating miracles out of molecules: hijacking the smallest bits and pieces of a child's greatness that you can observe and providing recognition and appreciation for them. Not past, not future: Just the truth of the moment.

Tragically, since 9/11, we all understand that planes can fly into buildings. We all now know that every last time a plane doesn't fly into a building, it's a victory and a blessing. We also now know that we don't have to wait until Thanksgiving to be deeply grateful – perhaps beyond any level we have previously experienced. Deeper levels of gratitude and 'great-itude,' for that matter, are continually available.

Feeling the *impulse* to do something wrong isn't a crime. When that impulse is resisted, it's a victory. Who hasn't had the feeling of wanting to break something? But as long as you haven't, you are still in the ballgame, with no consequence other than the glory of having made a great decision not to be destructive and of exercising wisdom, control and good judgment.

A child who seems on the verge of hitting or considers setting a fire, and then chooses not to, deserves recognition. In our society, parents or caregivers traditionally make a big deal only when rules are broken or appear about to be broken. By setting off the fireworks at these times, we accidentally provide a great deal of energetic recognition for the rule-breaking behavior.

Children measure the value of a behavior according to the energy it elicits from other people. The standard response of giving energy to rule breaking (past or imminent) inadvertently deepens that child's impression that unwanted behaviors are highly meaningful – and he'll keep returning to those behaviors to get that energetic 'hit,' especially as long as little to no energy is being offered in response to *desired* behaviors.

The truth to me is that, in every parent's heart, there is gratitude in some core sense when poor choices aren't happening – when lines haven't been crossed. Why not stick to the truth and gratitude of each moment? My approach puts words to that gratitude, framing the decision to *not* have a problem or break a rule as a great choice.

When a child's behavior reflects a value like cooperation, why not wax poetic about the positivity of that choice instead of assuming that this is standard-issue behavior not requiring recognition – especially when we make *such* a huge fuss over behaviors that are uncoopera-tive? Why, for that matter, shouldn't adults celebrate themselves for reflecting these sorts of good values?

As an adult who seeks to apply the Nurtured Heart Approach to yourself, you can't exactly fool yourself into swimming over the rope, so to speak. But you can create successes by recognizing each of the qualities of greatness you possess. They are there for the taking, in plain view, once you choose to hold the intention to recognize them and make them grow. ❄

Chapter 19

Pure and Present Greatness

The vast majority of adults value personal and spiritual growth. In most modern bookstores, the self-help section is the biggest in the store. If you haven't read any of those books, I'll fill you in on what most of them contain: some theory and practice for building self-esteem, for making better choices, or for being more loving, more for-giving, happier, more considerate or more assertive. They are about what we lack and how to get it.

If the advice is to tell yourself "I am going to be more loving," or "I am going to be more assertive," you are inadvertently telling your-self *I am not loving* or *I am not assertive*. The *energetic* meta-message to your heart and mind is that you are currently falling short. The message says "It would be nice if you could do better, but in actuality you are not at this moment." Certainly, you're going to try, but you might not even get there then, and for now, the truth is that you aren't where you wish to be.

Everything you think or say is energetically translated to the Now. When you hope or pray for a new quality, your computing system translates that to mean that right now, you appear not to be living up to your own expectations. A plan with all the smells and colors of positivity ends up merely strengthening the existing negative message of falling short. It's as if you are trying to row to the other side of a pond and you wind up going in the exact opposite direction. Your response is to row harder and harder, but you're still going the wrong way. As you pray, wish, hope and plan for your own betterment with increasing intensity, you row away with lots of vigor, but you're continuing to pour your energy into sending your boat away from the destination you wish to reach.

The way out of this quagmire is to *create a new way of talking to yourself about the qualities you would like to develop in yourself* – a new 'messaging system' that better serves your purposes.

How do you start the rope at the bottom? **By inwardly capturing a moment where the loving, or the forgiveness, or the assertiveness is *already happening*, even if it's to the most miniscule degree. Then, in that instant, you drink in the experience of that quality, telling yourself:**

"Here I am, *being...*[this quality]."

You are reflecting to yourself a quality of your irrefutable greatness. The evidence is in.

This wording is important to differentiate. These are not so much 'great qualities' like great talent, great skill or great friendship as they are 'qualities of greatness,' where talent, friendship or skill are aspects of who you are as a great person. This is a qualitative difference, and here's why: We are not revering the talent, friendship or skill, but the way in which these qualities are part of you. The reverence is essentially for YOU as the holder of this greatness. It's for you choosing to be this greatness. This greatness is who you are.

The present tense, too, is an important aspect here. When you say *you are* or *I am* rather than saying *you will*, the experience enters into your consciousness more irrefutably. You are claiming the moment with a greater assertion of the truth as you experience Now.

It's then not a question of whether you can or can't – YOU ARE!

As you begin to play with this, you'll feel your angels get excited. The universe begins to collaborate in an entirely new fashion. ❋

Greatness exercise. Select a single quality of greatness you admire in someone else – your favorite celebrity, your best friend, your partner. (Use your list from the Chapter 17 exercise, or refer to the lists on the following pages.) If you can see a quality in another, then it is already in you. If this were not the case, you could not see or discern it.

Today, as you go about your business, be on the lookout for even the smallest reflection of that quality in yourself. When you spot that reflection, acknowledge it to yourself.

For example:

If you find a way to see a moment of thoughtfulness in yourself, however fleeting, it then becomes a building block for a rejuvenated self-image. Start small if you have to. "By getting up to wake the kids for school before my wife, I'm letting her get a few more minutes' sleep. I'm being thoughtful, and that is a great quality."

Other examples of greatness you might see:

"I'm sticking to my original vision of this project rather than caving in to the demands of my co-workers to make it easier. I am embodying integrity, and this is a quality of greatness that I possess."

"In taking the time to give my daughter a hug and hear her talk about her day, I am the greatness of attentiveness and caring."

"I stood patiently in line at the video store and joked with people around me while the clerk struggled to keep up. Courtesy and consideration are great qualities I have."

Just think the thought. No need to say anything out loud.

Qualities of Greatness

"I am the greatness of…"

Accomplishment
Action
Activeness
Activism
Admiration of others
Agility
Alertness
Aliveness
Appreciativeness
Artistry
Attentiveness
Attainment
Attunement
Audacity
Awareness
Awe
Beauty
Being a good scientist
Being an advocate
Being extraordinary
Being in the now
Being a catalyst
Belonging
Boldness
Bravery
Brilliance
Building alliances
Calmness
Caring
Capability
Charisma
Cheerfulness
Clarity
Clear-mindedness

Collaboration
Commitment
Community-mindedness
Compassion
Connection
Conscientiousness
Consciousness
Consideration
Constructiveness
Courage
Courtesy
Creativity
Curiosity
Daring
Dedication
Deliberateness
Dependability
Determination
Dexterity
Differentiation
Dignity
Diligence
Directness
Discernment
Efficiency
Effort
Empathy
Encouragement
Energy
Enjoyment
Enlightenment
Expansiveness
Experimentation
Explanation

Faithfulness
Fascination
Fearlessness
Flexibility
Focus
Foresight
Forethought
Forgiveness
Fortitude
Friendship
Fun
Generosity
Genuineness
Giving
Good planning
Grace
Graciousness
Gratitude
Guidance
Happiness
Hard work
Healing
Hilarity
Helpfulness
Honor
Hope
Hopefulness
Humor
Idealism
Illumination
Imagination
Independence
Inquisitiveness
Insight
Inspiration
Integrity
Intelligence

Intimacy
Intuition
Inventiveness
Joy
Judgment
Justice
Knowledge
Laughter
Leadership
Light
Longing for/remembering God
Loveliness
Loving
Loyalty
Magnificence
Mastery
Meaningfulness
Mindfulness
Motivation
Nimbleness
Observation
Openness
Opportunism
Organization
Outrage (righteous indignation)
Passion
Patience
Peacefulness
Peacemaking
Perseverance
Perspective
Plasticity
Playfulness
Pleasantness
Positivity
Power
Principles

Productivity

Protectiveness

Purpose

Quickness

Radiance

Receiving

Rectitude

Reflectiveness

Refusal/opposition

Relationship/friendship

Resourcefulness

Respect

Resolve

Responsibility

Responsiveness

Reverence

Seeing the big picture

Self-control

Sensitivity

Sensuality

Service

Setting a great example

Sexuality

Spiritedness

Spontaneity

Steadfastness

Strength

Support

Synthesizing

Tact

Tenderness

Tenacity

Thankfulness

Thoughtfulness

Thriftiness

Togetherness

Understanding

Uninhibitedness

Uniqueness

Uplifting

Valor

Values

Wakefulness

Warriorship (the positive side of power)

Warmth

Wholesomeness

Wisdom

Zest

Chapter 20

Cleaning House

A friend of mine has an eight-year-old daughter who almost never breaks a rule. She's a straight arrow, eager to please and easy to get along with. There's only one thing that sets her off into "difficult child" territory: being told to clean up a messy room. When faced with a room strewn with toys, clothes and junk, this child is immediately overwhelmed. She doesn't know where to begin. In the face of a seemingly endless task, she becomes hopeless and dissolves into tearful hysterics.

This child doesn't have the wherewithal to make the following choice (at least, not without skilled adult guidance), but *you do:* You can walk into a messy room and be overwhelmed by the enormous mess, without a clue about where to begin, or you can just make the choice to start somewhere and *give yourself recognition for every step taken toward completion as you go.* Being able to start somewhere entails the heartfelt assumption that you are already full of light – that you are already great.

For example: Let's say that one day, watching the *Oprah Winfrey Show,* I find myself enthralled by her collaboration with car companies that enables her to give a car to each member of her studio audience. I'm moved by how influential and generous she is in this. So I pick related qualities and *take ownership* of them by saying to myself on the inhale "I AM powerful. I AM kind. I AM influential." If I see even a bit of it in another person, then on some level, it relates to or resonates in me. If it didn't, I would have missed it entirely.

I can say to myself that I AM anything I can imagine. Whether I currently believe this to be true or not isn't really relevant...*because you have to start somewhere.* It's always by degrees that we transform something, whether it's a sloppy room full of crumbs and toys and dirty clothes or the house of our minds, hearts and souls. This process is not about what is fully true or fully false. It's always by degrees that change happens – an unfolding process. *A messy room is in the process of transforming into a clean room even if you've only picked up one out-of-place item.*

Equally true is the fact that you already possess degrees of power and influence, whether you are awakened to that yet or not. If you didn't, you wouldn't be able to get out of bed or make a phone call or decide what foods to buy. What you do influences others in many ways. The way you choose to spend your dollars, for example, influences what companies choose to produce. You indeed have power.

Your mind and heart and soul are in the process of transforming into more powerful, kind, influential versions, even if you've only taken one breath into this transformation – *even if you are simply saying that this is what you are.*

And even if you are already extremely powerful and know it, this is only true by degrees. Room still exists for further unfolding. Always.

Owning any of these qualities, or even trying them on for size by *pretending* to own them, creates at the very least a fleeting glimpse of that luminosity – of that clean, sparkling being that inhabits each of us at our core. ❄

Chapter 21
The Toll Taker: My Intention Wins

Another illustration I use to teach the foundations of the Nurtured Heart Approach is the story of a toll taker on the San Francisco Bay Bridge. This tale has been related to me by several people with small variations, but the gist is this:

A man commuting across the Bay Bridge pulls into the lane of a toll taker who happens to be dancing animatedly to music coming from his boom box. The driver remarks that the toll taker seems to be having a great time, and the toll taker replies: "Yes I am. I have the best job in the world – an incredible view, lots of nice people to talk to, fresh air to breathe. I get to listen to my favorite music and I can even practice my dancing while I work and earn a living." The driver then looks over at the other tollbooths and comments that the other toll takers don't appear to be having that kind of great time, to which the toll taker replies, "Oh, those guys in the stand-up coffins? They're no fun."

The world is what we choose to see in it. Do we choose to see the glass as half full or half empty? If we choose the former, all we have to do is amp-up our intention.

Shamu didn't intend to learn to go over the rope, but those around him – his trainers, his keepers, those who run Sea World – held this intention for him. When a parent or teacher uses the Nurtured Heart Approach with a child or a classroom, that adult is holding the intention of guiding the child to a new realm of success and inner wealth. When you use these techniques on yourself, you get the responsibility and the power that come from holding your own intention for yourself. What do you want your life to be like? Do you want *less than good?* Do you want *good?* Do you want *great?* How do you wish to enter into your experiences? You can absolutely choose how to see things. Making this choice in a conscious way and holding the intention of seeing and being in greatness are the foundations of the Nurtured Heart Approach and the greatness practice.

Another story, this one from an e-mail written by a grown daughter to her mother, illustrates this point – you are what you intend to be – with more complexity. We might call this one 'The Mattress Dancer.'

"On the way home from work, I saw that 50-ish lady who stands on the corner and dances with the sign for the mattress outlet. For years, I've seen her on that street corner, rain or shine, with a big smile on her face, just dancing her behind off – working it and loving it. She radiates joy and happiness. She spreads it to everyone who passes. A lot of people don't even notice her, but she fills me with joy. She made me smile and laugh and wave and dance along with her while she blew me kisses that day. She has no reason to be so happy, dancing on that street corner wearing a wooden sign for a mattress outlet, but she chooses to love herself and what she's doing. She chooses to love each and every person who passes her on the street and to share her joy and love through her smile and her ridiculous, hilarious, uninhibited, fabulous, happy dancing and waving. She radiates goodness, joy and oneness with herself.

"I believe it's a choice. I believe it's a difficult, difficult choice that we all need to make. I believe most choose not to choose, and remain numb, dumb and distracted with meaningless B.S. their entire lives. Others feel, see, think and know too much – and choose to either destroy themselves (one way or another) or become great, enlightened, evolved, happy, whole people.

"I think the latter is so incredibly rare, because it is probably somehow easier to stifle that true self and live in misery than it is to be true and do the work that it takes to become who you really are. I am becoming more aware of my power and seeing that I have often been reckless with my energy. I can't imagine how much work it would take to rise above all this and find myself, and then have the strength and resolve to live my life being true to that self. I haven't decided yet. But at least I am acknowledging that it is a choice I need to make. I know I have the potential to become someone I can stand to be alone with – someone that I can love and respect, who can love without judgment or resentment and without expectations."

We are all constantly, moment by moment, making these choices already. What if it *weren't* harder to live in who you really are? The writer says it's "easier" to stifle one's true self and live in misery, but I maintain that this is more a function of habit – of the defaults we tend to sink into. Although it is sometimes even *harder* to stay mired in 'yuck' than it is to choose moments of greatness, habit often flexes its muscles to keep us in those patterns.

When I work with parents to teach the Nurtured Heart Approach, I tell them that no one is to blame for their child's situation; that the problem has been with the parenting tools they have been trying to use. You can't use a rubber mallet to knock down a solid brick wall. You can't use conventional parenting techniques with a difficult child. And you can't use conventional 'self-esteem building' techniques with someone who is struggling to believe, deep down, in his or her own worth.

Like so many people, this young woman is (at least, in part) using the wrong tools to try to be happy. Her poetic mulling over the problem – and there is no denying that she writes movingly and beautifully about her predicament – seems so innocent and so right to the eyes of people who are accustomed to inadvertently giving more energy and relationship to what's wrong than to what's right. However, as long as she urges herself to have that greater strength and as long as she hopes to do the work she imagines it takes to have it, she continues to send herself the energetic message that right now, she isn't living up to her own standards of greatness.

Until she tries a different approach that confirms that she is already great in the present moment, she'll probably continue to feel as though she wants to be more like that mattress dancer but has no clue how to access that kind of uninhibited joy, that total lack of self-doubt, that loving generosity. The mattress dancer somehow already understands this, and so she has a joyous magnetism that both attracts and baffles others.

You do have the choice to live in your greatness. You can do far more than tolerate yourself: You can love and respect yourself without judgment, resentment or expectations, and you can make the choice to do it in each and every moment, starting now.

Rather than being reckless with your energy or misusing or failing to tap into your own power, you can channel that energy and power into seeing greatness in yourself and in others. You do this by setting your intention and choosing exactly where to put your energy: into creating, acknowledging and propelling all that is good and powerful and already magnificent in you and in others.

The part that this young lady already has gloriously right is that she can see the greatness in the mattress dancer. In seeing it, and in thoroughly enjoying the qualities of greatness held by that joyous and brave soul, she is energizing the networks of greatness in her own being as well. If I could talk to her, I would encourage her to acknowledge that she couldn't even begin to see the greatness of this woman if those same qualities of joy, hilarity and lack of inhibition were not in her as well. When you add this awareness to purposeful choice, moment after moment, to *not* give energy to what is wrong, you have the greatness of faith and daring. As priest and author Henri Nouwen said: Joy does not simply happen to us. We have to choose joy and keep choosing it every day.

Let's say you are listening to a co-worker tell you about an issue with another colleague. You can stand there and think about the problem being described; or you can zone out and think about your upcoming weekend. You can think about how that other guy is so strange for causing this issue or, conversely, about how right he is to be causing trouble for your friend because the friend actually deserves it.

Most people, in exchanges like this, will at least consider commiserating with the person who is complaining – or at least will try to figure out whose side to take in hearing the story. This is the default behavior we are accustomed to – i.e., getting sucked into the drama, into the negative energy.

But consider this: You don't have to give your energy to his problem to be there for him and listen to him. You can appreciate the positive. You can stand there and admire the glory of having a colleague who cares and who wants to spend time with you, even get your feedback on something important to him. You haven't alienated him in any way, yet you do not need to get sucked into the default setting that brings on negativity. Where else can you find greatness in the cracks of light between the frames of the footage?

You are the producer and director of this film, and you get to have the voice-over. The bubbles over the heads of everyone who appears in each frame are blank, and you can write the script, regardless of what they are saying, because the words spoken play second fiddle to the energy beneath them. You do not have to give any energy and relationship to a problem, even if people are begging you to do that. ❄

Greatness exercise. Notice how you put your habitual filters in place as you go about your day. When you are stuck in traffic, or dealing with a touchy issue at work, or talking with your spouse about something controversial, do you tend to drop into the gears that focus on what's wrong? Practice shifting your focus and seeing what is right and good and beautiful about your situation in any given moment. Whenever you feel yourself going down the road to worry, misery and doubt, take a breath and set your intention to look at what is great in the moment. Make the effort, even if it's huge; it only gets easier with practice.

Chapter 22

Video Game Therapy

When I was counseling families with intense, difficult children, parents would often mention that this child who could not sit still in a classroom for five minutes without causing a disruption was somehow able to sit in front of video or computer games for hours straight. And these children did not typically just play these games; they played them with singular focus and determination and with strong motivation to hit level after level after level. "Why can't my child be this way about school work, or about behaving well?" these parents would ask.

This was not hard for me to explain in terms of the approach I was developing. In fact, it gave me additional clarity about why what I was doing seemed to work so well with difficult children. I saw that these games offered players a few things that don't tend to be available in the rest of life by way of traditional methods of parenting and teaching. One, they have consistent expectations and rules, with immediate and reliable recognition of rules broken or mistakes made (momentary loss of the energy given by the game). Two, they give immediate and reliable recognition of success (a profound level of energy transpires via points scored, sounds and visual effects). Third, there is an immediate default setting back to success: When a game ends or a penalty has been exacted, the player can get right back into the game, starting completely fresh.

Some children with sufficient inner wealth can tolerate inconsistency and lack of recognition in their lives quite well and seem to naturally bounce back from perceived failures. Others – and these were the kids I was seeing in my practice – seemed to have a strong, abiding need for the same kind of structure found in standard video games. Without it, they couldn't handle their own energy, so they acted out and had other problems that were essentially a call for adults to give them a different kind of structure. As with playing a video game, once they had that structure, they were able to focus and handle their intensity well.

Wouldn't it be great if children could live their lives from a place that gives them such powerful ability to remain focused and committed when working toward a goal? Where all they want to do, as in the video game, is manifest level after level of greatness? Wouldn't it be great if, as in the video game, no one needed to twist their arms to *not* break the rules? If instead they held fast to not breaking the rules of their own volition? For that matter, wouldn't it be great if we could all do this? Kids certainly aren't the only fans of video games. Some teens and adults get hooked into these games just as powerfully.

The player has absolute freedom to break the rules of the game, and when he or she does, the game gives that player what amounts to a simple reset. It doesn't freak out or offer lectures about how the player could have avoided this consequence. It doesn't give ominous, verbose warnings when players seem about to break a rule. Adults watching the games may see the consequences as drastic and punitive: heads rolling, bombs bursting. But really, who's back in the game in a second or two?

In actuality, the game gives what's tantamount to an energetic illusion of a consequence and then moves the player briskly on to more play – and to the DEFAULT SETTING of more success and greatness. The player doesn't have to go to his room or sit in the corner or otherwise move from his spot in front of the screen to have this experience of a consequence. The game's consequence is really a built-in 'kiss' of forgiveness that leads straight into the next moment of success!

The concept of "video game therapy" became central to the Nurtured Heart Approach. I sought ways in which to bring the three points above into the manner in which adults deal with the children in their lives: to foster consistent and powerful recognition for success; to use only a brief 'time-out' or reset in response to rules broken (more on this later); and to follow this immediately by recognizing the next foray into success – a completely fresh and enthusiastic start with every expectation of good things happening. Through these three steps, the need or inclination to give energy to negativity automatically disappears.

As you cultivate your own greatness, think in terms of these points. Constantly recognize yourself for even small increments of success. When something goes wrong, instead of falling into WMDs, you'll learn to give yourself a brief time-out or reset and to set the stage for the next level of success. This way of living cultivates enthusiasm by making the evidence of your own greatness incontrovertible and present in every moment.

Winston Churchill said "Success is going from failure to failure without loss of enthusiasm." Enthusiasm is a word derived from the Greek word *enthousiasme,* which means "possession by a god." To be enthusiastic is to be in possession of your God-ness, to be seated in your inspiration. In this context, failure, like in the video game, is no big deal, and enthusiasm springs from a deep understanding and awareness of the greatness in you and all around you. This brings you from level to level, endlessly deepening and expanding – without ever asking the ages-old question "Are we there yet?" Inspired living becomes your default as you return, again and again, to awe at the endless possibilities. ❄

Chapter 23
Strategies for Acknowledging Greatness

Intention is crucial in shifting your defaults from worry, misery and doubt into greatness-thinking. Setting this intention probably won't happen all at once. Like any other habit, changing habitual defaults requires setting your intention often and returning to that intention when you find yourself back in your old patterns. This is where techniques become helpful, giving you concrete tools with which to get yourself back on track and to give energy to your own successes rather than pouring it into your 'WMDs.'

Following are some techniques to support you in changing your defaults. These are "voice-over" techniques that enable you to catch yourself in successes at any given moment. They are tools for channeling your self-talk – that monologue that rumbles incessantly through your mind, sometimes without your awareness – to build inner wealth.

Essentially, these techniques are easy-to-use tools that help you learn how to effectively praise yourself – how to give yourself *positive, evidence-based reflections aimed at your heart and your character.* You will learn to notice and nurture yourself not only for what you *accomplish,* but for who you *are,* while always staying in the essential truth of the moment.

You can call this practice praise, acknowledgement, appreciation, recognition or anything you wish, but in the end it's all about seeing, cultivating and growing your own garden of greatness.

1. Active Recognition

In this technique, you give yourself a verbal 'snapshot' of what you observe yourself doing. It is only about observation, not about judgment or evaluation. Active Recognition (also known as Kodak Moments) can be used to reflect actions or feelings. Examples might be:

"I'm washing the dishes right now."

"I feel annoyed about having to sit in this traffic jam but I am staying calm."

"My mood seems pretty good right now."

"I am trying to figure out how to assemble this toy tractor for my son, and so far I am staying patient and being careful to follow directions."

When parents or teachers who are using the Nurtured Heart Approach with children apply Active Recognition, the purpose is simply to let the child know that she is *seen* and *appreciated* in times when she's not breaking any rules or clamoring for attention in other ways. For adults engaged in using the Nurtured Heart Approach to propel greatness, this method is a way of putting yourself squarely into the present moment.

Using Active Recognition with children is about taking everyday and ordinary moments to the 'editing room' and bringing them forth in a way that makes the child feel meaningful, valued and worthy for simple life moments. When you use this technique on yourself, you'll find that it is a great way to transform ordinary moments into internal messages about your own value by way of an internal narrative of noticing and appreciating everyday actions and feelings.

2. Experiential Recognition

This technique expands on those Kodak Moments by tacking on a recognition of how your behaviors are a reflection of values you wish to cultivate in yourself – in other words, an illustration of your greatness.

"I'm washing the dishes right now. I'm taking responsibility for keeping my space clean and neat. Being organized and self-respecting are qualities of my greatness."

"By getting to work on time, I'm showing respect for my co-workers."

"Here I am, at exercise class, taking good care of my body, and afterward I'm going to eat a big salad for lunch instead of a burger and fries. I'm showing myself love and keeping myself healthy. My awareness and caring are growing parts of me that make me great."

Values Worth Acknowledging

A *value* is a quality of behavior, thought and character regarded by a society to be intrinsically good; it is regarded as having desirable results and is worthy of imitation by others. Holding and living your values inspires others as you live your life in your particular meaningful manner. Here is a short list of values you might look for in your day-to-day actions:

Compassion
Consideration of others' needs
Collaboration
Courage
Creativity
Determination
Fairness
Freedom of expression
Friendship
Good judgment
Good manners
Honesty

Humility
Kindness
Patience
Peacefulness
Respect
Responsibility
Self-control
Thoughtfulness
Tolerance
Wisdom
(Add your own to this list if you like!)

---

3. Proactive Recognition

This strategy builds on the first two techniques to give you tools to proactively recognize how you are *not* behaving badly.

What someone *isn't* doing wrong is a topic that rarely gets play time in parenting or in our self-talk. But consider the greatness available for recognition in any moment that you are not giving in to your less constructive urges. For example, when I'm irritated or frustrated, I am capable of extraordinary rudeness. Therefore, when I am feeling irritation or frustration and I am *not* being rude to others, this is a victory. A *big* victory! In those moments I am living restraint, power and wisdom.

This isn't about self-aggrandizement; it's about enhancing my ability to see and reclaim my inheritance of greatness.

At a presentation I gave on the Nurtured Heart Approach, I illustrated an extreme version of this technique by role-playing a teacher telling a student "Wow, you *didn't* burn down the school today! You're showing great restraint and respect." One attendee found this to be ridiculous. And it is! Congratulating a kid for not burning down the school? Insanity! But honestly, who does it hurt to point out what this kid, who might be a total handful, is not doing wrong? Do we really want to wait until this child shows up to school with a lighter or even a weapon to start appreciating the bad choices he could be making but isn't? (By the way, I've had tremendous success with fire-setters when I was simply able to get his or her parents to express the gratefulness they felt for each day their child didn't set a fire. Many other appreciations were added, of course, to round out the picture – the child felt successful not only for not setting things on fire, but for lots of other good choices being made throughout every day.)

You have to start somewhere, proactively crafting moments of success for that child. And the reality is that there's so much success to mine from, if we only look for it. Think of the enormous range this gives you in acknowledging your own successes. *Today, I didn't yell at my toddler when he poured his milk all over the floor on purpose. Today, I didn't smoke.* (You can even acknowledge this if you've never smoked in your life. It's something you're doing right!) *Today, I didn't eat food that was bad for me. In the last 15 minutes, I haven't given energy to worries, misery or doubt, although I was so tempted to go there.*

Even if tomorrow you revert to doing the things you're congratulating yourself for *not* doing today, you will still have the benefit of having felt the greatness of accomplishment. You will have deeply cherished, even if only for a few moments, the great power and control and wisdom that is necessary for these and other victories. These moments pave the way for many more victories to come.

It's a way of using ordinary moments (via Shamu/the toll taker) to download a meta-message to yourself that you are meaningful – without expending your energy on troubles or problems, and without needing positive feedback from others to feel valued and great. Here, the inner self feels acknowledgment and recognition for simply being. One more time: You are producer and director of the footage, and you have rights to the voice-over.

"I feel annoyed about having to sit in this traffic jam, but I'm not honking my horn or yelling at anyone. I'm using restraint to keep my cool, and that helps everyone."

"I'm standing patiently in line and being friendly instead of complaining or yelling at the sales clerk. I am respectful and calm."

"When my child broke the window with a rock, I could have really gone ballistic, lecturing and punishing him, but I didn't. I gave him a reset, then set up some community service requirements so that he could participate in fixing it. I felt angry, but I didn't take it out on him or energize his bad behavior. I am demonstrating compassion and forethought."

With each of these techniques, allow yourself to see and acknowledge how greatness is reflected in each of the qualities and actions you are recognizing. We will address this 'amping-up' into greatness in more detail in following chapters.

As you begin working with these techniques for self-acknowledgement, they may seem incredibly formulaic. Don't let this stop you. Keep in mind that you are only going to consciously use these techniques until you catch enough glimmers of your own greatness to make this practice more intuitive. Feel free to use all of these techniques in the ways they best fit you.

Nurtured Heart trainer and school principal Eric Dueppen beautifully describes the way these techniques support us in bringing out the greatness in ourselves and in others at the same time:

> The approach brings to light mistakes we've made in the past in teaching, parenting and all other relationships. What some people see in that mirror can be frightening. This is why it can be difficult for some people to implement this approach... and it helped me see that as a school, we have to collectively acknowledge that fear and celebrate the courage it takes to continue to move forward with the approach – despite our fears of inadequacy and the mistakes we have made in the past. Imagine being able to confront the past, acknowledge it, and move on with new techniques and strategies to create true inner wealth in every future interaction! How liberating this can be! ❄

Greatness exercise. Begin to apply these techniques as you move through your day. Begin with Kodak Moments so that you can develop the habit of re-centering yourself in the present moment. Next, begin to introduce reflections of the positive values you are embodying. And finally, begin to see how you are being great not only by doing right, but also by not doing wrong. Five to 10 of these kinds of reflections per day will begin to shift the way you see yourself and the way the world responds to you.

Chapter 24

Resets to Greatness

"Sometimes, when I'm overwhelmed, I give *myself* a time-out!"

I've heard variations on this theme from many parents. This is an excellent parenting instinct: to step out of the picture and take a breather when anger, fear and worry threaten to shift a situation into dangerous territory.

Adults who choose to engage in this greatness practice need to figure out how to give themselves a way out of the worry/misery/doubt trip and a way back into greatness. They require tools that will enable them to make this shift as often as necessary. And it needs to be done in a way that's as seamless and as unceremonious as possible so that the energy out of the reset is dwarfed by the energy of success, gratitude and greatness that flows in during the next new Now.

When the Nurtured Heart Approach is used with a child, it goes something like this: The child breaks a rule; the adult says "that's a reset;" and then the adult simply withdraws his energy and attention briefly. It may be only a matter of seconds. For the child, it's simply about sensing that a consequence has happened in response to the broken rule.

The adult then creates closure, relayed by a quick shift to welcoming the child back to time-in. Here, the adult conveys that the game of positivity is back on: it's all about pointing out the child's successes again. "Wow, Michael, you did that time-out beautifully. You accepted it gracefully and did what you had to do, and now you're not breaking any rules – you are being successful!" In this creative way, the reset always leads purposefully back to gratitude and greatness.

These time-outs can provide both adults and children with a straightforward way to notice and change their habitual defaults. They are, in essence, a reset of the inner compass.

Energy goes where attention goes. I talked with a friend about a time in her past when she had sent out a deep, heart-felt prayer that she would not lose her husband to divorce. Despite the end result she prayed for, she had given lots of 100-dollar bills to the worry and fear around losing him. She did lose him, and I wonder whether focusing her energy and gratitude on having him in that Now might have led to a different outcome. Maybe not. But we do tend to hold on tighter out of fear of losing something, whether it's a marriage or the last 10 dollars in our checking account – and the tighter we hold on, the more energy and relationship we expend around our fears and doubts.

Energy equals love. When we accidentally love our fears by way of giving our energy to them, more fear is invoked and delivered by our infinitely benevolent universe, which always gives us what we seem to want. What we worship is what comes our way. We can say we hate fear all we want, but if fear is what we dance with, then the songs will keep playing. More fear comes to aid us in maintaining our misguided intimacy. The 'reset' and return to greatness give you a way to stop that avalanche the moment you realize it's headed in your direction.

Parents who scoff at time-outs, saying they don't work, often turn to other kinds of consequences when rules are broken: grounding, lecturing or so-called 'natural consequences' (for example, when the child refuses to clean her room, the consequence is a messy room where she can't find anything and her laundry never gets done). Bottom line: all of these are time-outs. The child is temporarily out of the game, out of the flow of life – the place she really wants to be.

When an adult constantly defaults to worry, misery and doubt, that adult is in a self-imposed time-out with no end in sight. The WMD version is a self-punitive and self-imposed way of keeping yourself out of the game. The alternative is to boil it down to its essence, keep it simple and consistent, and have it rather be a version of reset that's about moving through to the next greatness – getting back 'online,' so to speak.

The metaphor of being online or knocked offline resonates quite well with most adults. We're so accustomed to our constant, easy access to the World Wide Web, our e-mail, and all those other instruments of connection that come through our computers. For most of us, being unable to get online when we need to work on the Internet is a big issue. If this were to happen, you would notice right away and do whatever is necessary, immediately, to get back online. The reset is an internal equivalent.

Words have a great deal of power, so choose your time-out word with care. After years of experimenting with various terms for time-out, I prefer to call them *resets*. *Time-out* sounds punitive; a *reset* is all about the next set of possibilities. Some parents like "red light/green light" or "pause/play." Perhaps you'll come up with some other term that speaks clearly to you.

A reset isn't a punishment, whether it's given to one's self or to one's child. It is simply a moment to breathe, to regain footing in the Now and to set your sights on the next manifestation of greatness.

You might even think of a reset well done as 'saving your soul,' in the sense that you are *saving it for greatness*. You are turning your soul or your life force away from the problem that's pulling on you for energy and relationship, just as you might turn your back on the prospective mate you know is wrong for you – magnetic or sexually attractive though he or she may be. You refuse. You detach. You know that going down that road ultimately will be bad for you, despite the quick thrills it might offer in the moment. And you use the energy that might otherwise be focused on the problem to intentionally zoom your soul/life force back to greatness.

Think of a reset as a way to put your foot down – to draw the needed line and to guard it once you see that the boundary has been exceeded or is about to be exceeded. The negativity is *de-energized* at this crucial moment of rule-breaking or WMD.

If you are a sports fan, consider the reset as having the same energy as a "turnover" following a rule violation in basketball. There's no drama, no angst – just an un-energized time-out, with a rapid return to time-in. It leads directly to the next success, where you see and acknowledge to yourself your own greatness and that of others.

Here's a brilliant example of a self-imposed reset from a school counselor and Nurtured Heart trainer:

> I started my day by heading off to work with a huge book bag, a cup of coffee, a thermos of coffee and a yogurt and cottage cheese breakfast in hand…only to have everything take flight, including myself, as I descended the garage stairs. I was covered in coffee and dirt and went down a nasty psychic road, and it was more than a few minutes before I caught myself. However, I then made a choice to reset, and I had

one of the best clinical days of my life! I was so energized by noticing other people's greatness. I had many personal wrenches thrown in my day but they did not destroy all the greatness I got to witness and experience. At day's end, I celebrated with champagne!

Gandhi, when asked to summarize his philosophy in a few sentences, said he could do it in three words: "Renounce and rejoice." Not far from "reset and enjoy." Reset to greatness. ❄

Greatness exercise. Choose a reset word for yourself. Choose carefully and don't be afraid to change the word if it isn't working for you. In the next chapters, you'll learn how to apply this word to your greatness practice.

Chapter 25
More Reasons to Build Inner Wealth

In his book *Blink* (Little, Brown & Co., 2005), Malcolm Gladwell writes about a study performed by Dutch researchers. The subjects were asked to answer a long series of tough questions from the board game Trivial Pursuit. "Half were asked to take five minutes beforehand to think about what it would mean to be a professor," Gladwell writes, "and write down everything that came to mind….The other half of the students were asked to first sit and think about soccer hooligans." The group that thought about the professorship and its implications got 55.6 percent of the answers right. The group that thought about soccer hooligans? They scored 42.6 percent. (page 56)

As I stated in Chapter 13, your thoughts *can* change your brain. The simple act of thinking about what it would feel like to be a person with the intellectual clout to be a professor *made the subjects of this study smarter.* For the other group, the converse was true. This study affirms, for me, what thinking, seeing, reflecting and being greatness can do for a person. It helps explain why, when I refuse to go negative and instead make a concerted effort to stand in greatness, more and more greatness comes my way. And each pearl of greatness I can burnish in myself and see in others contributes to the cause of my inner wealth.

With inner wealth as developed by the greatness practice:

- You stop categorizing people. Instead, you come to see them as worthy, unique and enjoyable for what they are as individuals.
- Your negative judgments transform to judgments pertaining to greatness.
- You can give from a vast place of inner abundance, without fear of losing yourself.
- You find less separation of beings at the soul level – a separateness that leads to so much day-to-day strife.
- You become increasingly attuned to your own gratitude and intuition – like a musical instrument attuned to a higher-frequency vibration. The universe then collaborates at that exact frequency, dialing it in like a radio station.
- You feel the universe jumping with you into a new gear: "Okay, if you're going to be great, I'll support you in that, because I enjoy greatness."
- You become more open to real intimacy, as you are in better touch with your own greatness and not fearful of exposing your divine essence. ❄

Chapter 26

First Thing in the Morning

To get up each morning with the resolve to be happy is to set our own conditions to the events of each day. To do this is to condition circumstances instead of being conditioned by them.
– **Ralph Waldo Emerson**

One morning not too long ago, I lay in bed zonked, having taken a melatonin (a mild natural sleep remedy) before bed. The phone rang. It was a social worker, and she was not having a good day. She was calling at an early hour from the East coast, which meant it was even earlier in my time zone on the West coast. She wanted to talk to me about my 90-plus-year-old mother's return home from the hospital.

My initial impulses were to be grouchy; be weird; be scared. Instead, I took a breath and said "My ex-wife is in New York visiting Mom at the hospital for this very reason. She knows a lot about this kind of situation. Let me get you some numbers." I did so, hung up the phone, put on some favorite music (Deva Premal) and got back in bed.

I resolved then to awaken myself into a mode of greatness to pull out of the shock of the awakening I had already experienced. For five minutes, I meditated; I used the emotional push of the situation to give that meditation a little trajectory. Then I called the social worker back. As soon as she picked up the phone, I could hear her energy had shifted. She had already found my ex-wife, and I was in a place where I could add to the upswing in her day by delivering a good, grateful and helpful message. Just taking that reset for myself and not falling into reactivity altered the course of my day, of her day, even of my ex-wife's day.

In retrospect, I see that I didn't necessarily have to go back to bed to meditate nor sit cross-legged on a cliff overlooking the ocean (not that there's anything wrong with either) nor otherwise remove myself from the raging river of everyday life. I could have done it in a flash, à la Tiger Woods hitting a bad shot: feel the angst quickly and vividly, then let it go and move on to yet more greatness.

Use the energy of the frustration, disappointment or anger to take greatness even higher. That's the reality of all things anyway, once we politely refuse to let impulsive 'not-greatness' take over. ❄

Chapter 27

Energetic Experiment

Susanna Bair has an adult son named Gerred. When I first met them, he and his mother and stepfather, Puran, had a challenging, sometimes contentious relationship, and Gerred was having many problems adjusting to adulthood.

At an advanced Nurtured Heart training, I did a role-play with Susanna and Puran. In it, I was asked to play the role of Gerred. No one instructed me about how I ought to play this role. I found myself drawn to using my body – without speaking at all – to respond in a pure way to the energy of their statements.

Their job was to talk to me as though they were talking to Gerred. When they said something that was truly in the moment and real and positive – "this is what we like about you!" – I allowed that energy to draw me closer. As long as they did it right, I even let that energy draw me right up onto the table on all fours to get closer to them. I couldn't get close enough. It was, at times, hilarious; and like just about anything that's hilarious, it was funny because of its core of incontrovertible truth. The energy running beneath our words doesn't lie, and I felt I was able to express that energy with total honesty. Like a magnetic force, it drew me in.

When the energy started to go critical – and this happened in very subtle ways – I felt myself pushed back. I kept moving away until they went back into that real and positive mode again, when their statements were purely grateful and appreciative, without any 'ifs, ands or buts.' This visualization of the impact of their statements helped them gauge where they were leaking negativity in their interactions with Gerred, which ultimately helped them navigate a healthier relationship with him over time.

That 'critical thing' is so alienating. I'm not referring to the kind of criticism that happens in a classroom with a teacher, or in a writing workshop or from an employer; nor the kind that pertains to meeting specific educational or work-related goals. I'm talking about the criticism that so typically emerges between parents and children: A dynamic that involves the parents making the biggest deal over the ways in which they think their children are falling short or making mistakes.

Because most of us learn this critical dynamic in childhood from our own relationships with parents, we bring it – subtly or not-so-subtly – into a negativity that creeps into any kind of interpersonal relationship.

Sure, our parents were critical out of a desire to help us be the best people we could be as we grew up. Most of us have the same good motives at heart with our own children. But I believe that an emphasis on mistakes and problems is a misuse of the energy of love and support. It never serves anyone – not the child, not the parents, not anyone else in the mix.

Isn't it obvious that when you lecture someone or when you are being lectured, the person doing the lecturing really is trying to help the other person move more into his or her greatness? Criticism and nagging are forms of helping, but they are energetically upside-down. The more energy we pour into these upside-down attempts to create greatness, the worse problems become. We are watering weeds. While we are urging the other person to do the right thing, energetically we are showing we highly value them in relation to the problem or the shortcoming. No one would ever do that on purpose but energetically we do it all the time.

At every stage of life, we learn from experience. Advice taking the form of criticism and nagging – really, almost any advice that comes in response to a problem or as an attempt to fix an issue – is almost guaranteed to backfire in the long run. It creates energetic distance in the relationship. In most cases, it throws a wrench in the spokes of the intended download of information from parent to child, and it stands to deepen the recipient's impression that quality time and connection best occur by way of rankling interaction.

Unless the parent-child bond is very strong (with a high presence of inner wealth and a real skill, dedication and desire to process to solutions), criticism can easily backfire. Criticism leads to defensiveness, which leads to head-butting arguments that go way off course from the adult's original intent. Arguing, as unpleasant as it may be, is a highly energized mode of communication and often becomes a default – a place where people subconsciously plunge because the outcome so predictably results in heightened and intense connection. For some people, this is the only kind of intimacy they are comfortable with, and so they are drawn into replicating it over and over. And then, following each of these negativity-soaked exchanges, each person walks away with intensified internal dialogues of worry, misery and doubt, further magnetizing their proclivity for these kinds of interactions.

Parents who put energy into criticism or nagging no doubt care deeply about the welfare of their children, but that energy will serve everyone better if it is used to teach the very same lessons and make the very same points in a way that helps the child remain open and receptive. This is done through recognition of success – recognition of the things children do to demonstrate their greatness in the Now.

Anyone taking the time and trouble to criticize has the desire, on some level, to move the other person to something they perceive will be useful to the situation. In the past few years, I've learned that, if the critical person knew how to speak to the other person's greatness, he or she would do so. I have come to see that underneath the rough exterior of nagging and arguing is a desire to take the higher ground of positivity. My work is about going straight to that positive place.

When we lecture *ourselves* to try harder to fix a problem, we are inadvertently pushing *ourselves* further into the quagmire of the problem. We wind up just raising the energetic charge in the wrong direction. The harder we try, the worse the situation gets. We inadvertently deepen the pattern and the suffering. Instead, we can choose to purposely energize further adventures of greatness, creating within ourselves a sense of safety, intimacy and nurturing. ❊

Greatness exercise. If you're open to this exercise, try it with someone close to you. Have him talk to you about you – perhaps about a problem the two of you face in your relationship, or a problem about which you'd like to ask his advice.

Tell him to give you advice or to tell you to try harder at something. Allow your body to silently reflect the energy of his statements. (Climbing on the furniture is optional.) You may be surprised at how readily your body responds when you remain in your heart space and how you can stay in a sense of humor once you awaken to the energetic side of the equation. Switch sides and see where your own statements of greatness 'spring leaks' by watching your partner respond to the energy of what you have to say.

Chapter 28

Staying Online

There are many ways to go online. You can visit the library or an Internet café to intermittently access that connection; you can have dial-up access from home, which is excruciatingly slow; you can have DSL or cable that comes in through a wire; you can have wireless Internet, where your laptop picks up a wireless signal that it can sometimes access, whether home or away; or you can have mobile Internet through a cell phone or a cell phone signal adapter you plug into your computer. At each level, you get more access, and some offer better download capacities and speeds than others. We can be certain that in the future, we'll have even better and faster services that will make our present ones seem slow.

As for me, I want a dedicated, high-capacity, always-online, lightning-fast connection to the Internet...and I want the same kind of connection to my own greatness/God-ness. The latter – let's call it the 'Intranet' – has come to me through these greatness practices.

More and more of us are seeking some way to connect with an energy beyond the humdrum grind of daily life. We desperately want that energetic connection to the mystery, spirit and greatness all around and within us. Some of the lucky ones end up falling into it by accident, getting just a fleeting, delicious taste before losing hold of it again. Very few of us have a reliable roadmap to lead us there over and over. Even if we have moments of clarity, insight or enlightenment, we stand the real possibility of falling off that horse without even realizing it. Then, we might find ourselves waking up from this days, weeks or years later, realizing we've been 'offline' for all that time – living in defaults of worry, misery and doubt and stuck in past and future rather than present. Life can so easily sweep us into the vortex of not remembering.

If you were online on your computer and got knocked off, you'd be utterly aware of this. You'd do whatever was necessary – call tech support, reboot, jiggle wires – to get back online. For most of us, a few days offline at the computer would be unthinkable, let alone a few months, but we can all so easily fall offline in how we live our lives for far longer than that without even realizing we are offline. Imagine being equally aware of being offline on the Intranet as you are for the Internet. You'd tenaciously find a way back – quickly and efficiently, every last time. Forgetting would no longer be an option.

Being offline, in this context, means falling out of touch with the greatness and God-nature of yourself and all that is around you. The fallout from this usually involves mounting problems and difficulties in one's life. We can actually attract this kind of fallout when we hold the subconscious belief that we need a crisis just to get God-energy into our lives.

When you fall offline – that is, when you find yourself moving into the internal vortex of WMDs or feel attracted energetically to the external whirlwind of crisis and difficulty – see it as a reminder to reset and *get back online*...to remember that we are greatness, and why. If you develop the ability to do this, you can find your way back online in an instant. And each time around the block, the greatness becomes more compelling and more alive. We are climbing back into our God-nature – the God-nature that was never absent; the God-nature that was always beckoning, just waiting for us to dial it in; the God-nature that becomes so evident with every new moment of seeing and being greatness.

The next time you find yourself going offline, use it as an opportunity to get even better 'connectivity.' Heart-rhythm breathe gratitude and greatness until they are one: *Great-itude.* ❊

Chapter 29

I Am (Appreciating)

A few years back, at a week-long advanced training for the Nurtured Heart Approach, I was chatting with my fellow facilitators as some breakout groups were finishing up. The participants' assignment was to take turns being appreciative to one another in a way in which the facilitators had instructed them. In the background of our chat, many people in different small groups were saying "I am appreciative of [something in that other person.]" However, from my perch in the distance, all I could hear was a humming, continual "I am." In the blur of it all, I had the sense that appreciation was the sound of the universe.

To me the "I am" sounded distinctly like a chant of "Om," the Sanskrit word often intoned in yoga and other spiritual practices (which also happens to mean "I am"). It took me in its spell. Once I had made that connection, "I am" became the sound of appreciation in action: gratitude, great-itude, love of being with simultaneous acknowledgment of the greatness in self and others.

Leah Henningsen, a friend and an art therapist who works at a Tucson mental hospital, had this to say after I shared this story with her and its impact on me:

"I really like that 'I am' is the sound of appreciation or gratitude in action. 'I am' reminds me of my true self because it activates the part of me that is able to consciously remember – despite all distractions! – that I exist, I am real and unbound. If I am unbound, then I am connected and capable. If my existence remains true despite something that has seemed to threaten it, then the threat must be less real or less powerful than it has seemed – perhaps not real or powerful at all.

"Remembering that 'I am,' and experiencing that activation of consciousness, makes true the things I most wish to be true: the truth of inclusion, potential, empowerment, abundance, creativity, inspiration, restoration, compassion, connection, peace, power, innocence… and I AM these things. They are no longer something separate from me, to be sought. And the more I can visit that space of I AM, the more these truths come to light.

"When I stand in knowing that I AM, I am not defending or energizing the illusion that I Am Not. We can spend time entrenching ourselves in proving what we are not, which of course never leads to anything other than more illusions: that I am not what I had hoped to be and am instead lacking, separate, incomplete, weak, bound to fear, unworthy of love and incapable of creating."

This analysis led me to another version of the reset: Instead of using the word "reset," I can say to myself "I am." This serves the dual purpose of momentarily preventing myself from running off the tracks of greatness while reminding me quickly and effectively who I really am. So far, it feels like a seamless, graceful way to get back online. ❄

Chapter 30
Adding the Greatness Piece

Let's briefly review the techniques for acknowledging your own successes, first described in Chapter 23:

Active Recognition/Kodak Moments: Simple observation of actions, feelings or thoughts.

Experiential Recognition: Kodak moment plus acknowledgement of the values displayed in one's self-observed actions, feelings or thoughts.

Proactive Recognition: Self-acknowledgement and praise for not breaking the rules/energizing WMDs.

Now let's add what I call *the greatness piece*.

This is where we return to the concept of greatness introduced early in this book and incorporate it with these techniques. Here is where you find avenues through which to factor in *the ways in which your successes reflect your own greatness*. In doing so, we are supported in seeing how the successes of others reflect *their* greatness and seeing ways in which those characteristics of greatness are reflected in ourselves. (Remember: If we didn't possess at least some glimmer of those aspects of greatness, we could not see them in anyone else.) What you end up with is an ever-growing, ever-shifting, ever-expanding realm of greatness in you and in those with whom you interact.

You might imagine the self-acknowledgements you give yourself with the techniques listed above as an e-mail you send to yourself. To these e-mails, you will begin to create attachments that reveal to you facets of your greatness.

If you are like most people, you are starting out with limited capacity to recognize yourself for being *good,* much less *great.* But you need only to begin to catch the most basic glimmer of goodness to send your energy there and open it into a recognition of your own greatness. From there, you continue to build yourself into a mindset/heart-set of greatness for both yourself and others.

Living in your own greatness means that:

- You find yourself moving into an immovable belief in the God-ness of your being.
- You have an unflappable, heart-centered understanding of knowing who you really are and what inspires you.
- You have a positive influence on those you encounter.
- You consistently make great choices that enhance rather than hurt your relationships and endeavors.
- You have abundant inner wealth (the kind of self-esteem that comes from repeated instances of being held in esteem). If inner wealth were actual dollars and cents, you'd be a billionaire.
- You have vast and congruent self-worth (*congruent* meaning that your worth to yourself is equal to your worth to others) because you prove to yourself over and over that you are worthy of deep connection in regard to matters of goodness and greatness, large and small.
- You take responsibility for your life – and hold all the power in your life.
- You can be in touch with, pursuing and living your dreams, rather than being frightened by them or stuck in other ways.
- You can stand tall in your greatness as life calls on you to stretch into more demanding responsibilities.
- You can intentionally influence the world around you, with confidence that your influence has value and meaning.

- You are not tripped up by or afraid of problems – they don't stop coming, but they are no longer impediments.
- You are fundamentally optimistic and have positive expectations.
- You have a renewed access to the intuitive stream the universe has to offer.
- You have the knowing sense of what you want to accomplish and who you want to be in the present moment.
- You have a deep faith in the great and wise unfolding of life on every level.
- You can reset back to greatness easily because you have such a deep connection to enjoying being 'online.'
- You can stay in your heart, the seat of greatness, and attune to the transmissions of truth that the heart so readily accesses when open.

Greatness is always there for the picking, like a bountiful grove of fruit. You can bring it forth with fierce power and commitment.

Adding the Greatness Piece to Active Recognition

Let's say you were going to add this 'greatness piece' to a Kodak Moment (Active Recognition). You are calling your own attention to the Now through conscious acknowledgement of where you are and what you are experiencing. Here's how you might add that 'attachment' of greatness:

"I'm feeling annoyed by this problem at work, but I'm persevering in trying to work it out. Perseverance is a great quality I have."

"Taking this new yoga class is scary for me. Still, I'm going in there to do it, and this bravery is a quality of my greatness."

"I'm mopping the floor, a job I really hate doing. I know it's important to keep my home clean as a way to take care of myself and my family. I am the greatness of caring and concern."

Adding the Greatness Piece to Experiential Recognition

This technique is for self-recognition wherein you are acknowledging yourself for "walking your talk" – for living in accordance to values that are meaningful to you. You're sending yourself an e-mail that honors you for living a specific important value. In adding the greatness piece, you are adding an attachment that reminds you that you are living a quality of greatness, right now.

For example:

"Although I'm not getting along with my sister right now, I am continuing to try to reach out to her and heal our problems. I'm demonstrating how much I value family and good communication. These are all qualities of greatness."

"Although I felt like not telling the truth in this situation, I did because honesty is important to me. Being truly honest, and being careful to do so in as sensitive and non-judgmental a way as possible, are qualities of my greatness."

"In giving part of my lunch to the homeless man who hangs out near my work, I showed unselfishness and compassion. This decision reflected my greatness."

Adding the Greatness Piece to Proactive Recognition

Proactive Recognition, where you acknowledge yourself for NOT breaking rules or doing something that could be harmful to self or others, builds inner wealth and guides you to an inner sense of greatness.

Rules can be confining. Acting in the interest of the common good rather than doing something completely selfish or self-gratifying can be difficult! When you choose to follow the path you know to be the right path, you are demonstrating wisdom and power. You are reflecting ability to collaborate and cooperate. Go ahead and acknowledge yourself for doing so. Who does it hurt? Have you figured out an answer to that one yet?

Confront yourself with the fact of your own greatness when you are practicing a Proactive Recognition:

"I'm in a hurry but I'm choosing not to speed on these dangerous roads. My concern for others' safety and the safety of myself is a quality of my greatness."

"When that checker made a mistake with my items and had to start over, I felt like making a rude remark, but I didn't. Instead, I made a friendly joke and she smiled. My ability to lighten a tense moment is a quality of my greatness."

"When my daughter gave me attitude, I wanted to start screaming at her, but instead I reset myself, gave *her* a reset and then dove in to support her next positive choice. I am the greatness of patience, determination and gentleness."

All of this might seem like a lot of words – a lot to ramble through and think about in moments when most of us are accustomed to numbly moving forward through the day. However: Think about how eloquent and long-winded you tend to get when things are going wrong; when you make a choice that you're *not* proud of having made; when you are getting mired in the muck of negativity, anger, blame, shame and other WMDs. Those moments bring out the poet in most of us, don't they? All I suggest is flipping your eloquence into moments where you're making the choices you want to make – the choices that dovetail with your best intentions.

Think how often our bodies cry out in hunger for physical nourishment. What makes us think our hearts and minds are any less hungry for the nourishment of gratitude and greatness?

Any excuse for a feast! You can see any moment as an excuse to nurture yourself. Are you going to ruin anyone's day by doing this? Even if you were to enact this practice simply by walking down the street every day saying to yourself "We are greatness," do you doubt that things would get sweeter and sweeter? ❄

Chapter 31

Epiphigasms

> There is a vitality, a life-force, an energy, a quickening that is translated through you into action and because there is only one of you in all of time, this expression is unique. And if you block it, it will never exist through any other medium and be lost.
>
> – Martha Graham, American modern dancer and choreographer

Biblically speaking, Epiphany describes the Twelfth Night – the sixth of January – when the infant Christ received his visit from the three Wise Men and they reveal his divinity to the world. The word 'epiphany' comes from a Greek word that means *to manifest*. Before the time of Christ, it was used to report the appearance of gods and goddesses on the mortal plane.

Irish author James Joyce, whose books were first published in the early part of the 20th century, shifted this term to a more secular use. In several of his books and stories, his characters were said to have epiphanies, which Bernard Richards of *The English Review* described many years later as "sudden flashes of perception and insight." Joyce described them in a letter to his brother as "little errors and gestures – mere straws in the wind – by which people betrayed the very things they were most careful to conceal." He also saw these epiphanies as potentially beautiful, lyrical, mind-stopping: an experience that puts one directly and totally into the present, a momentary recognition of the greatness of life, wholeness and radiance. This usage of the word 'epiphany' has become its main application.

This is a word I adore, but I wanted something less heady to describe the full-body, full-soul, heart-centered experience of being in one's greatness. One day, I had it: a combination of epiphany and a perfect orgasm: an *epiphigasm*. (Joyce scholars would wince, but I like it!) This is where everything, for a moment, comes into alignment, and the bigger picture of the greatness of self and others falls into place like the cascading last pieces of a completed jigsaw puzzle. In these moments, the next dose of knowing is fully revealed and it feels ever so sweet.

Let's try an exercise where you can bring on your very own epiphigasm – a master integration of sorts. Maybe even multiple epiphigasms! ❆

Greatness exercise. Give yourself the luxury of settling in to a sweet space and allow yourself to drop into slow, deep, rhythmic breathing.

Once again attune to your heartbeat and feel it as the drum that it is, pulsating out from the middle of your chest to every last corridor of your body and declaring your aliveness. Let this pulsating beat dictate the cadence of your breath. Sip in the precious energy of life on the in breath and fully give it back on the out breath, in time with the drumbeat of your heart. Experiment to find an even number of beats upon which to time your in breaths and out breaths. Feel the beauty of this life force entering your bloodstream. Feel the breath like a second drum that aligns with that of the drumbeat of the heart.

Now, give your heart a voice and let the knowing come. Let your heart tell you truths of your greatness and allow the breath to carry that message to your entire being. This is the sacred vault of who you are, where the real treasures reside. This is your divine inheritance, an inheritance that you alone can bring to the world. Take a few of these gifts in your loving embrace and allow them to be the music of your Now.

"I am the greatness of wisdom." Sweet in breath, sweet out breath.

"I am the greatness of truth." Sweet in breath, sweet out breath.

"I am the greatness of aliveness." Let the message dance in your being.

"We are great compassion." Send whatever messages of greatness are there for you to the cells of your inner world on the in breath. Send them out to the world at large on the out breath. Cycle your greatness through your own being, and then release it out into the universe. There is always more.

If you run out of specifics, go with "I am greatness," or "We are greatness," or simply "Greatness."

If you get stuck, refuse to get sidetracked in any random other thoughts. Reset immediately to a little more greatness. Just a little bit louder now...a little more greatness now... And let it come!

Chapter 32

Michelangelos Everywhere

Go ahead, tell the absolute truth of your greatness. Don't be shy – be brazen! Be absolutely, ruthlessly opportunistic with how great you are, even if at first it feels like it is only the truth of who you hope to be. Even if it feels pretend, unreal or surreal.

Imagine Michelangelo standing in front of a rough, two-ton block of marble. Then imagine the works that came from those moments: the 17-foot-tall statue of David preparing to slay Goliath, or the monumental and breathtaking Piéta. The vision he held became a more visible truth in tiny increments with each small alteration of that big piece of stone. Certainly, there were days when he got stuck. I imagine that, on those days, he simply held that vision until he knew where to begin carving the next shape.

Some days, I can be so specific about my own qualities of greatness or that of others; on other days, it's all I can do to force myself to remember generalities. If you have days where you can't think of specific words to reflect specific qualities of greatness, just tell yourself "I am great," or even better, "We are great." In a pinch, "I am" or simply "greatness" will do.

Hold a vision of magnificence. What does it look like to you? Feel the vision; smell the vision; make believe it's on television! Because you are, in essence, broadcasting your greatness, even when you are not totally clear about how its qualities manifest in you at this moment.

This isn't about ego, any more than Michelangelo's sculptures are about ego. They are both manifestations of the divine that come through human beings. It is said that Michelangelo held as his truth that he was only chipping away what wasn't the beauty already buried inside every stone. How fortunate are we to get to have that experience of revealing our beauty that is already there? Will it hurt anyone for each of us to amplify this, to embrace it, to radiate it within – or out to the world? ❄

Chapter 33

Be Here kNOWing

What's fascinating about yesterday is that it's *so over*. Even better, the moment before this one, too, is *so over*. No need to hold on; couldn't do it even if you wanted; could try, but truly, it's *gone* – even if yesterday was the best day of your life. If that's what you hang on to, it inevitably gets in the way of Now, and it's all downhill from there, isn't it? Even savoring the greatest past moments interferes with being truly open to the present Now. So let's consider playing with the Nows we have at our disposal.

Instead of "Be here NOW," I suggest going with "Be here kNOWing."

Embrace and direct each Now, knowing how you want to be in the world, how you want to cultivate and direct your power and influence, and living that out with pure, clear and immovable intention. As you *collaborate* with the Now instead of merely inhabiting it, the Nows get even sweeter. You get to color your world with the cosmic array of the tones and hues you experience, fully embracing the moment and bringing new splendor and meaning into whichever frames you choose.

I never had what I would consider full-tilt success with "being here now." I could get there and be there, but on some soul level, I always felt something beyond that was elusive and disappointing. Then I realized that this Now could have multiple layers of realization, and I got so excited about the possibilities. I can choose the way I shoot the picture on the Now; I can choose the frame for it, or where I hang the picture, or how I talk about the picture while I'm hanging it on the wall.

Once, after co-leading a Heart Rhythm Meditation/Greatness five-day intensive workshop with Puran and Susanna Bair, I immediately attended a weekend-long Gabrielle Roth Five Rhythms Movement training. There, I found myself dancing in a room with over 100 people in it. Most of these people were strikingly beautiful, though a few seemed either a bit rough around the edges or even a tad strange-looking.

The dancing was a wild expression of the inner self – something that isn't exactly Fred and Ginger material. But there I was, moving around the room, dancing silently and from the space of my great previous week's attunement. I was cherishing each and every person for the greatness I perceived in them. From time to time I got stuck in judgment, but stayed aware and reset myself internally. Then I was able to change the trajectory and find a place where I could honor whomever I was currently looking at. I didn't need to speak to anyone or even know anyone to see the bounty of the greatness that surrounded me and came from within me. This was such an exhilarating success because I was able to actively remember that I was the producer, director and editor of the footage and that I had the exclusive rights to my own voice-over in each and every frame.

You can be here knowing every single living and inanimate thing... See, sense and project knowing the greatness, goodness, God-ness of all... Feel gratefulness for all. Experiment with ways to experience how you might be in that space: so very present to the moment, with an inner voice-over of greatness, gratitude and God-ness. Like a program that runs smoothly in the background as you work on your computer, enhancing and enriching your experience...like 'Photoshopping' greatness into every picture!

This activates a world of fascination and wonder. Nothing is ever the same again. Even that which remains the same is imbued with the differences brought by the evolving, ever-new you to the equation. Instead of calcification, replication, sameness, blandness and boredom, *everything and everyone is lit up – stimulated and catalyzed with your intention of appreciation.* Every new Now is imbued with your evolving version of love. And in each new Now, you evolve further as a lover of life and everything in it.

Every time you arrive in the Now, heart first, and inhabit it, you have a direct experience of *being your God-ness.* This is, I believe, why people who stay in this place more or less all the time are so captivating and compelling. We are seeing God come through them. As we move into this space of kNOWing, we can be equally captivating and compelling gateways to God. ❄

Greatness exercise. The next time you make a trip to the store, bring this awareness with you. As you go about your business, make it your intention to see everyone and everything with a heart-set of greatness. Breathe and reset as needed.

The programming to perceive greatness in others is there all the time. It's in the hardware. You're just activating it through your intention. If you've already been someone who does this, today make it your mission to take the trajectory to a higher level, and/or challenge yourself to see the greatness in someone who might otherwise have gotten past your radar. When you get deeply into this, you'll see that there really are no exceptions. If you find yourself feeling there are, reset and give it one more try, climbing a bit further into your heart, where there are some amazing vistas with plenty of scenic angles to choose from.

Congratulations on bringing greatness to an eyes-open meditation.

Chapter 34

Great Expectations

A friend from England told me a story about a boy who got a favorable note sent home from school, but it wasn't until months later that the discovery was made that it was sent home with the wrong child. Meanwhile, it changed the life of the boy dramatically. He and his family all thought that he was finally being appreciated at school.

Our expectations of others are revealed in subtle ways. Take, for example, the phrases customarily used to check in with a friend or family member: "How are you doing?" If the person looks like he or she isn't doing so well, we ask "Are you OK?" Questions like these can open dubious files, the quintessential can of worms. If the person on the other end actually feels like answering the question honestly (instead of automatically saying he or she is "fine"), you may have opened the door for that person to wax poetically about his ills.

These questions seem so much like the right ones to ask. They feel so compassionate on one level – even therapeutic. Many therapists train extensively to learn to best aid the process of helping a person who needs to express – or, as the case may be, vent – what's going on for him or her, in a safe space. This practice is recommended in self-help book after self-help book.

However, questions like these in reality *set up an expectation that the person is not OK.* By their very nature, they open that classic can of worms of complaints and problems and set our own energetic expectations for more of the same.

Wishing, hoping, wanting and even praying can easily be turned energetically upside-down. We often put ourselves in a place of lack, where we madly scramble for union or reunion with God, joy, money, better health, a better relationship or whatever it is we are wishing/hoping/praying for. In doing this, we add dimension to the energy of NOT having it. Drawn to a trace memory of having been whole, we remain in a shadow of lack.

When we approach another person or ourselves with a statement like "I hope you get it together!" or "I wish for things to go better for you," our expectations are obvious. Energetically though, these are not positive statements. They create an inverted sense of relationship with self and others – a sense of lack, of holding out the carrot of the future instead of appreciating the Now.

As you shift your attention to recognizing greatness in the Now, you send a message to the universe that you are grateful for what is happening in this moment. The universe gives you more to be grateful for in the next Nows…and more Nows full of greatness to be great-full for. This loving universe provides more of what you express gratitude for and more of what you energize.

Certainly, your life will not be void of challenges from others or from yourself. It is not necessary or productive to fear those challenges or to have anxiety over them. There will be people and circumstances that will want to abrade your courage and your will, dim your light, dampen your power. I used to fear this myself, but this changed once I realized that *no one but me is in charge of my spirit and greatness.* Only me. Ironically, now that I really get it, those kinds of challenges don't seem to turn up on my doorstep anymore.

In the presence of negativity, I can say to myself "No! I'm going to stand up for greatness. I'm going to take this negative energy and use it as jet propulsion back into further positivity." Instead of getting into a mindset of trying to figure out what I am doing wrong, how I've done it better in the past, or how I can emulate past successes by walking meticulously in those same footsteps, I choose to trust in the moment and expect to inhabit greatness there.

The word on the street back in the days of Jesus Christ was that his birth heralded the coming of a great teacher. This must have affected his ability to step into and live in his own greatness in each moment. Conversely, many people have gone their entire lifetimes without ever having their greatness recognized. Nurtured Heart teachers and counselors, in their work with children in schools, YMCAs, girls' and boys' clubs and elsewhere, tell stories of how they've just experienced touching a child's life so profoundly – simply by seeing her greatness clearly and telling her how great she is.

Expectations are powerful drivers of success, moment to moment. You could consider this a frustrating which-came-first-the-chicken-or-the-egg scenario: "So in order to have success, I have to be successful?!?!" Or you can see that you can create successes with a simple shift in perspective – by seeing that *you are already successful* in so many ways. You don't have to simply trust that this is the case; this book is about giving you strategies for developing that all-important positive expectation of yourself by knowing and seeing that you are indeed already successful and already great.

You get to use your imagination here. It's the preview of life's (great) coming attractions. Your greatness practice is about stretching your imagination wide to create an exciting vision of the Now, which then sets your expectations for the next Now. You're exploring the power of your imagination to find ever more detailed, fascinating and subtle permutations of greatness in yourself and others, progressively opening the door to more of the same.

This is not a formulaic practice, but a vastly creative practice that will be different for each person. You take the basic techniques and set your creativity loose to find out what the expanding universe of greatness is for *you*. It's all in your hands, in your mind and in your heart. ❄

Chapter 35

3 Refusals

Think like a queen. A queen is not afraid to fail. Failure is another
stepping-stone to greatness.
– Oprah Winfrey

As you embark on this journey to greatness, know that you will be challenged in this process, and that taking specific stands – described here in the form of refusals – will give you a rock to stand on in the tough times when you are tempted to default back to worry, misery and doubt.

Talking about refusals may run counter to your notion of positive thinking. Here's my reasoning: By being very specific about what you will NOT do, you leave yourself huge vistas of what you CAN and

WILL do, and you can then recognize yourself for any quality of greatness that exists in that broad spectrum of actions.

I advise adults who use the Nurtured Heart Approach with children to couch rules in negative language. Instead of making a rule of "be considerate," the rule is spelled out as specific things to avoid doing: no hitting; no pushing; no kicking; no biting; no shoving; no interrupting. Any time the child is not breaking rules, she can be better seen and recognized for it in colorful language: "Stacy, you are not pushing Jen out of the way, even though you are feeling impatient for your turn. You're being considerate right now." This way, the child knows exactly where the line is drawn. She has the freedom to make the choice to cross that line. She knows there will be a consequence if she does, as in sports, and also knows that the adults will celebrate her when she *doesn't* cross it.

These refusals are a form of rule-setting for yourself. Their clarity becomes a great advantage. Tell yourself:

1. **I REFUSE to forget to deepen and propel my own greatness. I will fiercely energize and nurture nothing but greatness in myself and others.**

Although this is a nurturing approach, it's also quite fierce. You are signing up to play hardball with yourself – to set your intention on greatness and stay there with the tenacity of a warrior until it becomes your default. As this becomes the new default setting, the greatness practice moves from the realm of improvement into one of transformation.

2. **I REFUSE to accidentally energize negativity – that is, experiences other than greatness.**

When we make a big deal over problems, we are energizing negativity. Most of us default to a place of essentially celebrating problems by way of how we spend our energetic capital, while under-energizing or failing to acknowledge successes. This refusal is about turning this habit on its head: energetically acknowledging success while refusing to put your energy into worry, misery, doubt and other negative feelings or situations.

Obstacles are inevitable. When you give your energy to an obstacle, however, you are energizing it. Giving energy to an obstacle is equivalent to loving that obstacle.

Row against the current if you need to, but don't give any energy to cursing the current or hating it or wishing it would go the other way. Give yourself acknowledgement for every inch your boat moves in the direction you want to go. Give yourself acknowledgement for knowing which way you *want* that boat to sail!

3. I REFUSE to look the other way when I cross the line into negativity. I will actively remember to reset and use that as an impetus to go further into greatness.

The time-out/reset works much like a penalty in a video game – you're out of the game for a moment, reset your intention to win, and then you are invited back into the game without reprimand or lecture but with renewed opportunity and evidence of success. With a child, it's a win-win when a limit gets pushed: if she doesn't cross the line, she is applauded, and if she does cross the line, she gets a brief 'penalty' (a time-out/reset) and then a push to the next moment of success and more applause.

For you, this means resetting yourself when you start to go down the road of negative thinking. You are going to have problems come up in your life. In Nurtured Heart-speak, you're going to *leak negativity*. Give yourself permission to do this! In the Nurtured Heart Approach, one crucial point comes up again and again: that you cannot stop a child from breaking a rule if he or she wants to. We give the child *carte blanche* by saying "If you're going to break a rule, you have the freedom to do so...but know that there is always a consequence when it happens." Sooner or later, the child comes to see that all the juice comes when they *follow* the rules and that there's nothing to dread when a rule is broken because consequences are simple and designed to ultimately lead to even more success. This effectively drains the energy the child has grown accustomed to receiving in return for breaking rules (or even for just threatening to break them). There are no attempts to stop the rule from being broken. There is plenty of positive reflection of the child's every movement *away* from breaking that rule, or for his deftness as he skims right along that line between rule followed and rule broken; but once the line is crossed, that's a reset, followed by a move back to time-in.

Think of how this might apply to the greatness practice. Let's say you get reprimanded at work by your boss, and you are angry and bitter about the whole thing. You could go down the long, aimless road of talking about the episode to others in your snarkiest tone; or of thinking about mean things to do to your boss (spit in his coffee? steal his fountain pen?); or of sending him a furious e-mail. You might *so* want to indulge in your vitriol for a while. But instead, you could catch yourself, *reset* yourself and get to the next success. It isn't about trying not to be negative, but about deftly catching yourself in that negativity, resetting and moving on into your next success. In doing so, you capture the vast energy of negativity and put it to work to farm further greatness.

For example, you might silently reset, then think "I dealt well with this reprimand. I listened respectfully and did not get defensive because I knew that doing so would cause the problem to grow and might get me fired, and I like my job. I made a choice to listen, and if at some point I feel that my boss is receptive or that I am in the right time and place to explain my point, I trust I will do that. For now, I am comfortable moving in this other direction of greatness. I dealt with my anger well. I am the greatness of self-control and of seeing the big picture."

When these refusals prove difficult, use that difficulty as a reminder – an indication that it's time to increase your trajectory into greatness thinking; to more aggressively find examples of your own expressions of greatness; and to more enthusiastically recognize them. Over time, you will get better and better at resetting and not giving energy to negativity. This is what I mean by *changing your defaults*.

If you encounter another person or a part of yourself that poses resistance to messages of greatness, consider that this indicates a need for *even more* inroads to that greatness trajectory. Don't back off when someone says "Leave me alone with that greatness stuff," or "That's not true of me," or "You're just saying that," or when you find your inner voice saying things like this while trying to acknowledge your own greatness. Instead, *go even further into greatness and gratitude*. We all know that the person who is always rejecting compliments is actually in great need of positive acknowledgement. But getting those compliments through takes a more concerted effort with some people. From the point of view of this greatness practice, the breakthrough to receptivity for greatness might be just on the other side of a small, babbling brook; for someone else, you might have to span a raging river. It's a simple matter of a grander, more energized trajectory. ❅

Greatness exercise. Either wait until the next time you start to feel worry/misery/doubt creeping in, or purposely think of something that typically makes you anxious, like money, an issue you are having with someone or a work or health-related issue. Then, purposely refuse to give it thought and energy. Do it again and again until you come to see how consciously you can choose to not give the gift of your life force in any way you don't want to. It really is always a choice.

To whatever extent you are able to do this, you have shown the greatness of your wisdom, determination, courage and power. These are truly great qualities that you have.

Here is the formula when you find yourself sliding offline or into WMDs:
1. Give yourself a reset and get right back online.
2. Tell yourself: "I am refusing to energize negativity" and
3. "I am refusing to forget to propel and deepen my own greatness."
4. With purposeful intention, find anything from a glimmer to a groundswell of greatness in yourself to recognize.

Repeat as often as necessary.

Chapter 36
The Internal Workout; Or, Greatness Yoga

If there's an item in your house you want to be able to lift, you can go to the gym and work out a few times. At some point, if you build adequate muscle, you can lift that item. This is how the greatness work goes, too. You awkwardly lift and carry these self-acknowledgements of greatness, learning the vocabulary and feeling like you couldn't possibly heft some of these words onto your own shoulders as descriptions of yourself (words like clear-minded, courageous, creative, extraordinary, magnificent, enlightened, nimble and other qualities of greatness listed elsewhere in this book). But with repeated 'workouts,' you find ease.

When suddenly it's easy to bench-press that 50 pounds 10 times whereas it once felt virtually impossible to squeeze out five reps, the weight didn't get lighter, nor are you "cheating" by throwing the weight up and down with momentum (risking injury in the process). You got stronger by utilizing proper form and executing the exercise many times over. You exercised your wherewithal to lift that weight over and over again until your muscles were up to the task.

Similarly, as you do these exercises in finding and amplifying your greatness, you are building inner wealth – a kind of strength that eventually means you will no longer have to turn to old, self-destructive patterns.

Have you ever walked by a class at the gym or yoga studio that looks intimidating but fun? Have you kept right on walking and not given it real consideration, thinking "That's too hard for me. I'm not strong enough or flexible enough or dexterous enough. I'd end up looking like a fool!" Let's say you had this experience and this self-talk but nonetheless went in there and did only what you could. You do only about an eighth of what the rest of the class does. The next time you go back and do about a sixth, then a half, and then before you know it you're attending class number 10 and riding high with everyone else, giving it your all and feeling capable and confident.

In yoga practice, some teachers talk about going to your "edge" in any given pose. For example, let's say you are in the pose known as 'seated forward fold.' You're sitting on the floor with both legs stretched out in front of you. In the far distance, your toes loom, and you think "I've just gotta reach those toes, then I'll *really* be doing yoga!" You lurch forward, and before you know it, you're shaking and straining with effort, your back is complaining, and you're at risk of injury.

If you went about this by honoring your edge, you would breathe slowly into the pose, tilting forward a bit further as you exhale in each cycle of breath, accepting at each point that this is the body you are in today and it's great just as it is. You would let yourself go deep enough to feel a tugging in your legs that is significant, but not painful. You would let yourself linger at that edge, only moving through it when the breath and the muscles allow it with relative ease. In each increment of deepening that pose, you mine your greatness. Where is the greatness in just touching your toes? Appreciate greatness all along the path.

When we see certain qualities of greatness in others and want them for ourselves, we also often think we don't have enough of it. *If you can see a quality of greatness in another, it is there – at least residually – as a quality of greatness in you.* Go ahead, try it on for size! Even if it feels phony at first, you might be surprised at how quickly it comes to feel, authentically, like *the real you.* Affirming the presence of the quality over and over makes it wriggle to life and grow. ❄

Greatness exercise. Go about your day with a new mission: to see, construe and mention to several others an aspect of their greatness.

After each exchange, check in with yourself: How do *you* manifest that quality? Make a point of energizing these aspects of greatness for you as well, seeing ways in which you stand in that quality.

If I give gratitude to the cashier at the market for the considerate and thoughtful style he uses to make customers feel welcome, I can dare to "accuse" him of that greatness. At the same time, I am going to dare to accuse myself of those very same qualities. Perhaps I'll start by simply saying "I love that I can see and appreciate the greatness of being considerate and thoughtful. I am so grateful that it is important to my being. I hold that greatness as meaningful."

Trust me, the heavens are celebrating.

Chapter 37

The Hardware of Greatness

You will notice that I use a lot of metaphors and analogies involving computers in this book – Googling greatness, for example, or the time-in as being online and the reset as a temporary loss of Internet connectivity. These metaphors have turned out to be such a perfect reflection of the way the greatness practice works that I find them irresistible.

Here's another one: Life 08, the Apple software package that came out in 2008, comes with a bunch of bundled programs. These programs, when downloaded, upgrade every program in my computer. The greatness work operates in a similar fashion. Life itself constantly offers bundled upgrades that, when downloaded, will conspire with you. These upgrades offer tremendous support to you in your life's quests.

Another example of a comparison with computers is this: The heart is like the wireless modem on your computer, receiving and sending all the time, always online. It is the place that accesses and receives messages of recognition and greatness, and it is a transmitter of these qualities. You need only to click on your Internet or e-mail icons to access a whole universe of information. This awareness of the heart's capacity has helped me find incredible resonance and openness. When I give acknowledgment to myself or others from my 'head' (a place where thought dictates my words), the impact falls short of the recognitions I make that come purely from the heart.

Here's another one: *Greatness is in your hardware.* Once you recognize this and sign on, you get constant downloads of new software. You know then that greatness is in everyone's hardware. You've got this great new software package for them to download. You don't even need their permission. (In this universe, there's no spam, viruses or software glitches.) Once they're online, they, like you, will get constant downloads and free upgrades.

When you do not acknowledge and tap into your own greatness, it's as though you are using only one tiny function of your powerful personal computer – the calculator, maybe, or the practice-typing program.

Once we are in the groove of greatness, a lot of things that once seemed to be a very big deal cease to matter. God is great despite the storms that ruin houses. Humanity is great despite its many problems. Oprah is great even when she weighs a few extra pounds and regardless of the ups and downs of her love life. We, too, are great no matter what is going on. Greatness is the fiber of the heart and soul and is endless in breadth, width, depth and scope. There is so much to honor and revere in all of this – and all of it can bring greatness into the world. Once you're signed on – once you capitulate to the fact that the hardware of greatness is in every being – those free downloads just keep coming. ❄

Greatness exercise. Go into your heart and resonate with your new, growing sense of greatness. Make the choice to feel it deeply, right now. Amp it up with emotion by revisiting in your mind a time when you felt incredible joy and sense of self-worth if this helps.

Add purpose. Feel that you are talking to your own soul or to the soul of another about a dedication to changing the world for the better. Be with the feeling that your unique blend of qualities of greatness makes you the greatest "you" there is – the perfect match to your dedication. This very combination has been created through your collaboration with the universe. Acknowledge that you are this greatness, and that more is always on the way.

If a voice contradicting these thoughts comes into your mind, don't do battle with it. Don't engage, dialogue or listen; simply reset and go deeper into your heart rather than your mind. Turn your attention back to this fantastic greatness dialogue. The heart so deeply holds this truth as self-evident. Refuse to give energy to negativity here – don't give your energy to anything that distracts you from the ultimate purpose in this moment, which is to raise and cultivate greatness and deepen and clarify your dedication to it. Use any discontent that comes up to further motivate that movement into greatness.

In workshops, participants have come up with some amazing journal entries following this exercise. After taking a few minutes to do this meditation, you might try journaling about it: write your 'Manifesto of Greatness.'

Chapter 38

Praise without Ceasing

In 1961, a novel called *Franny and Zooey* was published. Its author, J.D. Salinger, had already published his best-selling *Catcher in the Rye*, and *Franny and Zooey* was also an instant best-seller. It is still read by high school and college students all over the world. This book is a classic for many reasons, but I bring it up here because it has relevance to the greatness practice.

The story goes something like this:

The first section of the book is about a 20-year-old named Franny Glass. She comes from a family of many children, all of whom are highly intelligent. As children, they became celebrities due to their performance on a radio game show called It's a Wise Child. The eldest boys, Seymour and Buddy, introduced their siblings to many world religions and Eastern spiritual thought.

Franny meets her boyfriend, Lane, at the train station near his college, with plans to go with him to a football game there. At lunch, she talks to him about her frustrations with the shallowness, egotism, falseness and tearing-down she sees all around her at the college she attends. An aspiring actress, she has quit the play she had planned to perform in because she can't stand all the egotism she perceives. Lane personifies this himself, intent mostly on being in the right place with the right kind of girl and discussing, in academic-snob terms, an 'A' paper he wrote. Franny has no appetite and keeps breaking into a sweat; she's a nervous wreck. At one point she goes into the ladies' room to regain her composure.

She has been holding a small green book. After rebuffing Lane's questions about this book, she finally tells him what it is: It's entitled *The Way of the Pilgrim,* and was written by a Russian mystic who propounded a practice he called "prayer without ceasing." It involves repeating, over and over again, the prayer "Lord Jesus Christ have mercy on me" until it becomes automatic, synchronized with the heartbeat. At this point, the author says, this prayer becomes part of the subconscious, which leads to a spiritual transformation – to enlightenment, a direct connection between the person praying and God.

Franny then faints after lunch, and we find her next in her parents' cramped New York apartment, having been there crying and petting her cat for days. We meet Zooey, Franny's older brother, who is a handsome actor. And over the course of the rest of the book, Zooey – with the help of the wisdom of Buddy, a college professor and expert on world religions, and Seymour, a poet, mystic and genius who committed suicide three years earlier – convinces Franny that her embrace of this prayer without ceasing has to do with *her own* falseness, shallowness, egotism and judgment of others. Just as she judges others to be all of these things, she, too, is judging them in return. Zooey shows his younger sister how unconditional love and acceptance is the only enlightened response to the flaws of others.

He brings up a character created by Seymour called the 'Fat Lady' – a personification of the everyman/everywoman, the regular person, the average person who seems to be nothing special, who may seem stupid, self-absorbed or egotistical. Zooey tells Franny that, yes, everyone is flawed, but we all share an essential humanity that deserves loving respect. As she takes this realization into herself, Franny moves into a more peaceful place. Her lips, which had been moving silently in the Jesus prayer in her attempt to become enlightened, stop moving, and she lies still, smiling up at the ceiling.

This is a wonderful book, well worth reading if you have not done so already. Two important threads help illustrate the essence and practice of exploring our own greatness and the greatness of others:

1. In changing your defaults to praise (or 'prayze') without ceasing, you are in essence learning to talk to yourself

in a way that becomes an undercurrent in your mind and in your life. It becomes second nature – synchronized with your heartbeat and, essentially, with your being. You are not asking anyone to have mercy on you, but you are appreciating the qualities of greatness with which you have been endowed. You are giving yourself and others the mercy Franny sought. You are not trying to escape yourself or the outer world through this praise, but to embrace and uplift yourself and others, just as they are. You are *being* mercy.

It's a sort of *retuning to greatness,* where the orchestra goes from being out of tune to being exquisitely in tune. As you practice resetting from worry/misery/doubt and acknowledging your greatness, it becomes more and more effortless. You will eventually be able to invoke that greatness thinking in a heartbeat, on the spot, while walking down the street, not just on your meditation cushion. It may be methodical at first, but we are moving toward a place where it's automatic and always accessible – even mystical.

2. When we criticize, judge and otherwise inflict negativity on ourselves or others, we are not fixing anything; we are engaging in a battle that can never be won. When we appreciate greatness in self and in others, we are demonstrating respect and gratitude for the miracle that is this universe. We are *making* the best of everything we encounter – which will, ultimately, save us a lot of pain and suffering that can easily arise when we misinterpret life to think that we have to leap some abstract, externally imposed 'bar' to be truly happy. (Remember Shamu; he was celebrated for swimming over the rope, whether it was on the bottom of the pool or several feet above its surface.) With the former we can be happy anywhere because we always have what life has given us – the gratitude and greatness, the great-itude that sweetens everything.

Franny learns to see the greatness of those whom she had been judging and criticizing, and, by association, in herself. Although we don't learn where Franny goes next, we're led to believe that she is able to re-enter her life, just as it was before. She will likely pursue her acting career because she is good at acting, and this is what she can best offer to the world. There will likely be no renouncement of her education, no shift into a permanent state of silent mysticism, and no passage into numbness. She sees that she can direct the scene differently and see beauty in the people and places that had looked so ugly to her before. She learns that she can tell herself a different story than the one she has been telling herself and that her connection to the greatness of God comes through her connection with the greatness of humanity. ❄

Chapter 39
It's NOT the Money, Honey: Standing in Abundance

We all need money. Money is the form of life energy that allows us to meet our basic (and not-so-basic) needs. Even the daisies in the field compete for nutrients and resources. Money can behave like other forms of energy: it can either be a vessel for positive thinking and greatness, or it can be a source for avalanches of worry, misery and doubt.

We can choose to approach finances from the greatness perspective.

I had a crisis not long ago that had to do with money, or at least I thought it was about money. Money became scarcer in my life, and thoughts about being in trouble financially began to overrun my head. Even as I lamented my predicament, I was resetting the negative thoughts. But an undercurrent remained. I could feel it like a hum in my energy system. I was resetting and resuming greatness internally; nevertheless, I had a pretty good dose of "poor me" going on. I could see subtle leaks where I would catch myself acting wounded and failing to walk in my greatness. As a result of this energetic shift, I became much more careful in my spending. I had created a sad story, and now I was in the vortex, multiplying the negative spin-offs.

The interesting thing is that the universe picked up on my doubts about finances and presented me with several unexpected costs. It was as though the universe got the message that I liked worrying about money and lovingly handed me more to worry about. This was not a punishment, but rather a reward for what I was giving my energy to.

At some point I realized this whole dilemma was much more about standing in my greatness than anything else. If you invoke greatness, opportunities to stand in it will come. The universe will call these opportunities forth as containers for the greatness you already embody. It will feel like suffering to not take that route. It's so sweet when I seize that current moment of realizing that I'm *not* standing in greatness and subsequently step up to the plate. The great news is that there will always be subsequent opportunities. Whatever level of greatness we can currently generate and tolerate is the current level of greatness that we get.

From this experience, I emerged more determined than ever to give my energy to positivity and greatness. This means living big. This adventure in and out of my "poor me" story was a great lesson.

In self-help writings, when the concept of finances comes up, there is often much talk about *abundance*. Abundance is a lack of scarcity. It is an overflowing, where there is plenty of whatever is needed, and then some. Material or financial wealth is only a tiny aspect of abundance. Look around you at nature – there isn't much efficiency in those systems, is there? A fruit tree makes a huge abundance of fruit, and much of it might rot on the ground, but it feeds the soil and plants new trees, it feeds insects and other creatures that feed the birds and lizards, and so on. A fish or insect will lay hundreds of eggs and only a few of its offspring ever make it to adulthood. Plants make thousands more seeds than are needed to renew their own kind. Our earth has developed an outrageously abundant and complex allocation of universal energy that works quite well as long as we don't tamper with it too much. Abundance is in the hardware.

Your qualities of greatness are your true source of abundant wealth. How much you let your brilliance, respectfulness, wisdom and power shine out into the world says a lot more about your wealth than any balance in any bank account. For example, a child who has sufficient inner wealth will always find a way to make higher education opportunities happen, regardless of whether personal resources exist. Conversely, a child without inner wealth may never see such opportunities evolve even if that child happens to have an enormous college fund.

Financial wealth may offer more opportunities to spread your inner wealth out to the world, but you don't have to have a red cent to live in your own greatness or to shine it out through every pore. Intention to be in your greatness might bring plenty of money, but abundance comes when we use that financial fuel to further support the expression of greatness. As positive-thinking guru Norman Vincent Peale said, once you "throw your heart over the fence, the rest will follow." Oprah is certainly a great example of this.

The tricky thing about financial abundance is that it can cause us to close our greatness down – to entertain worries, misery and doubts about losing the elegant, expensive comforts we've grown so fond of and accustomed to, or conclude that finances are the only thing that counts. Some people who have plenty of money tend to live in a state of 'poverty consciousness,' where they feel consumed by worries about there not being enough to go around.

We also can become poverty-conscious and constricted by a feeling that we do not have enough time – we're time-strapped, stressed, racing around and feeling like we never have a moment to breathe. Many people feel they live in a resource-scarce world, and that time is one resource that is increasingly scarce. Actually, there is an abundance of time because we all have this moment and every next Now. If we can learn to stay centered within each Now, we can sense that we have all the time in the world, no matter how much we have to do in a given day.

Abundance begins with your own belief that an abundance of love, wisdom or other qualities of greatness are already within your heart and soul. You are just awakening them by resonating the energy of these qualities on your breath and radiating them in, through and from your heart. In any greatness meditation, you could replace the word "greatness" with the word "abundance": *I am the abundance of love. I am the abundance of wealth. I am the abundance of wisdom.*

Wealth doesn't count unless it's for everyone. I'm not saying that you should give all of your money away; just see how it feels to hold a vision, energetically, of everyone having abundance in their lives. It might be an abundance of love, an abundance of music, an abundance of health or wisdom. The dance of plenty is much better when everyone is included. If it's truly a dance of overflowing greatness, then it has to involve everyone.

We all are truly the abundance of love;
We are the abundance of wealth;
We are the abundance of wisdom;
We are the abundance of compassion and brilliance;
…and on and on. It's incontrovertible. It's in the hardware. ❄

Chapter 40

"Help Me!"

Help! I need somebody
Help! Not just anybody
Help! You know I need someone
Help….
– The Beatles

This classic song is obviously about asking or pleading for help from the universe, from a deity or from other unspecified sources. Nothing wrong with that, right? You're conjuring up collective energy, engaging a potentially helpful gear. However, from the energetic side of the equation, I question whether a generic plea like "help me" inadvertently creates and participates in an internal relationship based on lack.

As we are all so accustomed to respond to difficulty by invoking a plea for help, the suggestion that this may not be helpful will seem counterintuitive to most readers. I only call it into question as part of my personal attempt to always more fully align the *energy* of requests with their *intention*.

When energy and intention are in congruence, I gain in two ways: I become clearer about *what I want,* and thereby I have more freedom to play with the energy of what I want as though I already have it. What already *is* can be further and further imbued with the aliveness of my intention to have more of that particular quality.

The words "play with the energy" are chosen intentionally here. Let's assume that your greatness is already a given. This, then, is about the fun of finding more and more alive versions of it that continue to serve you better. If what you've been doing up until now hasn't served you, that's not your fault. If you've been operating from a problem-oriented, problem-energizing paradigm – even if you swore you'd never be this way but that software has attached itself like a computer virus in an under-the-radar energetic manner – now you are installing great new security software that comes with a bundled-in sense of humor about it all. So now you're relaxing into a new way that is more playful, that invites curiosity and fun.

I no longer want to call out to the universe for help. My choice is not to draw other people into my life based on what is missing, but based on what I already possess and wish to grow. It's one thing to ask for help with the housework, to seek out a repairman for my house or car, or to call 911 when there's a fire. But in other, more subtle instances, I don't want to confuse my relationship with the universe or the divinity in which I believe by pleading for help. My relationship with the energy of the 'great mystery' (the divinity of my belief) – an energy that also resides in every living being – thrives when I honor it in gratitude or when I see myself as a great manifestation of that energy and mystery. I honor it by exploring the horizons of greatness.

It's as if the universe celebrates those who awaken the qualities of greatness they have and take them as far as they can. Our universe is, by its nature, creative and curious, and it celebrates creativity and curiosity in its inhabitants.

If you have the greatness of being thoughtful and considerate and you honor and own those qualities with gratitude and courage, you will see how the universe celebrates your doing this. The universe rejoices in growing beyond where it is now as reflected and embodied in you. People will appreciate you more and more (and more) for the things you do and the example you set. Great opportunities will just come your way.

Explore the growing edges of all the qualities of greatness you have, and I promise you: The world will dance back at you with a great big smile. ❄

Chapter 41

The Bone Pile

No problem can be solved from the
same level of consciousness that created it.
– Albert Einstein

To live in your greatness, you do not need to go to the bone pile: the place where all of your past issues, successes, resentments, victories, problems, achievements and mistakes are buried. You do not have to laboriously deconstruct or reconstruct your life. You do not have to relive your past successes in order to have more success now. You do not have to dissect your past failures and traumas in order to avoid making the same mistakes again. You are totally free from everything that has happened before this very instant.

I am well aware that this runs counter to tons of psychological theory and practice, including some of the models in which I was heavily trained as a therapist. It may run counter to fundamental beliefs you hold dear. But consider it deeply before dismissing it, because this is a fundamental aspect of the greatness practice.

Going into that bone pile can be the very thing that stops you from living in the greatness you are manifesting in this new Now. The same goes for your relationships with others. For you to support them in living in their greatness, you don't need to fix, delve into or analyze their past errors or successes.

Consider, too, the 'CSI' typically performed in the wake of problems. Parents often mount a crime scene investigation before the dust has settled following a sibling conflict or the breaking of a rule. In all of this well-intentioned delving, in trying to dissect a problem, we are seeking a solution: a fix that will heal the damage and prevent a recurrence of the same problem.

In my experience, going into the CSI mode hands over that $100 bill – a wheelbarrow full of energy – to the child right after he breaks a rule. You are giving your life energy, your greatest gift, to problems. This very energy contributes to the child's impression that he gets more out of life, more aliveness, by way of adversity.

An excellent illustration of this concept came from Nurtured Heart trainer and author Tom Grove in a personal communication to Sam Healy, another trainer who had just completed a Nurtured Heart Approach training for 500 team leaders for the Americorps program. Sam wrote that he was learning, in his efforts to turn public schools on to this work, "about bureaucracies and threatened egos (fear)." Tom responded:

> I, too, am sometimes taken aback by some of the things going on in bureaucracies and by people that leave me feeling naïve or stupid. I've decided I can't/won't/don't need to know the underbelly of things. This fits for me with the idea that we do not need to know a child's story/background to move forward. If someone wants to act out, they will, and sometimes it is overt and sometimes covert. If I get caught in trying to figure it out as a way to dodge/prevent/stop them, then they have me....

We all have the urge to go back and sift through that bone pile. You will find yourself wanting to go there to try to understand something that is happening in this Now: a conflict with another person, perhaps, or an internal struggle or unanswered question. Consider this a leak of negativity. Reset yourself (literally, removing yourself from the *Not*-Now) and return to the greatness that exists in this very moment. Fan those flames, and your heart's wish will come forward.

Delving into the past to try to construct the appropriate Now is something like doing manual labor. For each error made in the past, you accrue experience and knowledge that you get to apply to your life today. You are locked in at the level compensated per unit of time spent struggling, making mistakes and suffering. The greatness practice is more like the entrepreneurial model, where you have an income stream with endless possibility for exponential growth. *Your past is irrelevant,*

aside from how it has shaped you into your glorious present manifestation.
Out of your core greatness and goodness flow all kinds of goodies.

You can begin to accomplish this through the simple techniques outlined in Chapters 23 and 30, but now you can add another dimension to continually return yourself to your birthright of greatness. It involves Heart Rhythm Medication, which was introduced in Chapter 14 and that dovetails beautifully with this practice. ❄

Chapter 42

The Greatness Channel

In meditation, dial into your own greatness as if it were a radio station: the Greatness Channel. The heart is the transmitter and the receiver. It can dial in instantly – and it will always tell you the truth about all of the qualities of greatness in your repertoire – the ones that have become luminous, the ones on the way and the ones there for the awakening. Tune in and receive. Give your heart a hundred votes. Give it a hundred million votes because the mind has a tendency toward amnesia. It forgets our essence. But the heart always remembers who you really are.

As we awaken from the collective amnesia about our greatness, a glimmer quickly triggers an avalanche of remembering. The soul really does want to remember, and it gets pretty darned excited to dance these new steps and to channel this energy into manifesting the lives we want. This is not serious, heady business. This is nourishing and fun. It truly becomes play.

There is sheer joy in seeing what new 'downloads' are available, or what's new on the Greatness Channel. This greatness practice is about that kind of *presence*, an invigorating aliveness that comes with seeing things fresh, being fresh in the space of your life and with whatever moves into that space. Staying in the heart amplifies and radiates your greatness out to others. Living your greatness will always be of benefit. There is never a shortage of real estate for anyone in this territory of greatness. It's collaborative play, not a competition.

The heart can get so developed, so big – bigger than the body itself. It can spiritually and energetically encompass what we think of as the physical brain, becoming the *real* brain, ruling the universe of the being with the energy of love. Your connection to the Greatness Channel is the beginning of this transformation.

This is your own personal 24/7 connection with the great greatness of your being and all beings. All you have to do is connect, breathe through your heart and listen deeply. This broadcast will always tell you the truth of the moment – that WE get to translate and CREATE our own greatness. We don't have to wait and hope for someone else to "catch us being good." Feeling like we can't be successful unless acknowledged by someone else is the definition of disempowerment.

Tuning in the greatness is the quintessential move to real empowerment. Spend an hour seeing the greatness in you and another, or both. Either way you will experience enormous power. Whether you express what you create or experience it silently, you will feel it loud and clear.

This Greatness Channel is always available to you. Tune in to it now. You may immediately find yourself connecting to truths about the qualities of your greatness:

"I am being courageous. I have the greatness of courage."

"I am being wise in taking this path, in reading this book. I have the greatness of wisdom."

"I am exploring new possibilities. I have the greatness of exploration and adventure."

Even a tiny shred of evidence of the quality in question is irrefutable evidence that it reflects one of the myriad aspects of your being. You can then claim this quality at ever-greater levels, making it yours in a bigger way by breathing life into it and by affirming the quality over and over in your internal monologue.

If something contradictory comes to mind, don't do battle with it in the usual way. Don't engage at all. Don't dialogue, or even listen. Simply say to yourself "reset," and then get back online and go even bigger into the greatness conversation with yourself. Get even more determined. Refuse to give your energy to negativity – or, for that matter, to anything that distracts you from your purpose here, which is to awaken and cultivate greatness. If discontent comes up, channel that energy, too, into even further levels of greatness.

In the story of Hercules, he cleans a dirty set of stables by diverting a river. In the same fashion, the breath acts as a river through the heart. With this practice you are literally channeling your life force. It cleanses and refreshes you to better online attunement. It always breathes you into this Now. Once channeled properly, this force will move you that much more quickly toward your life goals.

Take a moment after doing the meditation below to journal or talk to a friend about what came through to you. Stick to speaking of your forays into experiencing greatness and reset yourself if you start to feel compelled to discuss problems or obstacles. Be brave about telling your friend to reset, too, if he or she drifts into talking about problems, obstacles or negativity. ❄

Greatness exercise. Revisit the Googling greatness exercise in Chapter 9. Doing the exercise will take you to a page that lists your traits of your greatness. Each one is a link to another page.

For example: Let's say you find a listing that says you are a person with the greatness of intelligence. Imagine clicking on the word 'intelligence' to find that this trait is linked to a description. It brings up pages of evidence: One is when you wrote your History 101 term paper with creativity and originality. When your research into Roman culture initially seemed unsatisfactory, lacking depth, you looked deeper into writings by authors of that time to get more accurate, in-depth descriptions.

The page is full of evidence of your great intelligence. Read your fill, then click the 'Back' arrow to choose another quality of greatness: perhaps the greatness of awareness ("I was able to spend that day at the beach really staying present, taking in all the sights, sounds and smells") or the greatness of courage ("I confronted my boss about unfair rules about maternity leave, even though I was scared that he would fire me").

This courage, this sensitivity, this awareness, this intelligence and so much more are qualities of the great being that is YOU and that is becoming ever more great this very moment.

Connect with your 'breath beat' and use this pulsating network to 'heart-cast' the truth of your greatness further than ever before. Use the heartbeat-inspired in breath to bring it to every cell of the body, and use the heartbeat-inspired out breath to send more of the same message out beyond your being to all beings.

Chapter 43
Chakras and Greatness Work

At a recent workshop, renowned Los Angeles yoga teacher Jasmine Lieb handed out Post-it notes. She told students to write down a commonly used phrase about something or someone that bothers them. A few examples that came up:

"He's a pain in the neck."

"This is a pain in the ass."

"It gives me a headache."

"My gut tells me this is all wrong."

"I'm all choked up."

"That pisses me off."

"It blows my mind."

After collecting all of the Post-its, she put a large diagram of a human onto an easel. She began to read off the phrases written on the Post-its, placing each one in its proper spot on the diagram. When she was done, pink Post-its had clustered at each of the seven chakras from crown of head to base of spine.

When the ancient yogis developed the concept and map of the seven chakras, they understood that most of the discomforts we experience in the physical body are centered in one or more of these chakras. The system of yoga poses that is still used today was designed to shine energy into and through the chakras, releasing the tension that can bring on the feelings Jasmine Lieb's students described on their Post-its.

To those who do not study yoga, *chakra* may sound like an esoteric term. But a chakra is, quite simply, an energy center of the body. For those who would rather not deal in intangibles, know that modern science has demonstrated that each chakra correlates to major nerve ganglia – clumps of nerves that are central shuttling stations for life force that travels throughout the body. Most of them are also home to glands, the organs of the body that produce communicative chemicals called hormones.

The chakras are used as centers of focus in many kinds of yogic meditation. In the context of greatness practice, a chakra is a place along the spine within which we can hold negativity or that we can cleanse with greatness and positivity. Let's examine how you might apply an understanding of the chakras to greatness practice.

- The root/first chakra is located at the base of the spine. It is also known as the "support chakra" because its function is survival and grounding. Its inner state is stillness and stability. If something is a pain in the ass, something is out of balance in this chakra. Balancing the root chakra grounds, focuses and centers us, even in the face of life's stresses.

- The second/sacral chakra is at the level of the sacrum, the flat part of the very low back. It includes the genitals, urinary tract, lower abdomen, and uterus or prostate gland. Its functions include procreation, sexual desire, pleasure and sexuality. Balancing the sacral chakra brings sexual vitality, physical strength and fertility. When something pisses you off or turns you off, it's affecting you in the sacral chakra.

- The third/solar plexus chakra sits just above the belly button. Laughter, joy and anger are centered here. Balancing the solar plexus chakra helps us deal with tension, calm frustration and anger, and open up intuitive powers. When your guts are stewing with anger, they usually stew at right about the level of the solar plexus chakra.

- The fourth/heart chakra is at the center of the chest. It embodies love and compassion, and bringing balanced attention here promotes the health of the circulatory system and brings a sense of oneness with the universe. On the other hand, intense stress or overwhelming grief creates a storm of hormones that can (rarely) actually stun the heart into a spasm. Most people recover from this, but it's often mistaken for a heart attack. If a person dies of a broken heart, this is probably what has occurred. An ache in the chest – whether due to lost love or to actual heart disease – is about something amiss in the heart chakra.
- The fifth/throat chakra functions as a center of communication and creativity. Balancing this chakra improves communication skills and helps energize the brain's communication centers. When you're all choked up with emotion you can't convey with words, you are feeling your throat chakra in an imbalanced state.
- The sixth/third eye chakra is at the center of the forehead between the eyebrows. It has seeing and intuiting functions, and balancing this chakra promotes these functions as well as the function of thought. When something gives you a headache, you are experiencing blockage or congestion in the sixth chakra.
- The seventh/crown chakra is at the top of the head. Its function is understanding, and it is linked to psychic abilities. When your mind is blown by something, you are feeling it in your seventh chakra.

The Nurtured Heart Approach, Heart Rhythm Meditation and greatness practice all emphasize the heart chakra over others, but it can be interesting to breathe greatness into the other chakras as well.

Clearly, if we can lose our balance of any of these qualities, then we must, to some degree, possess all of them. Give yourself and others credit for having the greatness of stillness and stability, vitality and strength; of intuition and the power to handle strong feelings; of love, compassion and communication; of seeing and thinking things out; and of knowing and understanding.

Know, too, that any of these chakras can fall out of balance. It's like a leak of negativity. Give yourself permission to fall off that horse of awareness and balance, because you're going to, no matter what. The key is to have tools at your disposal to get back onto that horse. Understanding these chakras is just another one of these tools.

Knowing what you now know about the chakras, feel your life force passing through them from bottom to top, from side to side and from front to back.

Retaining balance is not so much about "keeping" balance as it is about enjoying the sway when balance is lost – finding the contentment in the constant rebalancing that is simply part of life. ✳

Chapter 44

The Forward Heart

In Heart Rhythm Meditation, the Bairs teach about the four elements or dimensions of the heart: height, depth, width and forward/internal. They teach that each of these aspects has different qualities and can be brought out through different meditations. These qualities can be felt deeply during their guided meditations. I strongly recommend deeper exploration through their books or workshops if this intrigues you. For the purposes of this chapter, I wish to focus on my own interpretation of their teachings about the forward aspect of the heart.

The forward heart has a sun-like quality. It shines out through the eyes. It embodies and radiates courage, radiance, creativity and generosity – important qualities of greatness. Here is an exercise taught at a Heart Rhythm workshop that cultivates the forward heart.

Begin with the basic Heart Rhythm Meditation – eight counts of in breath and eight counts of out breath, counting in time with the heartbeat. Add to that a heartfelt experience of the truth of your greatness. Breathe in with that intention, and breathe out fully with that same intention: to be in greatness. Sustain this as long as you feel comfortable.

Feel the breath coming in through your back. As you do so, feel, for a moment, as if everything everyone ever said to you – even the worst insults, slights or non-constructive criticisms – was that person's best effort to tell you that you were a great person. If they could have told you about your greatness in a direct way, they would have.

Breathe this in. Send the breath all the way down to the root chakra, up the spine to the crown of the head, and then send it back out the front of your heart. Breathe out all of what you would love to say about the greatness of others. Feel the awareness in your heart of the intention of greatness.

If, in a meditation like this one, nothing specific comes to mind, make up a general statement of greatness: "I am greatness" or "we are greatness." I have done this on many occasions to keep the momentum going in this work. Even if I were to use only this simple statement as a living/waking meditation, a backdrop to my day while I was going about my business, I would be making enormous progress. I have done this on many a day and can look back and see that this meditation has had glorious impact. At the same time, I know that this simple statement is not all there is to send you to your greatest heights.

I am always trying to stretch this practice further by making the statements increasingly more powerful. It is the spiritual equivalent of physical yoga, which progressively stretches and opens the body. Here, we stretch deeper and deeper into new qualities of divinity. It is this constant forward movement and unfolding that fascinates and intrigues me. ❄

Chapter 45

On Being a Jerk

Yes, even I, the guru of greatness practice, can at times be a jerk.

Fortunately, this tendency screams for expression only rarely now, but I have a few gears that I can still easily shift into – gears I know oh so well from the past. This is most likely to happen on the phone, where when pushed to my limit I occasionally get angry and rude. "Let me talk to your supervisor," I've been known to bark, the faint remnants of my New York accent making me sound like I am not someone to be messed with. Although this has not happened in quite some time – I believe as an indirect result of Nurtured Heart greatness practices – I still have it in me.

A few important people in my life have found this aspect of me a bit embarrassing. As I have worked myself up into demanding fierceness, they have cringed.

In the past, this kind of jerk-itude has been an accepted aspect of traditional male-female gender roles. In the more gender-equal environment in which this book is being written, the dynamics of power and receptivity can be shifted. A fair share of females probably have a gift for being a jerk that rivals my own. But what I'm finding is that *no one really has to act like a jerk to get their needs met.* We can support one another into greatness, embracing a balance of power and receptivity within ourselves that makes the external battle unnecessary.

Recently I was telling a friend about my journey out of the "land of the jerk." I concluded that although I may always, from time to time, feel the urgent pull toward that route, I need not spend any time in that space. I don't even need to make a pit stop there tempting though it may be.

Let me offer an example. The other day I left my car to get an oil change and a standard checkup. I exchanged my car for a loaner at 8:00 a.m. and went about my day, expecting the car to be ready by noon, as promised. Two p.m. rolled around and I still hadn't heard from the auto shop. I started to wonder whether I should go straight to where I pick up my daughter from school – though I anticipated she'd have a lot of homework (as usual) and though I had lots of other things to do in the afternoon as well. My plans to give her the time required to do her homework and to get my errands completed were going to be dashed. The first few calls to the service department only netted answering machines. I began to feel my inner jerk winding up. I was ready to give someone a hard time. I *wanted* to give someone a hard time.

All this led me to consider: Is it realistic to expect to get so squeaky-clean that I never feel the urge to be a jerk? Or is the bigger issue that we can feel the urge and segue it in a new and more upbeat direction?

I came to the conclusion that greatness is not about *not having the emotion* – the frustration, the anger, the desire to bitch at whoever finally picks up the phone at the repair shop. There are no Pollyannas here. Although I am going for "joyful all the time," true joy is not about having a one-note response to everything that happens. It wouldn't make much of a symphony if that's all we had to play. In the greatness practice, we can have and embrace the full range of human emotions. We are not trying to rid ourselves of the shadow side. The best part is that when we don't cringe, deny or hide from it, we can tap into the enormous fuel locked in the underbelly of life. Unlike fossil fuel, this kind of fuel is renewable!

I can *feel* that yearning to be a jerk, but I can also make the choice not to *act on that feeling*. There is an incredible energy in that feeling. Can we move that energy in a positive direction? Most definitely. In this, there is much greatness to be acknowledged – without any need to snuff out or defend negative events or emotions.

If someone else's behavior brings up anger or frustration for me, I can choose to tell myself: *I would not be so affected by this if I were sufficiently strong on the inside.* Then, I find myself led to renewed determination to make myself stronger – to expand my inner wealth. I do so in an inspired, self-coaching kind of way, without self-criticism. I see that the loving universe is inspiring me with a new challenge that will – with my enthusiastic participation – help me make myself progressively stronger on the inside. In acknowledging this, I take responsibility in the situation. And instead of feeling like a victim, I empower myself to move into a trajectory of growth. If I don't take responsibility for my own response in the situation, there's no impetus toward that trajectory.

In many conventional spiritual practices, the illusion of a higher reality is all that counts – as opposed to the 'lower' reality of the real, workaday world. But if we can let go of a division between these higher and lower realities – if we can see that in this very Now, we can grasp and channel the higher reality – that's where the greatness practice begins. Everything counts. Greatness is experienced in all, even in your own urges to be a jerk – YOUR 'jerk-itude' can inspire

'Great-itude.' A great, pervasive sense of peace is right there, all the time, even in the midst of all the difficulties life can bring. Instead of *seeking* perfection in isolation from the murkiness and messiness of life, we now experience perfection that is a given, already present, and there for the taking any time.

In my jerk-inclined moments, I consider that maybe, after all, there is no guaranteed default setting. Maybe this practice is really about a strong *tendency* to lean positive instead of negative. Maybe we never stop having to actually hold that intention and make the choice. Maybe we have to keep making that choice moment by moment.

In considering this, I see its beauty. There is an art to consciously being the gatekeeper for each next Now. This means that the Now is never automatic, but remains purposeful, even when you're deep into the greatness practice. More prosaically: You hold the camera that allows you to capture each next Now. YOUR finger is on the shutter. You can choose never to snap a photo of a proverbial "pile of dung" ever again…and if you find yourself pointed at one, you can, through purposeful presence and mindful intention, choose not to click the shutter…or you might even choose to see beauty in that steaming pile! What's more, you can spin 180 degrees and choose something else to snap – or even to turn the camera back and snap a shot of your own beaming face. That's the beaming face of someone consciously choosing not to snap the moment of something that won't ultimately serve them or others.

Instead of dumping our emotions on others and expecting them to behave in ways that make our lives easier or more pleasant, this practice is about deeply feeling our sadness, fear or anger (not to be confused with WMDs, which are NOT feelings at all, but construc-tions of the mind) and *knowing we can handle them.* Once you come to see by experience that you can indeed handle these strong feelings, you can let them wash right through you, pulling you into the next Now, where you consciously decide to do something with that energy that does not involve detrimental behavior. "I'm so annoyed! Man, I think I'll take a break to do some hard exercise and blow off some of this steam."

Or better yet, I can channel that same great energy of impulsivity into my mental gymnastics, choosing to go even bigger and better in the realm of seeing and being greatness. That, too, is always a choice in any next Now – knowing, with great purpose and clarity, what you want to do with those moments.

Psychologist and inspirational author Wayne Dyer writes: "If you bring forth what is inside you, what you bring forth will save you. If you don't bring forth what is inside you, what you don't bring forth will destroy you." To me, this has always meant "Live by your fire or die by your fire." The very same life force and intensity that can be such a gift can also be such a curse if not befriended. A person's life force can become muted by fear or washed out by denial or experiences of defeat. A child can come to despise his intensity because it keeps him hiding or running in circles or into walls. An adult who has come to hate her intensity can get caught up in self-medicating, making efforts to squash it with food, alcohol, drugs, sex or bad relationships. In these cases, that same intensity that can be so great can become a source of death.

On a day when you feel pulled toward dwelling on what is wrong with life, ask yourself: *Would it be a loss to refuse to go down that road? Whenever that road calls, am I required to say yes to it and start trudging along? Can I say no?* It's as though you have the old fire of negativity and WMDs going, and you've been tossing wood onto it even as you try to get the new fire of greatness and positivity going with wood from another pile. Why not put all the fuel onto the fire of greatness? You'll find that once it gets going, any kind of fuel will do the job; anything you throw in there will burn clean and hot.

Experiment with saying no and resetting to greatness. Five minutes later, you probably won't even remember what all that spin was about. ❄

Chapter 46

Willingness to Expire

In my own heart-centered breath/greatness practice, I find that the complete out breath enables me to trust that the gifts I have acquired, the gifts of which my greatness is comprised, can be released, sent out fully on the out breath. And then, when I refill/refresh myself through the in breath, I'm in essence *refreshing my browser to the next Now.*

When you hit that 'refresh' button, you don't lose your place on the Web or your previously visited sites or any of the other good stuff loaded into your computer. Likewise, when I fully expel the breath and inhale again, I find I haven't lost my settings to greatness. They only gain more clarity. Neither have I lost the gifts the past has given me or my visions/intentions for the future.

I know a woman who has a non-threatening heartbeat irregularity that tends to strike when she's tired, particularly during start-stop exertion. Her heart begins to beat at a rate much higher than her normal resting heartbeat – something like 100 to 110 beats per minute. Her heart feels like it's going to thump out of her chest. This accelerated heartbeat goes on for hours, sometimes only ebbing down to normal levels when she goes to sleep. It's not dangerous, but it does exhaust her and often ends her workouts before she's ready to stop. When she was evaluated for this problem by a cardiologist, he said he could do a couple of things to treat it: He could give her mildly sedating medication to take on a daily basis, or he could *ablate* (burn with a catheter to kill the tissue) what he said was an extra conductive pathway in her heart muscle.

She didn't think she should need to take a drug every day to treat something that came up so infrequently. And having someone scorch a part of her heart muscle with a hot catheter? That sounded pretty much out of the question.

She began to delve deeper, and in the process, tried a kind of breathwork called *holotropic breathing.* This involves lying on one's back in a darkened room, mouth open, and breathing hard and rhythmically, inhaling deeply and then blowing out fully on the exhale (basically, hyperventilating on purpose) for *one to three hours,* in time to loud music. She was stunned at how powerfully this affected her. It altered her consciousness, caused her muscles to spasmodically contract and released a torrent of emotion.

Afterward, she read up about this form of breathwork. It was developed by psychologist Stanislof Grof as a treatment for neurosis. Voluntary hyperventilation induces a state called *hypocapnia,* or metabolic alkalosis, which is the opposite of metabolic acidosis (also known as *hypercapnia*). In hypocapnia, the system is flooded with oxygen, and carbon dioxide levels fall. Intentional hypocapnia often induces altered states of consciousness. During these sessions, practitioners can experience a wide range of sensations and emotions, including euphoria, lightness, astonishment, catharsis, visions or vivid recollections of past events like their own birth or early childhood happenings.

In researching this, my friend discovered that chronically shallow breathing can lead to hypercapnia (high CO_2/low oxygen in the blood) and that holotropic breathwork had the opposite effect, flooding the body with oxygen and flushing away excess CO_2. She also found that heart rate could be bumped high in the way hers was by hypercapnia (high CO_2 levels).

Are you getting the big picture here? When she did, she concluded that she could prevent or cure her episodes of fast heartbeat by changing the way she breathed. As she began to observe her own breath, she noticed that she had trouble with deep *exhalation*. As she began to focus on exhaling more completely, she found herself having these fast-heartbeat episodes less often. She also felt generally more relaxed and energized.

The average person's breathing is shallow and constricted, especially on the exhalation (expiration). Exhaling is a letting-go. It can be frightening to let it all out and then some. In heart-centered breathwork, we focus specifically on the exhalations, consciously expelling all the stale air in the lungs. This can bring up discomfort, even fear in some people. After all, exhaling is the last thing we will do in our brief time on this planet. But trusting that fresh new inhalation of breath will return following that fullest expelling of breath is an exercise in trusting the Now. From there, we can learn to mine the Now for all its greatness and to expand that greatness exponentially.

When you focus on greatness with the in breath, you acquire more. You are drinking in all the universe has to offer. If you want to be more respectful, you can breathe in "I am the greatness of respect!" On the out breath, then, you have that much more to give. But to trust deeply enough to exhale completely – to release that great respectfulness out into the world – you must love yourself. In fact, it is an act of loving self and others without the necessity of thinking or stating that's what you are doing.

It is also tremendously cleansing to breathe in this manner. My own experience is that by trusting so deeply and by sending such greatness out into the world, one is expelling anything that is an obstacle to that greatness. In moving these obstacles and anything else that needs to move, we are making way for even more of the good stuff. ❄

Greatness exercise. Take a deep in breath and tell yourself "I am the greatness of the universe," and then on the out breath, tell yourself "we are the greatness of the universe." Feel your heart as the transmitter of that love. Let the breath come from the heart, with the exhalation moving love out at 360 degrees all around the heart. Experiment with the exhalation moving you to an experience of exaltation. After doing this a few times, settle into your heart-centered breath pattern (four, six or eight heartbeats per inhalation and exhalation) and add thoughts of greatness for self and others.

Chapter 47

Silver Linings

Imagine that every interaction you have had with another being on this planet has been an attempt to urge you into your greatness.

Imagine re-breathing/re-birthing all prior interactions from that point of view, regardless of how rough around the edges those interactions might have been.

Imagine that below the surface of another person criticizing or mistreating you is a place from which that person wants to ignite your greatness – but doesn't necessarily quite know how. Imagine looking into that person's essence, the person's core, and hearing the message he or she would send out to you if possible. Imagine that you could feel this even from someone who ridiculed, shamed, hit or abused you. Can you imagine that the message of greatness is what your parents, teachers and other important influences were really trying to convey to you?

Breathe this in fully, then breathe it out as loving support and encouragement of others' greatness. Know that you, too, even in your moments of being bitchy, despairing, angry, moody, depressed or prickly – you, too, seek to ignite the greatness of others. The more you get the WMDs out of the picture, the clearer and more straightforward these expressions will become.

You yourself become the one who removes obstacles. You do this not through brute strength or the changing of someone else who has it all wrong. You do it by the manner in which you choose to see things. You do it by remaining open-hearted.

You become a restorer of others and of yourself. *Re-story:* to tell a new story that is about the Now, not about the past or the future. That's a great form of restoration. ❄

Chapter 48

Wow-WE

There is only one human being.
– J. Krishnamurti, philosopher and spiritual teacher

Many of us, due to what we were taught as children, consider life on this planet to be a competition. To some extent, this is inescapable: on a globe with limited resources and too many people, there is bound to be competition. The good news is that we don't have to fight over greatness. There's plenty of that to go around. In fact, it's infinite and available to everyone at all times.

Consider that you don't need to make a distinction between your own greatness and the greatness of others. You can broaden, deepen and intensify this practice by referring not only to yourself – "I am the greatness of greatness" – but to the collective *we*: "We are the greatness of greatness." *Wow-WE* – what a difference!

Shifting from *me* to *we* carries with it a charge of universal energy. You're not alone, struggling in your little bubble, trying to navigate your way around the other humans in *their* little bubbles. It's not just you and your loved ones anymore. There really is only one human being, and you can tap into that collective greatness simply by shifting a single word in your greatness practice: by entering the realm of "we."

This does not entail becoming a bleeding-heart who constantly gives and seems unable to hold onto self or maintain boundaries. It's just a shift in consciousness. It changes the way you attach love to the in breath and out breath. It's about sweetening the ride.

Revered Buddhist teacher and author Thich Nhat Hanh writes about Inter-Being: the forest doesn't exist by itself, but needs the sun, soil, earth, insects and air. And we are becoming painfully aware that we are reliant on all of these elements ourselves as the environment is threatened. In the same way, we absolutely need others to be in their own greatness. You cannot be a great boss without great employees; a great husband without a great wife; a great parent without great children; or a great teacher without great students.

Fundamentally, we cannot engage in this practice alone. We need to see the greatness of others just as clearly as we see our own. We emphatically do *not* need people to be *less* great so that we can be greater – to the contrary! Others' greatness only amplifies yours, if you let it. By heart-breathing greatness into your life, you will find comfort and robust enjoyment in the greatness of others. You will contribute to this merely by standing in your own greatness.

Anyhow, what good is one person's greatness without everyone else? Do you want to be the last person on the island, great but alone?

Michael Franti, a singer-songwriter, has one song I love especially. It repeats the phrase *Everyone deserves music, sweet music...Everyone deserves music, sweet music.* Along these same lines, everyone deserves to sip at the cool pool of their own greatness. Music is universally available and a huge source of joy, pleasure and inspiration; so, too, is greatness – which is already within each of us, waiting to be realized and cultivated. Witness the miracle of seeing and reflecting another's greatness. Watch them shift toward this energy like flowers toward the sun. ❄

Chapter 49

Sideways Intensity

My life, for many years, has been deeply entwined with children and their intensity. When I look at an intense child, it is easy for me to see the beauty of that intensity, even when it's currently expressed in strongly negative behaviors. Even with that first glance, that first evaluation – as the child wreaks havoc and disrespects everyone in sight – I can see how that same life force can be re-routed positively to serve the child and the world. In fact, I can easily see how that life force can shift when the child is engaging in standard acting-out as well as when the child's negativity is expressed in worry, fear, doubt and other forms of misery.

My mother's intensity, however, was another story.

She was a very intense woman who died in 2008, literally finally letting go at the age of 96 – a monumental letting-go considering how she lived her life. While she was alive, I was stuck in a short view of her as someone whose life was hampered by a staggering degree of worry, fear, doubt and misery. She never saw herself as great, and I'm reasonably certain that she was never told that she was great. Having been so powerfully affected by this in my childhood and even in my adult years, somehow I failed to equate her intensity with an enormous wealth of life force…as if she were the one exception in the universe.

When she died, I felt my access to that life force blow wide open. I realized that the same tenacity, determination and intensity that drove me crazy as a child – usually manifested in the form of overwhelming anxiety – came from a deep well of caring. She loved so deeply that she could hardly stand it or contain it, much less express it.

In a flash, I got that the same intensity that came out of her sideways as fear and doubt was, in fact, a tenacity and determination that could move mountains. I got that her intense judgment of others was actually a greatness of integrity. She wanted things to be fair and equitable. She wanted what was right and fair for her family and for others she cared about.

Her life, to me, had seemed to be lived in lockstep with WMDs. But after her death, I was able to see differently the way in which her great life force had been kept hidden from view. Her positive qualities, woven into the fabric of worry, misery and doubt, had a greatness I had not been able to recognize before. For example: She was tenacious, single-mindedly focused. Once she had something on her mind, she would think of that and only that. This tenacity was misdirected into less-than-magnanimous pursuits and had therefore gone awry, but she absolutely had the greatness of that trait...and the greatness of many other traits. Might outward recognition of these qualities of greatness have relieved her of the burden of her anxiety and fears? How might her awakening to her greatness have opened life to her, enabling her to put these qualities to work in positive ways? I'll never know, but it's fun to imagine how this might have transformed her life. It's so easy for me to imagine the transformed intensity of a child who has these very same dynamics.

It was exciting to take a fresh look at her life and to see her greatness for the very first time. This close-to-home experience inspired me to ramp up my determined efforts to do this with others before it's too late, as it was in my mother's case. My intention is to use the energy of that loss to dedicate myself all the more to proactively growing greatness in myself and in others.

In those envisioning moments, as we pass out of this life, perhaps we are greeted by a vivid, ecstatic lightning bolt that illuminates the truth of greatness within and all around us. In those final moments, I like to think that we are met with a vision of who we are that we couldn't otherwise see – aspects of who we are that are just beckoning to be awakened. I also like to think that we can all "imagine" a death into greatness while we are still alive. ❅

Greatness exercise. Take as many deep breaths as needed to get comfortable and ready.

Now, bring the rhythm of your breath to match the steady rhythm of your heartbeat. Once you have found your right cadence of in breaths and out breaths – try for four to six heartbeats per inhalation, and another four to six heartbeats per exhalation – imagine receiving a call informing you of your own death.

Instead of being shocked or overwhelmed, you find that you are simply and purely fascinated. This childlike, open-minded fascination insulates you from any kind of regret, fear or sadness and transports you to a spirited illumination of who you have been as a great person. It's as if the seas have parted to reveal the greatness of the life you have lived.

Breathe deeply into the big picture of the person of great caring that you are.

Breathe that out in full acknowledgment.

Breathe deeply into the person of great love that you are.

Breathe that out in full acknowledgment as well.

See clearly the great choices you have made and the great judgment and discernment you have used.

Make believe you are finishing a eulogy dedicated to the greatness of your being. What else would you add? Imagine telling all those in attendance at your memorial service about your impact on the planet – all the greatness you bring to the lives of others and to all your endeavors.

If anything other than greatness comes to mind, reset to greatness without hesitation.

Lastly, imagine awakening to the reality that you are still very much here! Embrace the fact that all that has come to mind in imagining your life's end is the truest embodiment of who you really are. Once again, in this awakeness, fully accept all this greatness that is you.

Chapter 50

Greatness and Self-Care

In my work with children, I have found a curious side-effect of the Nurtured Heart Approach. Kids who have been drawn toward eating too much junk food or not enough healthful food start to feed their bodies better. Obese children tend to lose weight. Juvenile couch-potatoes get up and get moving.

These children are learning how great they are. And when they see the truth of their own greatness, they are drawn to take better care of themselves. They want to nourish their bodies. They are less apt to placate their unhappiness or frustration with foods that offer the opposite of nourishment. Girls who have acted out sexually at too young an age find themselves far more willing to "just say no" when they are in a situation that might have ended up much differently in the past.

In applying the greatness practice to myself, I find new love for my own body. I want to get rest and I want to play. I want to do yoga most every day and to otherwise nourish my body and treat it with reverence. I love how my body supports my quests and responds when I treat it well. I love how it reminds me of what is damaging to it by challenging me when I consume too much coffee or sugar or when I'm around influences that emerge as counterproductive. I appreciate how it ages gracefully as long as I remember that there is greatness in growing older. I recognize that wishing for some part of my younger self means I am living in the past – cause for a reset and return to greatness. And I'm pleasantly surprised that this greatness practice has me looking and feeling younger than ever, without any targeted effort on my part to turn back the clock on the aging process.

If you've struggled with weight problems or a habit of eating foods that are unhealthy, you know that this is almost always about a subconscious view you hold of your own worth. What's more impor-tant than what you feed yourself (notice that the word 'greatness' has the word 'eat' at its center) or whether you take decent care of your own body? This is painfully easy to forget in a world full of so-called "convenience foods" and mouth-watering junk. Almost everyone, including myself, falls into a pattern of poor self-care from time to time, and one way back is being in greatness – the building of inner wealth. When you recognize and appreciate your greatness, you are sending a highly charged message to your core being that you are worthy, you are meaningful and you are loved, without every having to directly utter those words. They come with the territory.

Children who have established a firm core of great inner wealth will also grow up better able to take good care of themselves in relationships with others. Those of us who didn't have this as children know how easy it is to get enmeshed in a relationship that doesn't work and maybe is even hurtful to one or both parties. Most of these worries, miseries, doubts and difficulties could be avoided or more gracefully ridden through by people who are secure in feeling their feelings – who, in fact, see their whole gamut of feelings (and the feelings of others!) as qualities of greatness.

Being able to hold on to one's self enables a person to really listen, to be present for another person even when that other person is having challenges. This is enormously healing for both parties and makes relationship strong and safe. When we are in our moments of greatest angst, we need to be heard and listened to and supported. Only the person with strong inner wealth can do this without being sucked into the angst himself or herself. Inner wealth prepares us to do this for others when they need it and to better ride out, support and express our own angst without blaming or shaming others.

The child who gains inner wealth will be well along the line toward being a whole person in relationships, rather than seeking a 'missing piece' to make their half a whole. Instead of entering relationships looking for something they lack, they can relate in joy and greatness. They are equipped to live the understanding that becoming whole is not about finding the missing pieces via someone else, but in reclaiming the existing yet unawakened pieces of ourselves – coming to terms with our own malleable, ever-evolving qualities of who we really are in our greatness.

Overall, the child with abundant inner wealth has a higher-order sense of what's right and of how to care for himself or herself. No longer a child yourself? Don't worry. It's not too late for you. ❄

Chapter 51

Greatness Contests

If other people's accomplishments cause you to sting with a feeling like you are falling short, you're not alone. This is a common issue for people who have been raised to believe that life is a competition.

There is no poverty of possibility. Everyone can be enormously successful. And you don't have to emulate others' talents to share in their greatness. All you need to do is recognize those talents. You are not only giving that other person a gift; you're also acknowledging the greatness in yourself!

Here's a new kind of competition for you: the greatness contest. How much greatness can you see in yourself and in others? Here's how to play:

Sit down with someone you care about. Tell him about his greatness. Feel free to go on and on. Then, have him digest what you've said and feed it back to you.

"George, I want to tell you about your qualities of greatness. You have an amazing capacity for caring. You let others know that you're there for them and that you can be strong for them if they need that. Your heart is so huge, and that lovingness really comes through your eyes!"

George might say: "Wow. Okay. I am a caring person. I am supportive of others. I have a big heart and you can see that when you look into my eyes."

Then, you relay back to the other person (George) how you reflect those same qualities of greatness that you identified in him: a reminder that you could not say the other person had these qualities of greatness if you did not possess them yourself.

Switch sides so that the other person starts off telling you about your greatness, you feed it back, then that person tells of how he/she reflects those same qualities of greatness.

This can be done with a large group by breaking the group down into pairs. Imagine doing this at your next work-related gathering instead of some of the traditional and conventional alternatives!

Some among us with the greatness of courage can easily imagine this and more and make it happen without blinking an eye. Most of us can imagine making this happen with a close friend.

My experiences of watching pairs of people in such exchanges have been extraordinary. Adults who have never before been told about their qualities of greatness immediately shine as if this greatness has been in their 'hardware' all along – as if now the secret is finally out. What a relief not to be carrying the burden of that great secret! ❄

Chapter 52

Get Your Heart-On

Love your enemies and pray for those who persecute you.
– Matthew 5:44

Love your enemies, and you won't have any.
– bumper sticker

What's your typical conversation like? In my observations, conversations frequently involve a dynamic something like this:

"Bitch, bitch, bitch, moan, moan, moan."

"Wow, I can see why you would want to bitch about this. Crazy. Awful. Terrible!"

"Yeah! I am so annoyed."

"OK, now it's my turn to….bitch, bitch, bitch, moan, moan, moan."

"Wow. Now it's my turn to empathize. This is a very bitch-able topic, and I can't believe you haven't bitched and moaned MORE, or sooner."

If I'm wrong about you, hooray. But let's accept that many conversations are about 1.) one person presenting a problem and the emotional baggage that comes with it, mostly negative; 2.) the other person listening and empathizing/agreeing/fanning the flames of negativity; and 3.) switching places. Sometimes there is an added element of dispensing advice.

Ever hear that saying about how you vote with your dollars? You also vote with your energy. *Every time you enter into a conversation like the one above, you are casting your vote for terrible, crazy, awful.*

In relationships, people want to express themselves. This is the way most of us have learned how to do this. The next time you find yourself faced with a person who wants to bitch, bitch, bitch, moan, moan, moan...try this: listen, but don't agree to fulfill the other person's expectation that you will bitch along with them. Breathe in whatever is being said to you that is tinged with negativity and then convert those comments with your internal greatness-translation software to statements of greatness.

Here's how that translation might go:

"My boss is so strict. I'm so sick of her looking over my shoulder all the time when I am totally working as hard as I can!" In translation, this becomes: "My boss is really focused on keeping everything in order at work, and she manages to be right there, ready to help and guide us, all day long. It must be so tiring – her attention to detail and drive are qualities of her greatness."

You don't need to correct the other person or try to change her way of talking about her boss. This isn't about changing the other person. It's about shining the light of greatness out of yourself. If you can get that inner translator going, you can respond to her comment as though she had been talking about her boss' greatness all along.

In essence, you're producing a 'heart-on': seeing the exchange through this mind-over/heart-over/voice-over of greatness. (If this borders on an auto-erotic experience, you may find yourself having an 'epiphigasm!')

After all, you are the director/producer/editor of the footage. You get 10 votes...make that 10 zillion votes. It really is *your* footage; *your* voice-over. Your heart gets to lead that discussion. Greatness is your heart's expertise. It always sees through to the core of the truth. And after all, under it all, we really *are* greatness. ❄

Chapter 53

Obstacles to Greatness in the Form of People

One day, a holy man was sitting near a riverbank when a scorpion fell into the water. The saint reached in to save the drowning scorpion. As he lifted it out of the water, the scorpion stung him. Moments later the scorpion slipped back into the water. Without hesitation, the holy man reached in again to rescue the creature.

A young man standing by saw all this. He approached the saint and asked "Why would you pull the scorpion out again when it stung you the first time?"

The holy man replied: "It is the nature of the scorpion to sting. It is my nature to help."

– from *A Single Blade of Grass* by **Ellen Grace O'Brien**

People who seemingly stand in your way as you shift into seeing and being greatness are often the greatest gifts. Not that a person can't be insurmountably difficult and toxic, but a person like this can also serve as a reminder that greatness is everywhere. Even that person who infuriates and frustrates you at every turn has greatness buried in her hardware, her core being. Holding this in your awareness can make a huge difference to you in relation to the person, even if that person never budges a centimeter in the direction of *who she really is.*

Engaging in this greatness practice is a choice. It's a big choice, a life-changing choice, and one that I am confident will never be harmful to anyone. And the reality is that many people aren't going to make the choice to go there. In the extreme, as you move into this, you will find that some people are just flat-out opposed – even toxic – to this practice.

When I use the word 'toxic,' I use it according to its broadest definition – not as a value judgment, but to describe something that is disruptive or damaging to something else. Water is needed and essential for life, but if you drink too much too fast, it can definitely be toxic; it can, in fact, kill you. If you're stuck in a large body of water without a way to get to shore, you can drown. Toxic is a relative term, and here I mean it to describe a person or a situation that can be an obstacle or even detrimental to the direction of greatness you are choosing.

The toxic person or situation is not necessarily bad by nature; it's just a matter of how he or it draws people in at this moment in time: through negativity. This is that person's current software program. No new downloads are in sight because the person is essentially offline.

In our world, this negative approach to drawing people in works, and it works very well. Some people are simply stuck in adversity because it has been their way of navigating the world and relationships, and there's often much to be gained with that approach. It's scary to try something new. Organizations can be toxically, tragically stuck as well. We all have known at least one such person or organization. (Maybe you have *been* that person or been in that organization but are choosing to change.)

We may be stuck in a relationship with such an individual through family or work, and their presence in our lives may feel like a real burr in the side of our movement into positivity, into seeing and growing greatness. While you may see such a person's great qualities, you may find yourself repeatedly drawn into his or her drama, to your own detriment.

With a person like this, you can empathize; you can try your hardest not to energize negativity; but you may find that this person has the doorway covered, or perhaps even nailed shut. This person has the deepest relationship with himself when he is steeped in negativity. This depth of relationship is important to him – maybe even central to who he feels he is. Letting go of this would be terrifying. Without negative relationship there would temporarily be no relationship, which can end up being perceived as intolerable isolation. You can see the terror in his eyes when that relationship is threatened. And your very refusal to go into that negative space with him may be threatening to him, bringing up all kinds of unpleasantness. In essence, the meta-message perceived by the toxic person is: *When I am in angst, I am more loved. I love myself more. I have hotter, juicier relationship.* If you fail to play into his routine for wringing as much energy as possible out of life, you may bear the brunt of his displeasure and criticism. Think of the fact that many people, particularly the kind of people who will stand in the way of the greatness of others, have never been told about their greatness, and they've always gotten their juice elsewhere.

When this kind of person is complaining, raging, judging, bitching or moaning, she has her most intensely intimate relationship with herself. She also has her most juicy moments of relatedness with others when diving whole-hog into this world of torment. She is drawn to this, over and over, and can't or chooses not to extricate herself. She will go to the mat arguing in favor of an approach to life that is steeped in worry, envy, fear, competitiveness, blame, shame, anger or other negative emotions. This is the way she is; it's just the way she operates. This leaves you, the person committed to greatness practice, with a small handful of choices:

- Give up the greatness techniques altogether in order to maintain/not lose/not rock the boat on this kind of relationship;
- Keep making the effort to relate essentially in greatness;
- Admit to yourself that you are not up to or interested in the task of sharing greatness with this particular person;
- Or, my personal favorite: Continually reset yourself to even greater greatness every time you encounter your frustration with this person, group or organization. This last choice actually 'converts' the energy of frustration to where it can propel a warrior-like stance and trajectory. In this, you can send spirited blessings to those who bring a more toxic energy. You needn't change anyone else, and you needn't lose yourself around someone else's 'inner jerkiness.' Just keep firing up your own blaze of greatness.

You can bring the reset into conversations with anyone. A friend told me about her 65-year-old Aunt Tess, whose life revolved completely around caring for her dementia-stricken 92-year-old mother, and the endless phone conversations Aunt Tess would rope my friend into. "She just goes on and on and on complaining about everything: The inept people at the doctor's office, the stupid people who won't fix the broken stuff in her apartment, how my mom is so mean to her. I never know what to say to her."

I told her to give Aunt Tess a time-out (not by saying it outright, of course). "As soon as she starts to complain, get quiet for a moment and take a breath into greatness. Then say silently to yourself 'reset!' And then, see whether you can find ways to tell her she's great. Like: 'Aunt Tess, I've got to tell you, you're such a good caregiver to your mom…I see how noble it is, how dignified, to devote yourself to taking care of her in these years…How great a person you are to make this choice!' And then, if she keeps on complaining, just tell her you have to go and end the call."

The great news is that, even if this person or situation remains impervious to your efforts, all this effort won't be for naught. You and everyone else you encounter will benefit from this higher trajectory and greater determination to see and be greatness. You may even look back and feel enormously indebted to this adverse person or situation.

If you do choose to go forward, the important thing here is to not see this challenge as an agenda of changing that person – but, rather, as an intention to enjoy and share the greatness you experience in that person or situation. If it's merely an agenda, then you will back off once it feels less egregious; if it's an intention, then you will derive even greater joy as it continues to unfold in greatness.

If you do not or cannot choose to walk away from the toxic person, keep in mind that he can have his angst, and you can bless him in it. Let this relationship be about you facing this angst and resetting over and over to your joyfulness and your greatness – or choosing to silently revere the greatness you know to underlie the current situation, even if it remains completely and forever inaccessible.

You don't have to announce to the person that you refuse to be drawn into his negativity because, energetically, you will be refusing to corroborate his sad story. He might get his cosmic jolt from anguish and WMDs, and that is what he will want to talk about…but you can gently, lovingly refuse to have that conversation. Instead, you can point out how great he is and refuse to have relationship with his problems. The only way out, energetically, is to create hotter relationship when angst is not happening. Give love, energy and relationship when the negativity is absent.

I have fallen in love recently with the expression "save your soul." Save your soul for when the problems and fusses aren't happening. That's when you can give the energy of your soul as fully as you wish in terms of gratitude or greatness or whatever feels right. You can refuse to give the precious gift of your soul's energy in response to the quagmire of negativity.

This being said, just because you open your heart and see God in everyone doesn't mean you can't say no and walk away. And just because someone does not choose this particular system does not make him or her wrong or bad. If a person or an organization has a system that is working, who am I to tell them that it's wrong? When people begin to seek new ways, it's because their current way isn't working any longer. This is often true of parents who turn to the Nurtured Heart Approach: They've reached the end of their rope and can no longer keep going on the path they've been on. It's often cumulative frustration that finally motivates them to change. It's nice to know that another approach is available when this point is reached. And sometimes, people are unwilling to go there until their frustration is completely unmanageable.

You can choose to walk away from a person like this. Even if you have to relate to that person because of a job or because he or she is a family member, you can absolutely maintain your separateness; don't get drawn into the person's negative drama. Let the energy of the toxic person push you into a squeaky-cleaner, higher trajectory with your own greatness practice. Seeing greatness. Being greatness. ❄

Chapter 54

New-Age Negativity and False Forgiveness

The traditional practice of yoga is changing and becoming more of a commodity in modern Western culture. This makes perfect sense; with changing times, ancient practices change and morph as well. For me, yoga is about maintaining a body that is limber, open and able to experience and send along the energy of greatness into itself and out to others. I choose not to go negative about how yoga is practiced today, but even a practice like yoga – designed to uplift, open and balance body and spirit – can be a stealth source of major negativity.

A friend sent me an article from Slate.com, dated March 21, 2007. The article, by Ron Rosenberg, is a biting commentary on the "rhetorical dumbing-down of yoga culture" entitled "The Hostile New-Age Takeover of Yoga." Rosenberg says that yoga, "once a counterweight to our sweaty striving for ego gratification...has become an unctuous adjunct to it." Ouch.

Rosenberg takes issue with the explosion of retail items (yoga mat bags and other accessories, pricey yoga clothing) and the way that this ancient tradition has been boiled down to "syrupy yoga-speak" that may or may not involve exhortations to sculpt your abs or butt. (Rosenberg quotes a friend who tells him that yoga is, for her, "less about Inner Peace than Outer Hotness.")

Rosenberg goes on to tell the story of a 36-year-old woman who wrote to *Yoga Journal* to get some advice in 2006. When she was 16, she had an "intense friendship" – not a romance – with a boy her age. This friendship had ended when she picked a fight with him at some point, then drew over a drawing he'd done on the back of her jacket. Then she tried to make him jealous by dancing with some other boys. She recalls that he gave her a "stricken" look.

Two decades later, the woman had found an old journal of his in her things. Reading it over had convinced her that she needed to apologize to this man and ask his forgiveness. She used a search engine to track him down and e-mailed him to say she was sorry and that she hoped they could talk. No response, which she assumed meant the e-mail address was no longer good. Then she dug further to find his phone number, called him and left a message on his machine. Still no response. Then she sent a letter "in desperation" to reach him and make her apology known, ask for forgiveness, and send a poem she'd written for him in the old days. He sent the entire thing back wrapped with a note that said "What part of no don't you understand?" She wanted to know, from the experts at *Yoga Journal*, how she should move past this 20-year-old experience, since the boy/man in question was unwilling to forgive her for her transgressions.

For me, this is where it got really interesting. The *Yoga Journal* advice-giver's instructions for "moving on" sported negativity leaks like the business end of a watering can. The magazine's experts (according to Rosenberg) "further encourage the hapless writer not to move on but to dwell endlessly, excruciatingly, on the microanalysis of the situation."

They tell her that she does not need his forgiveness, but to forgive herself; that the stress of not doing so could end up giving her a heart attack(!). They advise her to do a "five-step forgiveness ritual" that includes a ritual bath with scents and candles, journaling about her feelings, thoughts and memories, writing down all the patterns she wants to change in herself, then burning what she's written and sending herself flowers. If this set of rituals doesn't work, they say, she could try another four-step Tibetan Buddhist ritual. She might spend a lot of precious time ritually trying to make peace over an imagined slight 20 years past.

This is some serious digging into the bone pile!

It's all very self-involved, with the issue being about her relationship with herself, which causes Rosenberg to crack that this is "Whitney Houston yoga: I found the greatest love of all – Me!" He points out that the woman looking for forgiveness would be far better off getting out of her own head, getting on with her life and doing something for someone who needs help.

I'm in agreement with the author there. He is describing, fundamentally, a reset and a mining of the person's own greatness and that of others. I would add that she could then acknowledge generosity, wisdom and willingness to move on as aspects of her greatness, which will then further grow her proclivity to greatness. I'd venture to say that this is an even more accurate reflection of the true yogic tradition: seeing and being the greatness that we already are.

The *Yoga Journal's* so-called forgiveness rituals leak negativity, big-time. If the woman who wrote in with her forgiveness problem asked me what she should do, my response would not fill nearly as much space on the page as the *Journal's* response: I'd say "Reset and move on to greatness. Utilize the frustration of the past and that feeling of desperation to connect with this man as fuel to propel a greater trajectory of greatness than ever before."

Sometimes I feel as though I have to 'redo' my personal transgressions over and over again – eating foods that don't agree with me, for example, or arguing with someone – until I finally 'get' how to de-energize my response and how to move seamlessly into the next moments of success. This, to me, is true forgiveness, with no lingering negative energy. False forgiveness happens when I say "I forgive myself or another but I am still holding energy over this issue." Real forgiveness, a full deletion of the energetic charge, may take a few resets to greatness to realize. ❄

Chapter 55

Playing Hardball

Often, when people are first exposed to the Nurtured Heart Approach, their initial impression is that it's soft, sweet, syrupy, nicey-nice – like the grandma who could never imagine how you could possibly do anything wrong and is out to spoil you as much as she can.

Let me disabuse you of any conception that this approach involves anything but playing serious hardball. It is a tough approach. There's nothing soft about it. I'm ready to annihilate depression, anxiety and WMDs with greatness. I'm ready to smash negativity and hurl positivity all over the place! Show me your intensity, and I'll show you how the degree to which you have it is the degree to which it makes you great. And if you even *try* to go negative on me, look out, because I'm going to look right at you and see your greatness and reflect it back to you without the faintest hint of hesitation. I'm going to light it up like the Northern Lights. Like a supernova! I've got my blowtorch of greatness at the ready! Look out!

One day I was talking with the husband of a colleague – let's call him James – whose wife had told me that he was in a highly stressful work situation. She thought I could help him take a more positive tack and perhaps even create a more positive work environment for everyone there.

When we sat down together, James spent a lot of time describing the environment of his work for a contractor who did multimillion-dollar remodels on very high-end homes. James complained about how it was a sick system, sick from the top down. The yelling and cursing and anxiety that surrounded him were getting to him in a deep way. "Bosses get in guys' faces and scream and curse at them. My boss does this to me, and sometimes the purpose is to tell me that I have to get madder at and be meaner to the guys under me – that I have to make them afraid of me to make sure the job gets done."

But James also defended the system as he said: "It's about needing to be in reaction because without fast action, the dominoes start to fall. Things start to go seriously wrong. People can get fired just like that." He added with a chuckle: "Knowing what I know about you and your approach, I have to say I'd worry about you at this job site."

I responded, "I've used this approach with groups from the military, with the police and even with gangs. It's been used successfully with meth addicts. I play balls-out hardball with these people, but this doesn't mean I yell at them. Many times I'm the first person who has ever pointed out their greatness. And I get results with these people in a very short time."

James was more interested in talking about the problem – in defining it as precisely as possible, pressing me to comprehend how absolutely unique and difficult was his particular set of circumstances – than he was in hearing about an out-of-the-box solution. Although he was suffering from stress in his work situation, he was too jazzed from handing himself all those $100 bills for negativity to seriously consider any real change. He spoke with eloquence and wit, making me laugh sometimes, but giving me the overall impression that he was intimately married to the drama (read: negativity) around this situation.

He wasn't ready for a shift and walked away believing that, if I were to try to use the Nurtured Heart/greatness work to transform the way people interact at his job site, I would doubtless be eaten alive. As for me, I don't evangelize to people who aren't earnestly interested in making this shift, and there were no hard feelings in me as I walked away from that exchange. Indeed, what transpired for me was further commitment in my trajectory to continue 'Googling greatness' and magnifying magnificence more than ever.

With greatness work, you are playing hardball in the sense that you are absolutely refusing to back away from acknowledging and convincing yourself and others of your/their greatness, and you are absolutely refusing to buy into negativity in yourself or in others (see the Three Refusals chapter if you need a refresher on this). It is not a punitive approach, but it's intense, focused and relentless.

It would be a fun experiment, I think, to have James sternly gather all the guys who work under him and to tell them, with big energy and infectious enthusiasm, "Hey guys, sit down. I've got to tell you something. This client is very tough, and they expect perfection from us, and you guys all followed the rules today. There were no directives from above that were stringent or harsh. Thank you for being so mindful. That mindfulness is a quality of your greatness. Thank you for the beautiful work you did today. Every one of you took great care and used great diligence in making this project fit the client's vision of perfection." If and when James is ready to see that this is a reality – if indeed all rules were followed and there were no stringent/harsh directives from above – and to get excited about it, I've no doubt that this would be the beginning of a workplace transformation.

James, in his way of clinging to worry, misery and doubt, is not the exception, but the rule. Most people focus on problems and the energetic 'hit' they bring. But those WMDs spill out into his work and family life, and no doubt the same thing happens for many of his fellow workers. The route of negativity creates a path strewn with more negativity. The outcome of taking the route of greatness would be yet more greatness to enjoy and to applaud.

This is the energetic reality. You can say you are a positive person, but ultimately, you vote with the reality of your energy. If you entertain negative thoughts, feelings, people or situations, negativity is the music you are choosing to dance to. What we energize is what gets our love. The universe loves us back by giving us more of the same.

In the next chapters, you will find several stories from Nurtured Heart practitioners that show the approach's potential in extreme situations. ❄

Chapter 56

Addiction and Recovery

Back in the 1980s, I fell into a period of experimenting with various mind-altering substances – alcohol, marijuana, cocaine and more. Fortunately, I got out of the whole situation without any visible scars. Today I have a new understanding of both the roots of addiction and the keys to escaping its clutches.

I can trace it all back to my original childhood addiction, which was to get more relationship through wrongdoings, both external and internal. From very early on I noticed that creating chaos and havoc and drama got me the strongest forms of relationship and energy from others and from myself – a far stronger hit than any success I could manage. A later addiction to mind-altering substances seemed like a natural evolution.

Recently, after many years of drinking infrequently and lightly, I shared a bottle of wine or more with a friend. Although this may not sound like a lot, it was too much for me. The next day I found the wind had really been sucked out of my sails. I was, for all intents and purposes, *in recovery*, and I had to make a concerted effort to not have that conversation with myself about "why'd you drink so much…how stupid…you feel like crap today and it's your own fault!" It reminded me of being on the heels of episodes back in the '80s. *Get the drug, feel that feeling, come down. Blah, blah, blah, why am I doing this? It feels so horrible to come down! Blah, blah, blah, gotta get some more*…and so it would go. Then I would find myself seeking out my next hit in some dangerous place where there were people with firearms and other unsavory characteristics.

In the days of my old addictions, I found myself connected primarily with people who were complaining. My whole world was about misery and complaining when I was overdoing with substances; and as any intense person would do, I did the addiction thing full-tilt. I did a lot of whatever I was doing and often put myself in harm's way, risking getting arrested or killed or killing myself with an overdose.

Between descents into this place, I would enter a passionate aftermath where I pledged to take better care of myself. I would then have periods of deep health where I didn't use, ate well and got my life back on track. But they didn't last. There was only so much I could handle because I lacked the inner wealth to sustain that state of stability. Whether I was up or down, I was still essentially in relationship with these same issues – bumping into different walls of the same house.

Most people look at addiction as a two-sided coin: the bad part (when you're using) and the good part (when you're not). But the entire cycle of any kind of addiction and recovery – of not using and going back to using again – is a kind of full-frontal nudity with your misery, a perpetuation of a kind of internal dialogue that feeds the fire of problems with an intensity that can seem irresistible. Even in the midst of my healthy periods, I was still having the same internal conversation with myself. The theme was always the same: *problems.*

My energetic truth through all that time was that the qualitatively best intense relationship I had with myself and others was in relation to problems. We all want intimacy, and I, like most people I knew, was craving intense relationship in one form or another. This turned me into a magnet for situations where I had plenty of reasons to see myself that way and thereby keep the WMDs rolling. The loving universe saw how I had the juiciest relationship with myself when I pushed my limits or when I was hanging out in a risky situation and then subsequently kicked my own butt about how bad that was. The loving universe then, lovingly, handed me more opportunity for the same. I did not have the wherewithal to say anything but yes, almost every time. Energetically, I was demonstrating that I loved misery. I was misery; so I attracted more misery. That was my energetic reality.

I thought I was getting high, but in truth, I was getting misery. And the more I ran *from* misery, the more I ran right into...*more* misery.

Another level of addiction became clear to me in the years after I kicked all that stuff. The addict, it would seem, is seeking happiness. Any commercial or advertisement for alcoholic drinks will depict the quite pleasurable, usually social, side of having a drink or two. (At least I've never seen an ad for alcoholic drinks that depicts someone drinking alone and hiding multiple empty liquor bottles from concerned family members.) When you have a drink at a bar, sometimes you might end up feeling pleasantly giddy and meeting someone with whom you have a nice time. Then you come down, and you don't feel quite so good, and you stop meeting sexy strangers, and you think: *Hmmm, maybe what I need to do is go back to that bar for another drink.* And you have that drink, but you don't feel as good as you want to feel or as you remember feeling last time. No sexy stranger to chat with tonight, either. So, in search of some remnant of that past happiness, you have another drink. Soon you wind up exposed to all kinds of misery – not the happiness with which you had originally associated those initial drinks on that night when it all worked out. In the aftermath, you feel lousy, you have that conversation with yourself again...and before you know it, you're off to the bar for another handful of drinks.

Hanging on the past, regardless of how wonderful it was, is impossible. Any way you slice it, it is over. Attempts to relive it or fuel the present with its energy will quickly close the door to the wonderfulness of these present and next moments. We are miserable when we are not present. We feel that absence in our hearts and souls as a deep and ongoing loss. At those moments, whether we are conscious of it or not, we are energetically in relationship with loss. We are energetically loving our misery.

To me, the big question then is: How do we stop loving misery? There's so much energy in that tumble from grace that follows any form of barreling down problematic roads. The energy of the self-talk and the energy of the negative situations that transpire in relation to addictions is the perpetuating power that keeps this whole pattern spinning.

At some point you have to say "enough is enough!" You choose to love something more than your addiction. You pick something greater. You refuse to enter into those conversations that are essentially a seductive striptease for misery. Even if you screw something up, you feel it deeply but as briefly as possible. Despite temptation to give it lots of conversation, you opt out.

I'm reminded of a surgery I recently underwent to remove a non-malignant growth from my forehead. It was while I was writing this chapter, and I was on the phone with a friend, talking about how lousy it felt, how I hoped it wouldn't scar and so on. And then in mid-stream, I decided to refuse to go there. I told my surprised friend, who had jumped right into the bemoaning fray with me: "I need to reset here. I am a very healthy person!"

"I have to spur a better conversation with myself," I told her. "I'm going to energize a whole different realm of being. I'll still be in this 'Now' of fear but recognize where I want to go with it, instead of just being with my misery. I'm going to feel that alarm and fear and then say 'thanks, but I'm not camping out here.'" She was fine with the shift; I think perhaps she learned something, too, in that moment. I certainly learned that I could shift gears in a flash, even when the siren song of misery was calling my name.

I'm not going to pretend I'm some kind of Pollyanna who has no fear or dread. But when those feelings arise, I'm going to feel them deeply, efficiently and swiftly and then tap into that energy of worry and put it to work in a better direction in accordance with my highly accurate inner compass – a compass that knows what that better direction is. From that deep well of magnetism, I'll magnetize a force that will ultimately bring me to a more enlightened sense of who I really am. This is what I love now. This is what I'm addicted to now: climbing that trajectory of greatness.

I'm finding that if I choose to *switch addictions* – in this case, from the energy of worry, misery, fear and doubt to the energy of feeling and exploring the greatness of self and others – then there is no danger and ultimately nothing to recover from. I can enjoy the next Nows, and ironically, the happiness I sought in so many other ways is right there, smiling back at me.

Now the universe responds with further energy of greatness because I am demonstrating energetically that I love greatness. It's all in the loving. In its loving way, the universe gives me more to love. Now *that's* some good stuff…actually, some great stuff. ❄

Chapter 57

The Bridge to Somewhere

Susan Redford, a dual-licensed mental health and substance abuse professional, discovered the Nurtured Heart Approach in 2005, just when she was starting to feel like leaving the counseling profession. She was working, at that time, with Child Protective Services, dealing with parents who had become neglectful or abusive due to abuse of drugs (mostly methamphetamine).

Susan and a colleague formed a women's treatment group for these people with addictions. The Nurtured Heart Approach formed the foundation of the group treatment methodology but it incorporated another therapeutic method known as Seeking Safety. She vowed never to practice therapy again, but to practice *transformation*. (Susan's co-worker, having had no training in the approach, protested at first but was told "You're a natural – just follow my lead!") Three real-life stories from their group follow, as well as one from another Nurtured Heart practitioner.

Sophie's Story

On that first day of the group, in attendance was Sophie, a 19-year-old mother of two young children who had a history of crystal methamphetamine use dating back to the age of 13. Residential and outpatient treatments had both failed, with Sophie missing multiple appointments and occasionally having positive drug tests. If she didn't successfully complete her CPS case plan, she faced losing custody of her children. When it was Sophie's turn to talk during the group session, she lamented about living in an apartment full of black mold that was causing her children to become ill. Her many efforts to find better housing with her Section Eight grant (at the time, she had no income) had not been successful.

Susan turned to Sophie and said "Right now, I have to accuse you of being a good mother. Everything you have told us so far tells me that you are a good mother. You have taken your children to the doctor, you are giving them their medicine, you continue to clean your apartment, you are calling the landlord, and you are looking for new housing. I know because I am a good mother and you are doing everything I can think of that a good mother might or could do to make a difference for her children. I just have to accuse you of being a good mother."

After a silence, Sophie burst into tears. "Nobody has ever accused me of being a good mother," she told the group. "They just get in my face and yell at me and tell me what a rotten mother I am, that I am no good because I used drugs, and then they tell me I can never be a good mother." Everyone in the room was in tears. It was the start of a transformation.

One month later, Sophie had found better housing for herself and her children and her CPS case was successfully closed. Susan has not seen her since that time, and she feels sure that Sophie is just doing her thing now, being a good mother to her children.

Betty's Story

In another case, a big, strong mother of two named Betty had some problems with violent urges. She had 18 to 20 felony assaults on her record and took great pride in her aggression, anger and rage. Her children had already been detained (removed) once because of their mother's abusive tendencies and her addiction to crystal meth. There was no question that any therapist who wished to have a positive effect here would have to play serious hardball.

Betty had been in treatment so long that talking to her was like hearing a recording of Alcoholics Anonymous/Narcotics Anonymous literature because she was so fluent in that lingo. Betty had been sober for some years, but most people were terrified of her, including the CPS social worker who was responsible for her case. Betty would call that caseworker with demands she expected to be met "or else."

Following a relapse into drug use and placement into a 30-day residential treatment program, along with the removal of her children from her home, she ended up in the women's group. Susan wrote that "being in session with this extremely powerful woman was a combination of appreciating her brilliance while feeling as if I was in the midst of a rodeo trying to rope in an untamed, charging bull." Still, Betty was responding well to the Nurtured Heart Approach.

At one meeting, Betty had been ranting about her anger at various people and systems. Betty also said that, the night before, during a conversation with her almost 18-year-old son, she had made a choice not to be angry with him or argue. Susan saw an opportunity and jumped in: "Right now I have to accuse you of being a really gentle person, Betty. You have given us the irrefutable evidence of that today. And when I think about it, you have given us the evidence of being a gentle person all along. You are respectful in group; you listen to others and give them very wise feedback; you share your wisdom with others in such a gentle way, and you are an incredibly wise woman."

Betty covered her face with her hands and rocked in her seat. She told the group that she could remember having been a gentle soul before being sexually abused and said that, in the moment of Susan's compliment, she "remembered what it was like to be gentle again." From that point forward, instead of spouting NA and AA lingo, she began to speak authentically and to treat the people in her life more gently. Susan also noticed that Betty's transformation helped transform the CPS system as well: As she began to approach her social worker in a Nurtured Heart fashion, the social worker began to respond in kind.

Betty was clean thereafter. Her CPS case was closed. She dealt with her daughter's revelation that she had been sexually abused by her own father in a way she could not have before. Instead of killing her husband and going to jail herself, she focused entirely on taking the necessary legal steps and helping her daughter heal.

Angela's Story

Angela was in danger of losing her parental rights completely. She had a 20-year history of methamphetamine abuse and was about to be booted out of the CPS system altogether.

She was terrifically eloquent when it came to blaming others (parents, children, ex-husband, counselors) for her long string of failures at getting clean and straightening out her life. Susan wondered: With the kind of intelligence Angela obviously had, could she be shifted into a new pattern where she learned to give detailed reports not on her failures, but on her successes?

As Susan worked to nurture Angela toward this shift, she found that Angela was improving. She showed up consistently and on time and contributed brilliantly. Unfortunately, she was still testing positive for meth. When this happened, she would blame others or say she couldn't recall using. Her excuses were that she must have multiple personality disorder or that someone must have tampered with her sample. On one such occasion, unmoored by another positive meth test, Angela demanded to see Susan (her therapist), but Susan took a risk: she said she'd see her in Monday's regular group session, choosing not to energize Angela's negativity.

On Monday, Angela showed up and told the truth: she announced that she had used and had a dirty test as a result. Susan's response: "Oops, bummer – broke a rule. Surely you'll have consequences for using, but for now, I have to accuse you of being an honest person. Right now I am sincerely appreciating your honesty. I also have to accuse you of having integrity. You could have yelled and screamed and blamed everything and everyone for this dirty test, but you are not. You are taking responsibility, you are being completely honest, and you are giving me irrefutable evidence you are a woman of integrity. Now how many hours have you been clean and sober?" Angela responded that it had been about 75 hours.

After this, Angela had no more positive drug tests. She was reunited with her children four months later. The judge, amazed by her transformation, did not require the customary monitoring period of several months following the reunion. At this writing, Angela remains clean and sober, parenting her children lovingly and responsibly.

Tyrone's Story

Lisa Bravo, a therapist with extensive Nurtured Heart training, tells the story of Tyrone, a 16-year-old who had been a ward of the state since his mother's abandonment of him and his seven younger siblings a few years earlier. He had cared for his siblings for months before CPS figured out that no parents were in the home. The kids went into the foster care system. Tyrone became aggressive or violent in some of his foster placements and ended up in a group residential center. He was obese, had a speech impediment and often challenged the authority of the center's staff. Lisa was assigned to be Tyrone's counselor.

He would storm into her office, talking in a loud and demanding way, agitated and pacing. Lisa would respond with recognitions of his ability to not lose his temper and his great ability to articulate what was going on for him. Immediately, Lisa would see him grow calm. She saw that Tyrone was creating problems to try to generate an emotional connection with her and to remain in relationship with her. (If his problems went away, he would lose the daily connection with her and not get to leave his group home to meet with her.)

Lisa then tried a daring angle with Tyrone. She told him that they would only discuss his brilliance at their sessions and that, if he wanted to talk about a problem, he had to come in with a solution already figured out. From there, Tyrone began to reset himself out of negativity. He saw his own gifts. He began to treat his body better, eating well, exercising and setting weight-loss goals. In fact, he lost 100 pounds in the year Lisa was seeing him in therapy. The last time the two spoke, Tyrone was on his way to a pre-med program with the goal of becoming a pediatrician.

Accusing someone of greatness enters the heart on a pathway previously preoccupied with negativity and drama. In these people who ended up with therapists who nurtured their hearts, this pathway had been a circuit for circulating pain and aggression. These therapists were able to change this.

About her experience with her group of female recovering addicts, Susan wrote: "My co-facilitator and I are relentless in appreciating the barriers faced by and the strengths of each woman. We acknowledge what a miracle it is for a woman to merely show up for group – how difficult it was to get there. With issues about transportation, babysitting, mental health problems, we could write the book on problems, but we refuse to energize the negative. We reflect to them the fact they chose to be in group, what they are doing that's positive and what they could have chosen instead but are not doing…that they could have chosen to go out and use substances today yet they made a choice to be in group instead."

In the face of resistance from other providers of substance abuse treatment, Susan and her co-worker have relentlessly, fearlessly persevered in their use of this approach. They have shifted away from a method of treatment that is all about problems into seeing and reflecting the power, strength and goodness of the people they treat.

The truth of the matter is that those who are most violent, anguished, troubled or angry, who most identify themselves with problems and blame everyone but themselves for those problems, are the ones who *absolutely stand to benefit most from the Nurtured Heart Approach* – and, by association, from greatness practice. The harder, faster and more piercing those recognitions of greatness, the faster the needed emotional nutrition and first-hand experiences of success pile up.

Take this opportunity, right now, to re-affirm your Three Refusals. Commit to playing hardball with yourself. Accept nothing less than building yourself, day after day, to new crescendos of greatness. Reset any negativity into energizing greatness. I accuse *you* of greatness, and I encourage you to accuse yourself and others of the same. ❄

Chapter 58

Poop Happens

Another tale from the world of high-end construction:

A carpenter I know makes his living remodeling high-end homes, usually with the help of Mexican immigrant workers. The workers on these sites use Port-a-Potties for their bathroom business. And this friend of mine was, at first, blown away by the fact that the Mexican workers *never seemed to be able to get the toilet paper into the pit of the Port-a-Potty.*

Awful! To go into one of these claustrophobic, odoriferous chambers to do your own business and to then be faced with…well, you can just imagine…on the floor, next to the toilet, all over the place. The bosses hollered at them to stop doing this, and eventually they did, but then new workers would come in and do the same thing. Not surprisingly, this issue contributed to a hostile environment on the job.

This carpenter could feel himself passing judgment on the Mexican workers. *What are they* thinking? *Is this how they deal with things in Mexico?* But then, one day, an architect friend of the carpenter who had spent some time in Mexico explained this mystery to him. In Mexico, flushing *anything* down some toilets besides waste is a risk. Even the slightest clog can cause substandard plumbing systems to back up. These Mexican workers were, in fact, doing what they had been taught to do at home to prevent problems with plumbing. They were demonstrating the greatness of responsibility and caring for their surroundings.

This, then, was an act of being conscientious. Possibly the Mexican workers were thinking (en Español): *Why don't these people have a receptacle where we can throw this paper? What are they* thinking?

While we're on the subject of effluence, I'd like to tell you another story that deals with this topic, but in a much different way. A Nurtured Heart counselor told me this story about her 11-year-old son whom we'll call Travis.

He went on a long-awaited and exciting overnight field trip with his classmates. Something had disagreed with his digestive system, and as they rode on the bus to their destination, he could feel his intestines in an uproar. Afraid to use the bus bathroom – he didn't want to cause a stink and feared that he might be heard having explosive emissions by his classmates – he held on as long as he could. Then he lost control. He pooped copiously in his pants.

Now, I'm not sure if you remember being eleven. In this 'tween' year, on the cusp of adolescence, social acceptance and popularity are incredibly important. It was enough to ruin a child's life, to make him want to never return to school: the chaperones having to help clean him up, having to get new clothes from his suitcase beneath the bus, the bus reeking of a smell that had come from his body. At the very least, one would expect a child this age to elect to get mom on the phone and have her come and take him home.

Travis, whose mom uses the Nurtured Heart Approach powerfully with him at home, did call his mother. She did give him the option of coming home, but asked that he first consider this from his heart. The boy's sobbing began to dissipate, and then finally he said "Okay, I know what to do. I need to leave this moment in the past, reset and start over. I am deciding to have a great time." And this child was able to reset himself and move on to the next Now. He elected to stay on the trip and to shine his positive attitude out at his classmates. They didn't make fun of him; they were even supportive of him, empathizing and doing their best to be sensitive.

This a wonderful testimony to *inner wealth*. I know that if this had happened to me when I was a child, I would have let embarrassment and shame rule. My own 11-year-old self would have been incapable of making the choice to reset. At that time, I had nowhere near the requisite inner wealth to draw upon. I would have perpetuated the dialogue of negativity related to this incident long after everyone else had forgotten it.

Believe it or not, an inspiring thread runs through these two stories about excrement. As one reaches a point of having inner wealth to a significant degree, one can move to a mode of processing things differently with self and others. For the greater part of my lifetime I have had insufficient inner wealth. This meant that clearly processing within or with others was often obscured by a mixed agenda. Although I would have hated having an issue like Travis' on the school bus, in an unconscious and inadvertent way I would have actually "liked" having such an issue. It would have given me so much intense relationship. As a child, I didn't know how to obtain that relationship in a positive manner. Having such an unpleasant experience and the jolt of energy and connection it would have yielded would have fit my existing software/paradigm. In a convoluted way, it would have filled my desperate need for connection. Perhaps it would have made my day – for that matter, many days. For as long as this old software was all I had, it overshadowed my relationships.

This attachment to adversity can show up subtly. Like any person who is part of a community or a family, I have entered into contentious situations with friends, colleagues and others to iron out supposed issues. Today, I can look back and see that my subconscious agenda was to have the issue *not work out*. Sure, back then, if you asked me, I would have said that my agenda was to solve the problem. But now, it's infinitely clear that not only did I throw gas on those fires, but I attracted others who did the same. I drew people into my life who wanted to exacerbate arguments and differences because it was our current best way to get the intimacy of alive connection. I certainly didn't know how to do it in a positive way. Any glimpse I got at that time of positive relationship actually felt unappealing to me and failed to get my interest.

The clincher came after all those years when all of a sudden – due to reaching a pivotal juncture of sufficient inner wealth, I believe – I finally attracted a friend who was capable of an entirely different and better track. I saw that I was capable of living on that track of inner wealth and greatness myself. One day, we found ourselves talking about an edgy difference in how we viewed something, and it was clear and evident that we not only held the intention of working the process to a solution, but that we were both capable of this – and we did!

Now that I've felt the glory of this from the inside out, I've enjoyed this process numerous times. My faith in the ability of human beings to move through problems productively has been renewed and revitalized. With great intention and sufficient inner wealth, processing problems can yield huge rewards and can bring people closer together in any relationship context.

Lesser relationships – the kind that only feed on negativity and difficulty – fall away effortlessly as the new software takes precedence. Once you are really ready to see that glimmer of what is possible, it's hard to want anything less.

The child on the bus, with sufficient inner wealth, was able to process his difficulty to a workable solution, internally and with peers and his parents. So, too, can a carpenter nail any situation that comes his way by following the truth of the situation. All of this is possible assuming the hardware of greatness exists in each of them and they hold an intention to find solutions rather than jumping to conclusions. Even poop can show us the way back to our greatness.

One more thing I am certain of: that the 'sufficient' level of inner wealth, in my case, did not just drop from the sky. It happened as a result of the ever expanding 'accusation' I hold for myself and others regarding our greatness. That intention only grows greater and sweeter every day. ❄

Chapter 59

Baby, Baby: The Greatness of Feelings

A baby is the embodiment of the emotional roller-coaster. One moment she's inconsolable, screaming, red-faced and runny-nosed. The next, she's laughing and happy as a lark. As babies grow to become children, they lose the ability to let their emotions ride through them like the log flume at the amusement park.

Really, we have no choice. We can't expect to be able to let loose a torrent of tears or even a joyful outburst in the middle of taking the SATs or during class at school. There's a time and place for all this, after all. Displays of pure feeling make other people uncomfortable when they erupt from a person over the age of four or so. Once we grow up, we can't expect to be able to express our emotions whenever we feel like it…right?

In years past, human beings had rituals and customs that gave them safe spaces in which to experience their emotional heights and depths. Religious traditions and community rituals gave us culturally sanctioned outlets for this. In modern life, most of us have fewer and fewer places to "let it all hang out." On top of this, our culture has somehow transmitted the impression that we're supposed to sing only a limited number of emotional tunes: for starters, cheerful and lustful. (By lustful, I mean every kind of desire: the desires of your heart and spirit; the desires of your mind and body; the desire to buy consumer goods; the desire to have, do and be more.)

If we fail to feel cheerful, we are given the message that we are not OK. We may be offered all manner of advice, antidepressants, anti-anxiety drugs, and the like. If we fail to feel lustful, that's not OK, either – and there's plenty of pharmaceutical help for that, too.

The greatness practice is a way to allow a more fluid, healthy emotional expression. Instead of a noisy infant-style outburst, you can use the internal dialogue/monologue of the techniques described in this book to allow emotion to course through and be fully acknowledged.

A baby experiences emotion in his entire body. It courses through him from head to toe. As adults, we also experience emotion in our bodies. Remember Jasmine Lieb's Post-it exercise (Chapter 43), where physical experiences of emotion tend to manifest at the precise points of the seven chakras? We feel anger in the guts, joy and frustration in the crown of the head or in the forehead, sadness in the throat, fear in the chest/heart.

Try combining the greatness practice with an awareness of the physical sensation brought about by emotion. Practice Kodak Moments wherein you acknowledge the physical sensations of emotion in your body. Allow those sensations, and breathe them through you instead of trying to squash them down. Take a quiet few moments to inhale recognition for feeling your feelings and let it radiate with a companion feeling of greatness through the heart and into the place in your body where you are feeling emotion.

Simply appreciating that you are allowing yourself to fully acknowledge and experience your frustration, sadness, rage or fear is cause to celebrate. You are giving yourself the gift of feeling your feelings, including those that are difficult to tolerate. This is a quality of greatness. Fearlessly allowing yourself to feel and trusting that you can handle strong emotion is cause to celebrate. Allowing your 'feeling self' to do its thing greatly liberates wonderful energy that is now free to further fuel your new mission: movement into greatness.

Feelings can wash through you, taking you over; or they can come from a specific intention to overlay affirmations of greatness with positive emotions. Thich Nhat Hanh, Zen master and author, has been quoted as saying "Sometimes your joy is the source of your smile, but sometimes your smile can be the source of your joy." If you make conscious effort to add positive emotion to your affirmations of greatness, you can 'pop' the experience – make it vastly more powerful. You can intentionally overlay and imbue your recognitions with joy, gratitude, elation, excitement and other positive feelings. Unlike that baby who is completely overtaken by the emotion of the moment, you can consciously choose emotional colors into which you channel your energy.

The golfer Tiger Woods demonstrates this beautifully when he either hits a great shot and gets a rush of elation, or when he hits a poor shot and gets a rush of rage. In either case, the corresponding feeling appears to course through him like a bolt of lightning...and then, he quickly resets to greatness. When I see him doing this, I believe I can see him *capturing the energetic essence of the emotion* to help himself be ever more present and great in the next moments.

An exhortation to "feel your feelings" can be a gilded invitation to wallow in negativity. My suggestion when feelings come without being intentionally created by you is to feel your feelings *without accessorizing or pathologizing them.* Use them purely as a source of information. Feelings are so energized that, if you feel and use that energy without bogging it down in thoughts, you're going to prosper. Use the information in the energy of emotions to experiment with 'knowing.' Once you start trusting your intuitive sense of what the emotion is telling you, you will have your answers in a flash. Then move on and trust.

As soon as you ruminate on those feelings – surround-sounding them with past circumstances and worries about the future – you are digging yourself an energetic hole. Even if it is a negative feeling like sadness, you can amplify the greatness coming through it: "I love that I have this feeling and am so alive…I am not taking it out on anyone… and I'm not falling apart."

You can multiply the impact of building internal greatness by imagining that you are shouting your recognitions from a rooftop – on the inside. Adding great emotion of accomplishment, like Tiger Woods thrusting his fist in the air and saying "YES!," multiplies the impact.

Recently I had a gratifying opportunity to practice this myself. I ran into a friend at the golf course whom I hadn't seen in quite some time. He's a very powerful businessman. We always enjoy long, spirited conversations about our many shared interests but sometimes fall into competitiveness and some degree of mutual annoyance. In the past, when we were on some topic of mutual interest, I would find myself wanting to put forth collaborative suggestions for projects. Although I wanted to speak up with these suggestions, I felt anxious about doing so.

This time around the block, I was so much more conscious of the moment-to-moment status of both the fun AND my anxiety! I simply kept breathing and feeling my feelings. I stayed in the conversation. I stayed in the moment – a greater-than-ever level of consciousness that I believe to be the result of the further progress of this greatness work that I keep doing. Whenever one of the emotions got strong enough to get me to check out of the moment, I chose to see that as me going offline. In response, I consciously reset and internally said "We are greatness." This felt commensurate with going back online – being back in the game.

I didn't get thrown by the anxiety or the excitement, I just felt it non-judgmentally and kept breathing deeply and reset as often as need be. I had no judgments about how many resets I'd done; I just kept them coming as needed. At one point over a three-hole stretch, I must have reset several times per minute.

Resetting as often as necessary allowed me to stay fully present, to stay in the truth of the moment and to keep breathing fully. Most of us are conditioned to ignore our feelings so that we don't have some untoward expression of those feelings. We are conditioned to try to remain in the space of *reason,* of *rational thought,* and feelings sometimes threaten to ride that train right off the tracks. This practice enabled me to continually acknowledge my feelings – and like the elephant in the room, acknowledgement makes feelings much less frightening. I was able to end the round with a lot of fun and a renewed friendship, *and* with birdies on two of the last three holes!

And something about me staying in this online space of greatness gave him room to do the same. So instead of our old style of occasional competitiveness, on a level that can be a bit wearisome, we were both truly rejoicing in one another's successes. ❄

Chapter 60

Quit Praying for Peace

Every day, people wish, hope and pray. They pray from their hearts, hope on stars and birthday candles, and make wishes on eyelashes shed and blown off fingertips. They hope for the best and pray for prosperity and peace. What could possibly be wrong with that?

194

Let's say I wish for world peace. Translated to the Now, energetically, I am actually inadvertently energizing the lack of peace in the present moment. The energetic meta-message is that *peace apparently does not exist in this Now.*

When carried further, this line of reasoning illuminates another example of upside-down energy: In praying for peace, I actually contribute to that very lack of peace. I give my heartfelt personal energy, perhaps the most powerful gift I own and control, in an upside-down manner. I am trying desperately to row to the shores of peace...and accidentally, through no lack of motivation or energy, rowing in the exact opposite direction.

No one would do that on purpose, but we quite often do it inadvertently. Wishing, hoping and praying for something that is perceived to be missing is, energetically, upside down.

Prayers for peace often occur in response to news of non-peaceful, violent happenings: a stabbing, a riot, a school shooting, a battle fought in an interminable overseas war. When I pray or hope under these circumstances, I am acting under the belief that my talisman of prayer for peace can somehow fight, in the ether, the energy of war and destruction and violence. In my own experience, that prayer for peace sent out in response to news of war only serves to accidentally further energize the very stuff we wish to eliminate.

Philosopher and spiritualist J. Krishnamurti once said "Comparison is violence." When we compare circumstance A with circumstance B and then wish that circumstance B were more like circumstance A, that's bringing more violence into the world.

For the purposes of greatness work, I would like to reframe the concept of prayer. *Everything we say is a prayer.* Any time we speak to ourselves or to others, we are sending an energetic message into the universe – whether or not we ask God, Jesus, Buddha, Krishna, Allah or any other deity.

The traditional definition of prayer involves throwing a prayer out to the transmission center of the universe, with hope that it has some effect. Comments of gratefulness and greatness to self or others are energetically different: they are *direct transmissions*. With these "prayzes," you yourself embody that center, becoming its direct messenger. By directly giving self or others energetic transmissions of gratitude and greatness, you remove the iffy part of the equation. You remove the middleman. We are *being* God, relaying the blessing in a way that is 100 percent reliable. The benefit is that we get to experience for ourselves the power of that message fully manifested. We get to see and experience the immediate impact of that blessing on its recipient.

Here's a different mode that I have been experimenting with. Instead of wishing for peace, I can say "I am peace" or I can say "We are peace." I can find instances in my life where I can acknowledge peacefulness in myself and in those with whom I interact. This *builds* peace; it creates an energetic exchange that resonates into the universe. It praises peace. It "prayzes" peace. It prays peace.

I am *being peace* when I choose to get along with anyone; the same is true with those beings in relation to others. Peace is happening all the time. Thinking peace and visualizing peace become a great prayer of peace.

When we feel the grace and sublime splendor of peace, we are living the greatness of peace. Peace is not an accident. It is a distinct, evocable and replicable energy. It is a powerful prayer to harmonize with the energy of peace that is already widespread, visible and in our grasp.

Check the news and you'll be reminded that awful things happen in the world – on the other side of the globe and even in our own neighborhoods. But the news doesn't report nearly as often on acts of peace as it does acts of violence. It's easy to forget that these beneficial, benevolent acts and events outnumber the awful ones by at least 10 to one, maybe even by 100 to one, or maybe, in actuality, one zillion to one.

The truth is that there are billions of acts of "not being violent" going on right this moment. The truth is that every person not being violent this moment is indeed CHOOSING PEACE.

Since most people default to the negative, and since we are so drawn to dwell in pain, angst, worry and disaster, we can easily forget that peace is actually the predominant energy of most people in most places at most times. It is the predominant energy of most beings on the planet and of all beings at least some of the time. Giving the gift of our energy to anything else furthers that other energetic cause. Giving the gift of our energy to anything remotely peaceful furthers peaceful energy. That's the shore I am rowing to.

When you consciously refuse to give your energy to non-peaceful thoughts and activities, you are not condoning them. Saying no to violence is a clear energetic message, as is resetting to further iterations of peace.

Next time you feel the pangs of suffering related to violence, feel that feeling deeply – and choose to convert that same powerful, charged energy into deep and broad thoughts of peace. There is always room to take that cause further. Row to the shore of peace with greater intention than ever. Go from the powerlessness of *hoping* for peace to the powerfulness of *creating* peace. See peace and you will be blinded by how much light of peace is already there. In being peace, you will make the day of many – including yourself. ❄

Chapter 61
Left Brain, Right Brain: Judging in Greatness

judg·ment (n.): 1.) A formal utterance of an authoritative opinion; an opinion so pronounced. 2.) A formal decision given by a court. 3.) Capitalized: the final judging of humankind by God; a divine sentence or decision, specifically: a calamity held to be sent by God. 4.) The process of forming an opinion or evaluation by discerning and comparing; an opinion or estimate so formed. 5.) The capacity for judging: discernment; the exercise of this capacity. 6.) A proposition stating something believed or asserted.
– Merriam-Webster Dictionary

Judge not, lest ye be judged.
– The Bible

To sit in judgment of those things which you perceive to be wrong or imperfect is to be one more person who is part of judgment, evil or imperfection.
– Wayne Dyer, D.Ed., psychologist and inspirational speaker

Since the middle of the 20th century, science has understood that each half of the brain is, in essence, its own separate entity. The left brain is the center of language and speech. It is logical, rational, sequential, analytical; it does the thinking, analyzing and objective analysis, looks at parts instead of the whole, and checks for accuracy.

The right brain is the visual and movement center. It is random, intuitive, synthesizing, subjective; it looks at the big picture and is the seat of aesthetics, creativity and feeling. Most people are either predominantly left- or right-brained, but one side needs the other for balanced expression and thought.

At a social event I attended recently, I listened to friends discussing judgment – some new research demonstrating (not surprisingly) that judgment is a left-brained function. Their take on it was less than favorable. They were talking about judgment in terms of looking at the actions or ideas of another and judging them as incorrect or immoral; or in terms of the uniquely human ability to add the subjective ideas of "bad" or "good" to the reality around them rather than experiencing that reality as it happens in a fresh and neutral manner. Sometimes we even judge reality *before* it happens and assume that a certain outcome is inevitable.

In recent centuries, humankind has begun to put far more stock in reason than in feelings, intuition or knowing. We often rely more strongly on science than spirituality. This has gotten us a long way – into an age where technology, medicine, government, the arts and civilization in general are maintained at a level of complexity that in centuries past was unimaginable. Without highly refined powers of judgment and reason, none of this could have happened. As a result, we humans tend to rely on judgment and reason far more than we do on feeling and being in the Now.

Judgment is about weighing information at hand in order to make a reasoned decision. The ability to do this is important – there's no arguing with this. But humans display a tendency to decide what we believe and think about something – to pass judgment – long before all of the required information is available.

Believe me, I've been terribly judgmental in the past. I know how insidious and damaging judgment can be. My awakening happened in 1989 at a large week-long retreat on Whidbey Island, off the coast of Seattle, Washington.

Each morning, after meditation, I and about 200 other attendees would convene in a beautiful field to stand in a circle. Morning after morning, I stood in that great big circle, silently scanning person after person. Clearly, all of these individuals were magnificent people who had come here to further develop the goodness they already bring to the world. Then, however, I could barely see that at all.

At that time, I negatively judged person after person in that circle for a multitude of reasons – despite the fact that I knew not a single soul there. They were all part of a spiritual group dedicated to healing work, and I could have assumed they were all extraordinarily fine people, but I chose instead to make much less positive judgments. I did this despite the fact that we weren't speaking to one another at all: *It was a silent retreat!* I can't fathom a better illustration of the way judgments so often pour out of thin air. All of my judgments of the others at this retreat were a figment of a mental software program – let's call it Advance Judgment 1.0 – that caused me to download my experience of new people through this filter of negativity. This lingering aspect of my mind was now fully exposed. It was then that I realized beyond any shadow of doubt that all of this judgment was completely unfounded. I needed some new software.

At the time, I had no idea whatsoever what program I needed to download to achieve this end. All my previous efforts at self-therapy or professional therapy had been unproductive in this regard. Even as I stood in this huge circle of amazing people, taking part in a silent group meditation led by an inspiring and enlightened guru, I found myself more judgmental than at any previous time in my life.

And now, as I look back, I can see that what I did at first – which was to try more desperately than ever to *make the judgments go away* – poured more gas on the fire.

Inevitably, at times, we will snap to judgment about others or about ourselves. It's a necessary evil in our complicated world. This tendency seems to be programmed into our DNA, and for good reason – we'd never have survived as a species without the ability to quickly judge the safety or viability of a situation.

Although anyone reading this book most likely has an existence that is much safer and more secure than that of our prehistoric ancestors, we still have that almost overwhelming tendency to move out of the moment and into belief and judgment. But we don't have to turn off that part of our brains to live in the Now and to move into more positivity.

The solution actually found me, years later, as I started using my internal version of the Nurtured Heart Approach. Since adding my insistent attunement to greatness, I have shifted automatically to judging in a different way. I didn't anticipate this; it seems to have come as a free upgrade of the new 'greatness software' that I have been co-creating with the universe.

Now I have given the part of my brain that is responsible for judging a new and better job. Or perhaps a better explanation is that I have now gotten out of the way of the exquisite programming that was already there in the DNA. *That part of my brain is now responsible for judging people in greatness rather than in negativity.*

Now when I meet someone new, I prejudge them without knowing them at all: I judge that greatness is in their hardware. Even if they don't know it yet, they only need a few software downloads to awaken the greatness that's already there.

So my left brain gets to go hog-wild with the judgments, but from this far better vantage point of *knowing* greatness. My right brain then gets to balance this out by discerning the beauty of that greatness. I indulge my creative side through my fantastical, ever-expanding ways of seeing, recognizing and describing greatness.

In the end, I believe that left and right brains can merge within the expansive circle of the heart. The heart can get so developed, so big: bigger than the body itself. It can spiritually and energetically encompass the brain. Then it becomes the real brain, taking over the responsibility of judging and reasoning, but through the energy of love. ❄

Post script:
While writing this chapter, I was preparing to give a presentation at a conference in Tampa, Florida, at a meeting of the International Center for the Study of Psychiatry and Psychology (ICSPP.org). About

a week before my presentation, I received an e-mail about an event in Tampa at which a multitude of luminaries were scheduled to speak: Marianne Williamson, Wayne Dyer, Louise Hay and more. As I looked over the roster of speakers, I found myself feeling a more subtle version of the feeling I had at that Whidbey Island retreat. I was still judging with that negative tinge, only now it was about the speakers at an event I might end up attending.

This time, it came to me to first reset, then to consciously read the biography given for each presenter. With heart rhythm breath in place as I read each bio, I felt, saw and said internally: "Greatness." The healing was instantaneous and amazing. As I did this, I became able to deeply experience only the absolute beauty of each person and the inspired benefit they bring to so many.

During this incident, I saw that the remnants of that old, obsolete Advance Judgment 1.0 software still persisted in my hard drive somewhere. My response to this was to remain vigilant, maintain my Three Refusals, and continually search for further upgrades to new greatness software.

Most of all, I saw that no luminary – not even Williamson, Dyer, Hay or the others in that program – is luminous enough to stave off the scrutiny of my negative judgment when my ego is at the forefront. Conversely, no one can escape being great when that greatness software is up-to-date and running. As long as you keep it refreshed and running, it rules!

Greatness exercise. Go to any busy place: a store, a bustling avenue or a library for example. Purposefully breathe, see and be greatness in every last person's direction. Judge to your heart's content, but judge in greatness. Register how that feels. Go as deeply as you comfortably can into the experience; occasionally, go beyond your comfort zone. Have fun! Feel the joy of the greatness of others.

Chapter 62

Letting Go

I used to think that "letting go of the past" was about family-of-origin stuff: things like your relationship with your mother, your childhood woundings, the fact that your father didn't play catch with you in the backyard or that your brother used to beat the tar out of you on a more or less daily basis.

Today I see things differently: I see the cost of holding on to even the *very last steps* of the past – the weight of the baggage of even the last few moments before the present. Letting go of the distant past is good, but holding on to last week, last month or the last 10 minutes will continue to make it hard to let go of those WMDs.

Some time ago, I found myself in a 'stuck' place with an important person in my life. I so desperately wanted to talk it through, reach a place of mutual understanding and perhaps even get an apology. The other person wanted all of the same things, including an apology from *me*. (The *nerve!*) Clearly, the more we talked and delved, the worse the situation was becoming and was going to become. We had to both see that, at least for the time being, any amount of talking about the issues was putting more gas on that fire. It took tremendous resolve for us to let go of the background noise. Ultimately, I found it harder to let go of the last few seconds than it had been to let go of the stuff from my childhood!

Then I realized that it's just as deadly to go back a few steps – even a single step – as it is to descend all the way back down that steep mountain to issues sourced from childhood. After all: you can't get the last breath back; you can't get the last moment back. Better to use the energy of all those past losses and inspirations to infuse the Now.

The present is a natural outgrowth of every moment that has come before. Trying to consciously manipulate the disappeared past and the intangible future will only remove you from the Now – and with no guarantee of self-improvement, better relationships or greater happiness.

If you feel the need to process something that has already occurred, ask yourself the following questions:

1. Do you have the inner wealth to do it without getting buried in the bone pile?
2. Can you hold a sufficient quotient of intention to reach a solution, rather than flail around endlessly in the energized drama of the problem?

If you can answer each of these questions with an honest "yes," then by all means, dive in. But keep in mind that this very Now has all you need to solve your problem. Your entire past is contained in these present moments. In other words: You will be best equipped to solve problems from the past if you stay firmly situated in the present.

A huge tree grows to its present state from a tiny seed without any kind of machination, manipulation or application of past knowledge. It just keeps unfolding in the Now. Like that tree, you contain all you need to fulfill your potential and manifest all your greatness in the present. Whether you meant them to or not, the very last steps you took brought you to this moment and will motivate the ones you take in this very instant.

Even the idea of *potential* can tug us out of the present moment. If, as a child, you were ever told that you had *potential*, you probably don't have such great associations with this word. A child intuits that when someone is talking about your *potential*, it's because you aren't measuring up *right now. "Try harder!"* translates to *"You're not there yet!"* The implication is that you are not living up to what is required right now or not trying hard enough now. Since the heart deeply feels everything in the Now, this message enters the heart as a negative one.

The Nurtured Heart Approach works with the child's current greatness, pointing out how he is successful in the moment and reflecting that back in a way that fortifies his sense of inner wealth. Potential, in this context, is entirely beside the point.

In this model, you're always there. You're always living your current fullness, right now, with recognition that there is a delightful horizon of more fullness if you want it. Instead of seeing a lack and trying to fill it, you see the world as unfolding and manifesting in relation to the greatness you possess now – the greatness that you've awoken by this point. You can see where there's more to be had and how you can fan the flames – without waiting until tomorrow, without the implication that *maybe, possibly, perhaps you can eke a slight improvement from the depths of your self*...if you could just crank up the effort.

Is there something you can say to yourself to confirm and affirm your greatness in this very moment? How are you handling a situation, right now, in a way that shines your greatness out onto the world? This is the antithesis of potential, and that's a good thing.

Just reading this material shows your deep caring about this subject of growth and greatness. Caring is without doubt an important quality of greatness.

To not hold on to the past, you must relentlessly direct the energy and intention of WMDs and happiness/joy/ecstasy into propelling the Now. Use the energy of the last step, whatever energy it holds, to propel this current step.

Whether you are saying "That was so BAD" or "That was so NICE," you are staying in the past. If you use the energy of that experience, to whatever degree the energy of that experience exists, to support and inspire this current moment of greatness, then that last moment, good or bad, very good or very bad, is truly a gift.

Allow every encounter and experience – good or bad – to be a call and motivation to greatness. All of it serves to send you on that greatness trajectory with ever-increasing momentum. Remember: the last moment has nothing to do with this moment. You are riding a wave of energy that has come out of the previous moments of your life, but the context within which that energy arose is irrelevant in the Now.

There's a letting go of the future as well in this place. "Are we there yet?" falls away in this journey as we realize that we already carry greatness and that there's no limit to the creativity and joy available in this exploration. ❄

Greatness exercise. Imagine greatness to be the ever-expansive ocean of the heart. Imagine the breath to be the propeller that stirs this ocean of greatness.

Imagine that the prana (subtle energy) of life itself comes alive in your heart with each breath. Imagine the rhythm of your heartbeat dancing with the rhythm of each breath, embracing each new moment with love. Set sail on this ocean synchronized to each beat of this heart rhythm.

The heart is an ocean connected with all other oceans. All the rivers that connect all hearts consist of pure love. There is constant inflow into your ocean and outflow into all others. The substance and essence of each river, each stream, each drop of rain, and each trickle of dew and precipitation is holy spirit.

Meditate on the sweet purity of this experience for a few days, just for a few minutes each time. Once you feel you have gained access to a consistent experience of the vastness and beauty of this ocean and the love that flows within it, prepare for a cleansing, letting-go experience based on greatness.

Imagine greatness to be the ultimate 'heart cleanse.' Simultaneously envision the release of whatever no longer serves you from where it is held in the cells of the heart. Gently flush this material out by allowing the pure light of greatness to glow brighter than ever in the ocean of your heart space. Use breath synchronized with heartbeat. On each in breath, allow the entry of the pristine light of life-enhancing greatness into the cells of the heart. With each out breath, allow the exit of all that isn't greatness. Imagine the light of greatness itself making this process effortless.

The first time I did this, I visualized an amazing detoxifying and cleansing. An imagined steady, strong stream of toxic olive green and yellow energy surged out of my heart and out of my body. It felt so gratifying to see this go, and I could feel space opening up for my renewed heart growth – to have and to hold further iterations of greatness.

Chapter 63

Apologies Unaccepted

apol•o•gy (n.) 1.) a formal justification: defense b: excuse 2.) an admission of error or discourtesy accompanied by an expression of regret 3.) a poor substitute: makeshift
– **Merriam-Webster Dictionary**

Often, being willing to toss around the words "I'm sorry" like confetti makes you feel like you are coming across as a nice person, a giving person – a person who is exquisitely sensitive to and regretful for any damage he or she has done to another.

Let's look at Merriam-Webster's succinct definition of the word apology. It is a *formal justification, an excuse.* For what do you need to make an excuse? What do you need to justify? If you make thoughtful commitments (a big challenge in and of itself, but all it requires is 'Googling greatness' fully before making any commitment, large or small) and do your best to keep them, you don't have anything to apologize for.

If you show up late at an appointment, and you apologize for it over and over again, you're living in the past. That is not where your greatness lives! What if you decided that you weren't going to make excuses about anything anymore? That represents a good many reflexive apologies you will never have to make.

Next definition: *an admission of error or discourtesy accompanied by an expression of regret.* There's nothing wrong with admitting error or discourtesy. But expression of regret? More living in the past. Better to forge onward into greatness. *A poor substitute: makeshift.* As in: that fake designer bag you have is a poor apology for a Gucci bag. Are you a poor substitute for something else? Has one of your actions or efforts been a poor substitute for the real thing? If so, the greatness work will move you into a place of higher integrity. No apologies necessary here, either.

The reality is obvious upon closer inspection: A person who apologizes often and shallowly is not attuning to her own greatness or to the greatness of others. Once you start down the greatness path, you'll find you have little to apologize for.

I spent some time with a woman some months ago, and we were teetering on the brink of a possible romantic relationship. During that time, I realized that in years past, I would have been apologizing my butt off from the get-go: for not being able to commit right then and there; for not being more courteous, polite, giving, all-seeing/all-knowing, generous, sexy…you get the idea. But by that point, I felt *only like apologizing when I saw that I was not living in my own greatness*. Rather than casting myself as deplorable and placing myself at the mercy of this other person, I would simply reset when I fell out of step with my inner sense of greatness – a standard of my own making. Then I used whatever degree of regret I was feeling to propel the move onward. It was largely an internal process that kept clearing the jungle of entanglement and kept making space to go forward one step at a time – which is all we can ever do anyhow.

My 'best' at any given moment is tied inextricably to my current level of greatness and inner wealth. That's all I can bring to the table at any given moment. If life shows me patches where that is not quite the match for my endeavors, then all I need to do is go back to work invoking the next levels of greatness. For a person like myself who thrives on simplicity, this works, as it keeps things so very simple.

My deep belief and growing base of experience is this: If something is not manifesting the way I want it to at the current level of greatness, then all I need to do is turn up the dial. At some point, life will fall in line with what has been envisioned. This is not unlike going online to find just the right software upgrades for the job.

My overwhelming experience with 'greatness downloads' is that they come bundled with sufficient sensitivity to others, to society and to the world at large. The needs of the planet, the environment and the situation are all addressed organically. This takes the worry out of the equation (not that I would give that any energy anyway!). More good news: If my heart remains open (and it becomes more open with each subsequent download), it will tell me if my current operating level of greatness is falling short. When this happens, all I have to do is 'go online' to find the next upgrades.

You can do this responsively, when the situation or your heart demands an amped-up level of greatness; or you can do it proactively, just from wanting to go on the enjoyable exploration of the next horizon of greatness.

This being said, it may turn out to be appropriate to apologize from time to time to admit discourtesy or error. If you do so, do it consciously, and stop at "I'm sorry" or "I messed up here. I take responsibility." Treat it like a reset and jump back into greatness. ❄

Greatness exercise. Tonight, as you go to sleep, have greatness be your last thought before drifting off. Then, have it be your first thought upon waking.

Chapter 64

Breathe It

We should make all spiritual talk
Simple today:
God is trying to sell you something
But you don't want to buy it
That is what your suffering is:
Your fantastic haggling,
Your manic screaming over the price!
– Hafiz, ancient Sufi mystic and poet

If you think the severity of your problem warrants a certain level of whining, you miss not only the point, but the opportunity. Consider, instead, that the severity of a problem warrants a corresponding level of invoking the solution: not a call to escalation of whining, but a call to the invoking of greatness. A more severe problem evokes a more intense rate, grade and provocation of inspiration. All add up to a stronger invocation of stepping into and stepping up greatness/ God-ness. When you feel compelled to haggle and scream maniacally about all that is going wrong, recognize that greatness/God-ness is right there, at the burnished, beautiful surface of things, in this very moment.

When we deeply feel hatred, sadness, anger, frustration or other difficult emotions, we tend to hang on to it, allowing it to take over ensuing Nows. I love the idea of breathing deeply into the feeling and then, just as quickly, moving through, using this stronger-than-normal jolt of energy to propel the next new further excursion into positivity. Who is to say this is any less valid an approach than lingering on these feelings? Look at how swiftly and efficiently a world-class athlete like Tiger Woods moves to ever-greater levels of determination by purposely capitalizing on the intensity of his emotions – feeling them deeply and then moving on.

I believe that lingering has a serious downside: it deepens the internal impression that our juiciest relationship with self comes vis à vis problems. This ultimately sends a message to the universe that we like problems. So the universe, which loves us, gives us more to be sad, depressed and angry about.

Fear and worry cause the breath to become shallow and unfulfilling, especially as they cause your energy to tumble toward problems. Doubt is particularly good at directing your energy toward your troubles; it's a bottomless vortex that keeps on drawing your life force over time.

When a big problem rears its head, *breathe it.* In Heart Rhythm Meditation, there is an exercise where one inhales *receptiveness* into the left side of the heart and exhales *giving* on the right side of the heart. Take a few moments to feel this before reading on.

In my experience of this meditation, I have felt a great, continuous flow of energy that can envelop people and things that were formerly challenging. Receiving and giving energy form a circle that rhythmically wraps around me. When I practice this meditation, I come to believe that there is nothing my heart cannot transform. Giving away completely on the out breath allows ever more to pour back in on the in breath: more wisdom pertaining to greatness, or a deepening of what's already given. Then, when it's time for the out breath, there is that much more to breathe out into the universe. Each new breath is like a new train pulling into the station and out again, bringing greatness in and sending greatness out to others. I fully trust that there is always more to discover about greatness and juicier versions on the horizon. God is discovering the greatness and vastness of creation through God's extensions into this universe – that's us, folks.

It would be dangerous to chase after a missed train and draining to lament having missed it after it was gone. The great news is that there is always a next train, and a next train after that, and so on. What a relief! All you need to do, then, is forget and forgive energetically about past trains and hop on board the one that pulls up in front of you and opens its door.

Motivational experts give formulas about how to handle fear, worry and doubt. Formulaic ways of doing things might work at first, but they often become stagnant. Human beings don't usually take too well to formulas – we're too extravagantly creative for that! I've found that an energetic approach – an approach that works with the energy beneath all we say and do – is more flexible and conducive to flexing the creative muscles. In greatness practice, we practice being fully online with heartbeat, breath and greatness all at once. When we recognize that we're off line, we reset back to that space. It's that simple.

The best news is that we already have a heartbeat, we already breathe and we are already great. It's just a matter of coordinating the energetic pulse of all three. This will work anywhere along the continuum, whether these three elements are just barely beginning to coordinate or whether they are already exquisitely coordinated. ❄

Greatness exercise. Sometimes it's fun, just as a practice, to purposely go off line, or to make a game of finding the many times a day we wander off line. Play with whatever combination of heartbeat, breath and greatness best get you back online. Play with resets and feel the generosity and forgiveness inherent in the fluid movement right back to feeling and being connected.

Keep returning to greatness, and your problems fix themselves. It's the darndest thing.

Chapter 65

The Substitute Rabbi

On the day of my mother's memorial, the rabbi who knew her was sick. Another rabbi was asked to take his place. He didn't know my mother at all, and he had to be brave and intuit, with his heart, where the great qualities of this woman lay. He did it, and he did it beautifully.

This ability is there for all of us, all of the time. We can meet someone, and in a matter of moments we can see, feel and intuit that person's greatness. It's one thing to have someone who knows and loves you reflect that greatness back to you; it's almost more precious to have some brave soul meet you for the first time and see who you really are, in all your magnificent splendor, and to tell you what he sees.

I love telling a story I heard from the Champaign School District in Illinois. At one of the middle schools, a new child had arrived at the district well into the school year. He went in for his first morning at the new school. His teacher (whom we'll call Mr. Jones) is a master of the Nurtured Heart Approach, and that morning, Mr. Jones asked the class for two volunteers, arranging for this young man to be one of them. He asked that the two volunteers stand and then requested that the others in the class call out observations of their greatness. The class was able to give wonderful statements of greatness, even to this new student whom no one really knew. His courage, integrity, caring, thoughtfulness and other qualities of greatness were apparent to the others. A few adults happened to be observing in the room that morning, and there wasn't a dry eye among them. Then the teacher asked "Can I have two volunteers to stand up and hear about their greatness in class tomorrow?" Every child in the class raised his or her hand.

That's the clincher for me. The greatness is there, in each and every one of us. And each and every one of us wants to hear about it. ❇

Chapter 66

The Snoring Epiphany

At the Omega Institute, I participated in a Gabrielle Roth Five Rhythms dance workshop. After three days of dancing for hours a day, I was exhausted. But in the dorm, someone was snoring at a volume that totally ruled out my falling asleep. It was in the next room, but this person may as well have been sleeping next to me, snuffling and snorting directly into my ear.

To the credit of the Institute, they had warned that the dorms could present just such a difficulty and had advised attendees to bring noise-reducing gear. I had a noise-reducing machine and noise-blocking headphones, and I set myself up to try to get some rest. But the level of the snoring in the next room was so ear-splitting that, even with all this paraphernalia turned all the way up to 'thunderstorm' setting, I wondered if I might somehow actually be inside this person's nose.

So there I was in this world-renowned center for personal growth, ready to commit murder or suicide out of frustration. I could have done the Zen thing: breathing, feeling, letting my emotions roll in and out, letting go to the moment – and still would have wanted to slit my wrists.

As I fully experienced the next Now, I saw that I was doing a worry-doubt-fear voice-over, fully immersed in my WMD software. RESET!

I made a choice to flip the switch to splendor and greatness. I saw that life is what happens between the meditations – what we bring to each new Now. It's always what we bring to the moment. For me, the cosmic door to joy and peace opens when I remember to get back online and turn toward an active state of participation and collaboration with the unfolding Now. In this new moment, lying in my sleeping bag next door to the King of Snorers, as producer, director and editor of the next frames, I chose to intercede with a kNOWing of greatness.

I began by breathing greatness as deeply as possible, while also experiencing the reality as deeply as possible. Those realities included my inner state of fear of not sleeping; doubting and worrying whether I can function in the workshop the next day sleepless; and my anger toward the snorer. From there, I brought an additional condition to the editing room – imbuing each and every frame with a mindset of greatness. This meant using the energy of each bit of doubt, worry, fear and anger to further propel the trajectory of that instilling process, going deeply, steeply into greatness through the magic of that powerful energy.

And next thing I knew, it was morning. Somehow, miraculously, I had fallen asleep despite the rattling walls. Better yet, the journey that night into greatness was still with me when the sun came up. I awakened pre-set to a day of great greatness. And thus it was.

Sometimes it feels that the toughest moments have the greatest potential yields. I have been around for a few births, and I know I'd be on thin ice if I said this must be what it feels like – so I won't say that. I'll say that some of these most painful moments are there to tell us that a new download is ready to be delivered and needs a cosmic push of sorts. I'm sure many women have used the extra energy of fear, worry, doubt and anger to provide just that extra push that finally birthed a great gift into their lives. ❄

Chapter 67

Making Choices

Freedom is not the absence of commitment, but the commitment to whatever is right for you.
– **Paulo Coelho**, *The Zahir: A Novel of Obsession*
(Harper Collins, New York, NY: 2005)

Some people seem to be able to make choices effortlessly, seeing clearly what they want in a situation and making the decisions that will get them there. Others have a bit more trouble with this, and at the far extreme, some people seem to get so stuck on even the smallest decisions (chocolate or vanilla? red shirt or blue shirt?) that they enter almost into a state of paralysis when faced with a larger choice. By not making a decision or dragging out the process they default to juicy, negative inner dialogue. This is a kind of relationship, and it can bring a manner of self-nurturance to the situation – but not the manner that will best serve you in greatness work.

Many of us humans seem to have an inordinate, even overwhelming, number of choices to make on any given day. Old-school approaches to decision-making usually involve some amount of meditating on a problem, looking at it therapeutically, and weighing pros and cons. New-age approaches involve getting in touch with your dreams and visions, getting in touch with the pain that comes from not living those dreams and visions, and trying to mine any problems that seem to be stopping you from getting where you wish to go.

If you're thinking "Hmmm, that sounds like giving energy to negativity," you're thinking like I'm thinking.

For example, let's say you're struggling to decide whether to leave an unsatisfying, stressful job in favor of a different kind of work that is more satisfying and beneficial to the world but doesn't pay as well. You have a family to support and bills to pay. You have been agonizing over this, torturing yourself with WMDs: How will you make ends meet? Will you have to give up your health insurance, your college savings funds for the kids and so on?

In this greatness paradigm, what's needed is, first, a reset on the dilemma. Not a denial of its existence, but a pause that allows a moment of alertness in the Now. Then, call up a more amped-up version of greatness than you presently possess. The stronger the energy of the dilemma, the more energy will be needed to propel the push past the old horizon of greatness. Then, see where that leaves you in the next Now.

The longing for something different hasn't gone away. Neither has the fact that you have a family to feed and rent or a mortgage to pay. But do you really need to agonize and linger over these points of fact? Instead of lingering in the WMDs, climb into your new quotient of greatness and linger there.

Looking at 'pros and cons' from a greatness perspective is a difficult challenge. When you realize you can frame the picture of your Now however you like, those pro and con lists become less clear and drop off in importance relative to the growing truth of greatness that gives the heart a welcoming voice of clarity and strength. In every path, every option, there is abundant greatness. Recognizing this removes the fear of making 'the wrong choice.'

If you're struggling with the dilemma of whether to stay in your job or leave it, wait and linger in greatness until you know what to do – until no other path seems feasible. At some point, at some new and higher trajectory of greatness, greatness will always win out and illuminate the right path with absolute clarity, like an airport runway welcoming and beckoning beneath the night sky.

No matter how painful the state of indecision, we can be in 'greatitude' about the conflict as it's happening: it is the beauty of the conflict itself that maintains the current momentum toward greater greatness. If we had already reached the level of greatness the situation demands, there would be no conflict at all.

Keep in mind that you already make dozens of decisions every single day, with ease and without conflict. Trust me – even if these decisions seem simple, this is only because you have already achieved remarkable levels and landmarks of greatness. From this point of view, appreciate all the greatness you already have. And congratulations on all the greatness of wisdom, integrity, clarity and power you already possess! ❄

Chapter 68

Every Complaint is a Manifestation of the Ideal

If there is sin against life, it consists…in hoping for another life and in eluding the implacable grandeur of this life.
– **Albert Camus,** Nobel laureate novelist and essayist

We can complain because rose bushes have thorns…
or rejoice because thorn bushes have roses.
– **Abraham Lincoln**

Oh, how we love to complain! There's something so delicious, so satisfying about it. It can give us a warm, fuzzy, righteous feeling. So many people love to rant about problems, bemoan injustices, gripe about how something is being done all wrong – either by someone else or by themselves. Some people pour so much energy into complaining that they don't have much left over. We're so deft at seeing what's missing, what's wrong, and we talk about it…and talk about it…and talk about it.

Some of us can really wax poetic in the realm of complaining. A complaint could be viewed as the flip side of a prayer, but energetically, it's so often the very same thing. It energizes lack. It pours energy into what's missing or out of place.

The word 'sin' comes from a Greek word that means 'missing the mark.' To sin is to miss the mark. And when we complain, we may be missing the mark in a way that costs us more than meets the eye. We may not be doing outward harm to others, as when we fail to follow the basic commandments of *do not kill* and *do not steal* and *do not covet thy neighbor's wife*. But, as Camus so elegantly says in the first epigraph of this chapter, we are sinning against life. We're finding a discrepancy between the ideal and the current reality, and we are moving in there with all of our furniture and kitchen appliances and knickknacks. What good does this do?

I find the cost of complaining to be this: Not only are we 'paying' with our energy for the privilege of the flow of complaints, which is wearying and takes its toll, but we are further tainting our current relationship with self and others with negativity's toxicity. At the same time, we remain at cross purposes, radiating out to the universe an 'upside down' energetic message that we love complaining.

In plowing and fertilizing the field of problems, we reap a harvest. It consists of a deeper belief that problems bring us the juiciest relationship. As a result, we manifest this, both in our internal dialogue and in attracting and deepening further juiciness of that kind with others.

Perhaps worse, the universe – being kind and loving – will respond energetically to our problem-loving ways by giving us more to love (translation: more to complain about).

The good news is that we can turn this around at any time. Saying no to complaining in your conversations with others and yourself may not be the easiest thing you ever undertake, but it may ultimately save you from the undertaker. It is deadly to not start somewhere.

Starting somewhere is the key, and once you get on a roll, you won't really want to have complaining anywhere in your life. As you move that same energy into internal and external dialogues pertaining to greatness, the universe will multiply your efforts by giving you greatness and things to be grateful about at every turn. So it's only the initial move that's rough. It will ultimately get easier and easier. Eventually, you'll spot even subtle complaining a mile away. Walking away will be a piece of cake as time goes by. I promise you that you won't miss it. It will produce great-itude – an attitude of greatness.

We can begin to turn this around by seeing every complaint as the expression of an ideal. Pain is knowing, on some level, that we can benefit others and feeling that we are not doing that in our lives at the level we aspire to. Suffering is believing the energy of that pain can be released through complaining.

Practice re-directing that painful energy by turning the complaint upside down energetically. When you highlight the ideal that is that particular cloud's silver lining, you energize that ideal.

When you find yourself complaining or about to complain, take these two steps:

1. Internally say "reset" if it is an internal dialogue of complaint; or, if you catch yourself launching a complaint to another, you can stop and say "I am resetting myself. I'm not going to go there and give this any energy." You can even stop a friend, acquaintance or even a stranger by saying "I need to reset you here. I don't want to give energy to this issue." Several close friends of mine, and even my brilliant daughter, do this for me as needed – just as I am about to launch into some negative dialogue or monologue. Saved by their gentle reset, I can stop, thank them and redirect my attention and energy. Miracles happen!

2. If you're ready to forge brazenly into greatness territory, give some thought to what ideal you are seeing buried within the complaint and how you can find examples of that ideal in your current Now. Give your heart a voice and the answer will be there.

Let's say you feel like complaining about the bad attitude of a child (you can substitute anyone). What ideal are you seeking for her to live up to? Possibly, you feel that she ought to be respectful of others (or it might be any other trait of value). Rather than energizing the lack of that value, find ways in which she is already being respectful. To what degree is she respectful to her friends? To her teachers? To whatever degree she shows herself or others respect by following rules, doing the many things to get through a day on this planet, doing her class work and getting good grades, there then is that much opportunity to appreciate her respectfulness. Energize the ideal of what you wanted in the first place.

Now, take it further. Let's run with the example of the child who seems disrespectful. Even if she has crossed the line and earned a time-out/reset, this does not preclude teaching further lessons pertaining to her existing greatness of respect when the disrespect isn't happening. It also does not preclude seeing the situation from her point of view. Is her behavior demonstrating her respectfulness for her own need for individuation and separation from her parents? In so doing, she might be saying and doing things that are hurtful to you, but this may be necessary for her right now. She's drawing that line in the only way she can. Reflecting back your understanding can bring you closer at a time when things can easily fly apart.

You might say to her (or imagine saying to her): "Wow, you're growing up! You have your own ideas about how things should be. You're trying to stay respectful toward those ideas and that shows integrity and courage, even though you knew it would be hard for me to hear. Those are real qualities of your greatness."

If you ever feel like complaining about someone else's ill treatment of you, and you are having trouble getting past your own hurt feelings to see what kind of ideal you wish to see manifested, hold this thought: that even when others are unkind to you, they are, in some flawed way, trying to hold the mirror up to your greatness. They want *you* to be living their ideal. If they could express it better, they would, even if it doesn't seem that way now. ❄

Chapter 69

I Can Do Now; Or: Oh Maybelline, Why Can't You Be True?

Since I became single a number of years back, a few wonderful women have come into my life, and my relationships with them have helped me expand the greatness practice in unexpected ways. In particular, I've seen how intimate relationships can either push me out of greatness work and deep into WMDs; or can move me even further along that greatness trajectory *as long as I stay with that intention*. Intention is the key!

My relationship with one woman a few years back – let's call her Maybelline – was a real roller-coaster. It also was the fertile ground from which I harvested the idea of resetting myself when I caught myself giving energy to WMDs.

Did you ever have a beautiful sweater in your closet that you found yourself attracted to over and over – and then, every time you put it on, you remembered how itchy and uncomfortable it was? This was how my relationship with Maybelline felt. Try as I might, I could not get her out of my system. Unfortunately, it felt like the only way I could stay connected to her at that point in my life was to go with the flow – to do what I could to follow along and hang on for dear life. We had the kind of relationship where I ended up trying harder and harder to explain myself and where even silence gave energy to problems.

I would have never guessed that would describe me in relationship, but here I was immersed, in love, and in over my head. After the summer of romance, she accepted the dream job she had been searching for, which took her thousands of miles away.

I eventually went to see her in the remote area she now called home. During this visit, I felt transported back to my childhood: I couldn't seem to say anything approaching the truth because it would then be turned against me. As soon as I tried to talk straight to Maybelline, I felt she would misinterpret me and accuse me of being an awful person with awful qualities. It felt like a dead end, but I hung on; I'd like to think that this was because I saw in her the same kind of sideways intensity I often see in brilliant, intense children. She was powerful and just had trouble consistently directing that power in healthy ways. (The fact that she was quite stunning might have played a small role here, as well.)

Most of the time she was very loving and very positive, but there were times when even saying something as innocuous as "I have a headache" was enough to provoke an angry barrage from her. In those moods, she seemed unable to hear me for what I intended. If I was quiet, which I became more and more because anything I said seemed to amplify the weirdness and frustration of the situation, she accused me of being angry. Any explanation would create an avalanche of new issues. And at the same time, she expressed wanting me to stay, wanting me to be there with her.

As the visit went on, I came to feel hurt, raw and betrayed, cast constantly as the bad guy. But I also saw that responding to these feelings in myself would put me in the position of focusing on problems and on seeing Maybelline as the problem. Since we were in such a remote spot (unbelievably remote), I didn't have the choice to up and leave. There was nowhere else for me to stay, and planes left the island once a day on most days, but not all days.

An amazing opportunity began to beckon me like a neon sign: I realized there was a place in my life where I had a major software glitch; where in the past, I had come to believe that I was crazy, wrong and guilty and that everything was my fault. This relationship was bringing me back into that space. I saw that this was a perfect opportunity to strengthen my core being and belief in myself. I didn't have to go off and worry my wounds; I could use this opportunity to heal – to build my inner wealth and strength to where I could stop groveling or relinquishing myself, and I would be able to simply walk away with dignity and confidence, knowing I no longer needed to be connected to anyone in this way. This would not entail my convincing Maybelline that she was wrong, or that I was, in fact, a good guy. I could do this work on my own without her involvement. This could be the gift of this excursion.

As a child, I didn't stand a chance of not being swept up into the insanity. The price had been decades of not believing in myself. I saw that this was a great chance to change this. And since I wasn't entirely sure how to go about doing this, I began with a Heart Rhythm Meditation.

I felt like I needed something very concrete to hang my hat on, so I practiced a 'squared-off' version of the breath: breathing in to four heartbeats; holding my breath in for four heartbeats; breathing deeply out for four heartbeats; and holding the out breath for four heartbeats. As I found my comfort zone with this, I increased the counts to eight heartbeats.

Once this was set in motion, I began to put a prayer of appreciation on each aspect of the breath (in breath, holding, and out breath). A very simple and powerful prayer for me is holding the attunement of "I Am." This 'mantra' has held a special meaning for me for a few years (refer to Chapter 29 to find out why).

The day I decided to try to leave the island, no flight went out because of bad weather. I went back to stay one more night, resolved to hold on to my new little handhold/foothold of freedom. Honoring myself, I reminded myself that she, like my mother, was simply stuck. She couldn't help it. I could forgive and honor them both while remaining in love and in greatness rather than in unloving insanity.

But it was hard to stay in that place of greatness! My wounds were strong and fresh and my attention kept going back to them. My energy became muddied and my guard lowered. Then it occurred to me that I was giving energy to my problems and what I needed was to reset myself; and then, to consciously bring myself to new thoughts of greatness. Remembering to reset can seem so obvious after the fact, but so much can transpire until that moment of consciousness.

I realized I could make that choice in each moment, no matter who I was with. Doubts came and went; I fell off the horse of awareness and got back on; eventually I went forward and deepened my sense of inner wealth.

When it came time for me to leave, Maybelline told me she wished I could stay. I didn't change my plans but stayed in a loving place of wishing her the best and knowing nothing further was needed; no further insights could come from my staying another day.

All of this stuck with me for some time after our breakup. I saw anew how a fighting relationship can be so irresistibly *juicy* and that this isn't where the juice has to be as long as I live a life dedicated to the greatness of myself and others. Since then, I've seen how this intention causes fewer and fewer of these kinds of relationships to come my way.

These sorts of toxic relationships do come up, however; they do for almost everyone. So what does one do when this happens? Retuning to greatness involves having a tried-and-true way to interrupt the cascade into negative energy. Use resets as often as needed, and use the energy of the situation to fuel further journeys into greatness. Avoid trying to fix the other person so that he or she falls more in line with what you believe to be right. This is not about them. It's about healing the energetic side of the issue that you carry, the one that you now can tremendously impact.

Fast-forward to a couple of years later. While traveling and giving workshops, I met a new lady friend we'll call Rebecca. Not long after we met and talked a few times, we both felt a spark, and I said "So, what are we gonna do about this?" Being able to say this instead of something far less direct (like "So, uh, what are you doing later?") felt like a victory. I was telling the truth of the moment, and she appreciated it, and we were both able to stay in the joy of acknowledging our mutual attraction.

After a few dates, Rebecca asked me "Is this a lark or a relationship?" This is a sticky question, no doubt about it. On the one hand, I risked losing the enjoyment of her company and our togetherness if I told her it wasn't a relationship. On the other hand, I liked and respected her and didn't want to tell her any untruth just to prolong my enjoyment. And I didn't want to try to convince myself of any untruth for that purpose. This could have truly been a 'Maybelline Moment' where anything said or unsaid would have created hurt and havoc.

I asked for some time to hang out with this question. The subtext: "I'm going to go online and Google greatness. I'm going to hang out there and see whether there's anything there for me to build on." Doing this, I find, makes me patient rather than reactive. Going into that nice place in a moment of dynamic tension usually ends up transporting me into a place of further greatness without any effort.

Some people get really brutal with one another or with themselves in situations like this, letting the WMDs drive them into all manner of soothsaying. *Why doesn't he/she want to call this a relationship? Am I too old, too fat, not tall enough, not pretty/handsome enough, not a good kisser?* This kind of conversation with one another and with ourselves takes us out of the heart space immediately and completely, tossing us headlong into WMDs.

I don't want to be in relationship with another person's WMDs, nor do I want to be in relationship with my own. But I am willing to work to reset back to the precious Now and to hold that space personally and collaboratively. This is a space where anything can be accomplished.

Soon, there in the room with Rebecca, I felt an elevation in my radiance and resonance. Life itself seemed to be responding to this higher frequency. I realized that I didn't know the whole truth of the future, and it was hurting me to even begin to try to inhabit that future. So I told her my truth in that moment: that I didn't know what the future held, but that I could "do Now…and I can remain fully in the present with you and appreciate your greatness."

This seemed to allow for us both to stay in the moment – and to be very loving in the moment. Neither of us felt we were building a future in our connection. Not that we were ruling it out, but we weren't removing ourselves from the Now with plans, promises or judgments.

Holding what seemed to be this higher truth, we both walked away feeling clean and complete, finished with our connection and each loving where the other was. In years of greatness work I had not yet had this experience, and it was stunning and remarkable. I will always appreciate Rebecca's willingness to go there with me.

Please don't think I am in favor of intimate connection without commitment. That's not the point I am trying to make. What I am in favor of is embarking upon any new relationship with total honesty and sensitivity to one's own feelings and expectations and doing so holding the space of greatness – giving splendor form and function.

Imagine entering into a relationship while in this heartful, present space I've described. How much drama, turmoil and difficulty could we avoid by doing this? By being willing to lovingly say "no thanks" to plans for the future, without denigrating the present? How about just being with another person while saying no to the WMDs that will, predictably, roll in, and just staying in the space of the Now and greatness? If we can do that, we can also judge when we want to continue to have next Nows that include this person. In my opinion, these are the beginnings of conscious relationship.

A conscious relationship has to include *differentiation,* which is the ability to stay true to yourself when in close relationship with the actions and thoughts and feelings of others. The greatness work is, I have found, a wonderful way to move toward differentiation. I struggled to create this with Maybelline; and I successfully found it, if briefly, with Rebecca. When you are able to differentiate, you can rest securely inside yourself without being swept away by other people's emotions, opinions or moods. At the same time, you can have an openness that WMDs prohibit.

Greatness transforms relationships to a truly loving place. In the great mystery of it all, we are given endless opportunities to move from stuck places of the past to unencumbered and exciting versions of being great in the present moment. Conscious relationships are an amazing way to move through huge issues that would otherwise be difficult to access. Many early relationships, for many people, include quagmires and crossed wires that promote negativity. This isn't a bad thing – on the contrary, it is the perfect gift of the universe to have these grand and perfect opportunities to heal old wounds and unfulfilled dreams in the company of another. We deserve to have relationships that are filled with the greatness of being valued and meaningful. Such relationships are exciting and gratifying. ❄

Chapter 70

Playing with Depression

This is my depressed stance. When you're depressed, it makes a lot of difference how you stand. The worst thing you can do is straighten up and hold your head high because then you'll start to feel better. If you're going to get any joy out of being depressed, you've got to stand like this.
– **Charlie Brown**, from Peanuts

Depression is widely regarded as a disease with biochemical origins. We hear phrases like "imbalance of brain chemicals," "serotonin deficiency" and "physical changes in the brain" when we try to learn about the causes of depression. Research has uncovered all of these elements in studies of the brains of people who are depressed. Tweaking brain chemistry with drugs that alter neurotransmitter balance can help relieve that heavy dark cloud of depression in some people. Seems like an open-and-shut case, right?

This is an example of *ex juvantibus* reasoning in medicine: where we reason *backwards,* making assumptions about cause of an illness because of the effect of a treatment. *Ex juvantibus* is Latin for "from which that helps," and it's actually an increasingly accepted method for figuring out what causes a disease: Keep trying different drugs until something works, and then you can use the mechanism of that drug to gain information about the mechanism of the illness.

I think modern medicine needs to use whatever tools it can find to work toward disease treatments and cures that make life better and more comfortable for everyone. When an illness is life-threatening or serious enough to make one's life basically unlivable, it's time to pull out the big guns, and sometimes those guns include medicines like antidepressants. On the other hand, antidepressants don't work for everyone. (According to studies published in 2008, they don't work *at all* for about 30 percent of people with depression.)

At this writing, science would have us believe it's most likely that depression's symptoms are, indeed, a result of altered brain chemistry and function. But I believe that those measurable changes in brain chemistry and function are just as likely to be caused by our thoughts or life circumstances as they are to be some effect of a biological disease state. Research into cognitive-behavioral therapy, exercise and yoga practices finds that we can, without a doubt, change brain chemistry without drugs. Research has demonstrated each of these interventions to have effectiveness on a par with antidepressants, at least for mild to moderate depression.

While the research isn't in yet on greatness practice, I have every confidence that it, too, can change the brain at a biochemical level. If greatness is really the truth of our 'hardware' – of our true divine inheritance, as I contend it is – then it is completely understandable that when one isn't living the greatness that one senses as a core truth, depression would be the result. The soul is calling, and up until now there's been no answer. Bringing greatness front and center into one's life and refusing to entertain anything less would be the most natural antidote for depression.

Let's look at depression from an energetic angle. Depression is often seen as a total loss of energy, a black cloud that descends, a chill wind that sucks out our life force. But there is energy in depression. In its usual manifestation, it suppresses and suffocates. A lot is going on in a person who is in a depressive episode. Often, a seemingly endless tape of despair and self-criticism runs and runs in the person's mind. There seems to be no future and the past is a string of failures or of successes that can never be reproduced. Depressive energy is the energy of smashing into a brick wall, over and over again. American philosopher George Santayana defines depression as "rage spread thin." It may feel numb or slow or tired or even boring, but there's energy there. If you've ever been depressed, you know what I'm talking about.

Believe it or not, you can choose to redirect that depressive energy. You can translate those energetic messages of despair into a new internal dialogue of greatness.

The energy of depression comes from making a big deal about what's wrong. So go ahead, *make a big deal* – go for it, only do so now in a way that will foster healing. But say to yourself, as you teeter on the edge of a depressive episode, "Oh! I'm about to have another bout of worry/doubt/fear. I'm just going to play with it. Every time it floats in, I'm going to say 'no!' or 'reset.' Or simply 'I REFUSE.' Just for the hell of it, momentarily leave it behind. Then, for the nine seconds or however long it is before it floats back in, I'm going to say to myself, 'I am great, I am great greatness!' or 'I am using my great power and control to not entertain negative thoughts right this second.' Or 'I am going to acknowledge that in this moment, I am choosing to not think thoughts of misery and despair.'" And if or when that depression floats back toward you, say "no" or "reset" again. Get your 14 seconds of greatness thinking in before it returns again. Use those moments to find and acknowledge your qualities of greatness, using the techniques described throughout this book.

You are taking the power and intensity of that depressive energy and *tapping it.* You're shutting the valve of the pipe through which you tumble into depression with each reset and sending that cool, clear water toward greatness.

Of course, you should only do this if you *want* to feel better. I love what Charlie Brown has to say about this. There's greatness in depression, too. If you want to stand in it, go into it, dive in all the way, that's your choice. Mine the greatness there, too, and you'll stand a great chance of coming through the other side feeling like a warrior. ❄

Chapter 71

Roles Royce

Be the change you wish to see in the world.
– Mahatma Gandhi

No, that wasn't a typo: the name of the chapter is 'Roles Royce.' Bear with me.

A role is a set of actions or activities, assigned to or expected/ required of a person or group of people. In their day-to-day lives, most people play various roles on any given day: parent, employee, employer, spouse, athlete, lover, teacher. Some roles carry more importance than others, but hopefully, they all reflect our core values and beliefs. When roles in our lives conflict with one another, we see how we are out of integrity with our values and beliefs.

Overall, most people are protective of their roles and the core beliefs and values those roles require. Greatness practice helps us give our various roles more breadth, depth and excitement, making these roles dynamic rather than static. As inner wealth grows, you become a 'Roles Royce,' able to fluidly move between roles as easily as you inhale and exhale your breath.

With inner wealth, you get to keep reinventing as you go. In the community where I grew up, we would commonly ask each other "What's new?" or even simply "New?" Today's norm seems to be to simply say "Hi." I think if someone asked me "What's new?" these days, I'd always have to answer "Everything." And that's the absolute truth – nothing, no role, no feeling and no action, is ever the same now as it once was. Nothing would remain the same even if I spent all my time trying to keep it the same. The beauty of this is that everything feels fresh. Every encounter feels renewed.

The dynamic of being a proponent of greatness adds the excitement of change and interest to the very roles that can just as easily sink into a funk of tedium. In my 10-year captivation with greatness, I find I am consistently excited by and interested in seeing what next iterations of my many roles will emerge in the next Nows. It keeps me alive and curious.

I am often surprised and delighted at how those very same roles evolve and change as I keep returning to gratitude and greatness. Each new time around the block seems to sweeten the deal as I revisit old roles. In the rare instances where I am disappointed with an interaction or situation, I use that feeling as fuel – an impetus for stepping into a great next Now. It's as if the greatness software comes with its own built-in inspiration to keep growing greatness further and further.

Another added bonus that gets better with each new download: Greatness practice helps us feel less judgmental of values and beliefs that are at odds with those we hold in our various roles. Instead of jumping into an argument over right or wrong, we develop the ability to marvel: "Wow, that's interesting. I get that this person really sees the world this way and carries his own consciousness through that interpretation." Period, end of story.

Just because you now see the greatness of others does in no way mean you have to give in to the demands or whims of others – to play the roles *they* want you to play in the way they want them to be played. Actually, the opposite is true: In knowing the greatness of others and yourself, you know the importance of your dreams and as well as their direction. In seeing the greatness of others and having a knowing of their strength, you become better able to handle your separate life and independent choices.

This greatness work also frees you from the pain of self-judgment over not meeting your own expectations at fulfilling your many roles in life and from judging others for falling short of expectations you might hold for them in their roles. Although you may see greatness that you or others do not yet embody, you can hold onto the knowledge that all parties and visions involved will grow further into fuller versions of greatness in due time. Out of seeing and being greatness, you can have a fuller sense of compassion without judgment toward self and others as you fluidly move within the various, ever-expanding roles in your lives.

When you take to heart Gandhi's exhortation to "be the change," you are, in essence, feeling the freedom to try on new roles for size. They may feel at first like new outfits, requiring alterations, accessorizing or just getting used to. If you keep returning to those new, desired roles, even for just a few moments of the day, you'll find that they start to feel a little more comfortable. Then, the whole picture of yourself in this role may come together in a flash of knowing.

That flash of knowing tells you that you are *being* your destiny of greatness. You are, perhaps, *pushing* your particular realm and components of greatness beyond any prior manifestation, expression or statement of its kind on the planet. Everything comes into momentary alignment, and the bigger picture of greatness of self and others is simply evident: a great 'epiphigasm' involving both body and soul. Experience it just once, and you will want it to be your primary way of being, seeing and knowing. ❄

Greatness exercise. Keep rowing to that shore of greatness – the greatness that is YOU, the greatness that you already are. Inner wealth will come effortlessly as you keep experimenting with seeing, being and knowing your greatness.

Now that you've reached this juncture, exercise your creativity. Let your heart tell you in the next few moments how it wants to direct you toward your next step of greatness. Give your heart a voice, a trillion votes, and the freedom to experiment. You already have the vehicles of your breath, the heartbeat and your heart's attunement to this realm of greatness. See where the journey takes you. Use this time to renew your dedication to being a person of inspired greatness. Give yourself the gift of inspired gratitude for all you have considered, conspired to and accomplished on this journey.

Chapter 72

Tough Love

You might have seen Randy Pausch's appearance on the Oprah Winfrey show. Dr. Pausch, a dashing 40-something professor at Carnegie-Mellon, was diagnosed with terminal pancreatic cancer. Before leaving his job, he gave his students a moving lecture about life and living one's childhood dreams, which was videotaped so that his three young children could see it later on. A YouTube video of this lecture caught the eye of Oprah's producers, and he gave a version of the lecture again on the show. Some estimated that the lecture received six million online hits in the weeks after it appeared on Oprah's program.

Dr. Pausch died several months later. He was a truly great man, funny and brilliant and inspiring, and a great example for others searching out their own greatness. Only one small thing bothered me about his lecture: it reflected, in some places, a 'tough-love' attitude.

In the lecture, he told a story about Jim Graham, a football coach he had as a kid. One day, Coach Graham…

> …just rode me all practice. You're doing this wrong, you're doing this wrong, go back and do it again, you owe me, you're doing push-ups after practice. And when it was all over, one of the other assistant coaches came over and said, yeah, Coach Graham rode you pretty hard, didn't he? I said, yeah. He said, that's a good thing. He said, when you're screwing up and nobody's saying anything to you anymore, that means they gave up. And that's a lesson that stuck with me my whole life. Is that when you see yourself doing something badly and nobody's bothering to tell you anymore, that's a very bad place to be. Your critics are the ones telling you they still love you and care.

This reminds me of a therapist named Michael Davis, whom I met in Boulder, Colorado, many years ago, before I developed the Nurtured Heart Approach. Michael was married with four children, and he was a sweet, soft-spoken, intelligent guy. I visited his house a few times, and I recall clearly how in the course of everyday life, he made a point of sitting his kids down and telling them such wonderful things about themselves. It sometimes brought tears to my eyes. I had never seen anyone treat children so well – and he treated his wife with the same gentle, tender positivity. Michael and I went one day to watch wrestling practice at his son's high school, and from up in the bleachers we saw that the coach had a style of riding the kids hard. Being totally used to this kind of approach from athletic coaches, I thought nothing of it, but Michael went down to speak to the coach.

When he returned a few minutes later, I asked what he had talked about with the coach. He told me he had said "With all due respect, my children don't respond well to being talked to like that. They respond much better when spoken to positively." And this coach, to his great credit, changed his way of talking to these kids. Everybody won. And the coach sought Michael out after the match and thanked him profusely, letting him know it felt so much better and it was so much more effective.

I'm not saying that the tough-love paradigm doesn't work for some people. It dovetails with the Western cultural paradigm of being ridden hard out of love. It's about having to suffer to find your bliss.

But what is bliss if not resting in your own greatness? Being and seeing greatness is the bliss that I have come to love and that really feeds my soul. As you practice touching down in that place of bliss/greatness, it is activated like a GPS system located in your heart. It becomes the home page in your inner guidance system: the Greatness Perception Service. This version of the GPS lends sacredness and miracles to every day. In greatness, our hearts will always tell us where that bliss is.

I love Dr. Pausch's message about choosing life, choosing fun, touching a lot of people and enjoying the ride. But when it comes to riding others hard, well, it feels a bit sad. The attitude that a person needs to have his or her shortcomings pointed out is an attitude that focuses on the negative – on problems. Let's ride those problems hard! Let's stick with them until they've been squashed! How has criticism worked for you? I believe there is a much better way to propel someone to greatness.

What if you've done well? What if you've done beautifully? What if you are inhabiting your greatness, and no one points that out? Perhaps they haven't given up on you, but they are probably waiting for you to screw up before they say anything. If you acknowledge another for each increment of success, each shred of any desirable quality, you're doing the exact opposite of giving up on her. You're fueling her trajectory of greatness. Reflecting your own qualities of greatness to yourself is the opposite of giving up on yourself. You're finding those buried gems, polishing them, and shining more and more light into their facets. ❄

Chapter 73

Invitation to Greatness

The Ten Invitations
1. You are invited to love yourself, others and life without condition – trusting that, in an evolving Universe, everything is unfolding perfectly.

2. You are invited to do whatever makes your heart sing and your spirit dance. Only that.

3. You are invited to live fearlessly and passionately – to step into your divinity, while embracing your humanity.

4. You are invited to treat yourself and others with extraordinary respect and kindness – reaching out with love towards all beings, and seeing the Light within everyone.

5. You are invited to honour everyone else's beliefs, feelings, values and choices – knowing these add to the variety of life, and that everyone's path or guidance is unique.

6. You are invited to honour the earth, your body and all creation as sacred and divine – and to celebrate life in all its richness.

7. You are invited to choose your own mission or purpose, expressing your creative gifts, talents and vision in whatever way feels most joyful.

8. You are invited to listen to the inner voice of Love, which always sets you free – knowing that your goodness and worthiness are never in question.

9. You are invited to trust in a loving and abundant universe. Ask and it is given. Seek and ye shall find. Knock and the door shall be opened.

10. You are invited to follow your dreams and desires – trusting your feelings, and using your imagination, to create your own heaven on earth.

– **Gill Edwards**, from *Life Is A Gift* (Piatkus, 2007)

Greatness is a debt we have to our soul to unleash all that is already there for each and every one of us. As we polish all the facets of the gems that we are, we become increasingly attuned to greatness within ourselves and a more open vessel to seeing and holding the greatness of others.

Have you figured out yet whom this is going to hurt?

Choose to assume and attribute greatness. Choose to sense that a little bit of greatness is evidence that much more exists, like the tip of an iceberg barely revealing the massiveness of itself beneath the surface. Choose to believe that there are always greater levels of greatness and that *you are already embodying them.* As German theologian Meister Eckert said: "A seed of God grows into God – so let yourself go."

As I look back on previous iterations of my life – my wanderings, difficulties, addictions and roadblocks – I see that I needed some sort of "password" to access an aspect of my being that I knew was there for the taking. My frustrations over those years sprang not only from not having the password, but in *not even knowing that I needed one.* Now I see that this password is *greatness.*

The question isn't "Are you great?" and it's not "How great are you?" It's "How much greatness are you going to allow yourself to birth and experience in this lifetime?" and "How much greatness are you going to send out of yourself to others in this lifetime?" Trust that, as you find pieces of your greatness, it will open up with ease, like a flower that is perfectly ready to bloom. The rose doesn't discriminate whom it is fragrant for. Have you ever seen that bumper sticker that says "God bless everyone. No exceptions"? Today, let your greatness radiate out to all, *no exceptions.* ❄

Chapter 74

We Are the World

We share the world's resources. They are global. If one country's water supply disappears, who isn't affected? When a disaster strikes anywhere, we realize anew what a small world it is, after all. But we don't need tragedy to bring us together.

We share the same global energy system. We share the same global heartbeat. Think of the billions of people who are breathing the same air as you and I, in this very moment. Each of them has a beating heart, each in breath followed by an out breath. This is worth celebrating in each Now. Why wait for calamity in order to come together and recognize our shared heart?

The Internet is an embodiment of this enormous shared energy. Words, images, ideas and sound all travel in a flash throughout the World Wide Web, giving virtual shape to the connection we have always had. Energy changes forms but is neither created nor destroyed. We ourselves are embodiments of the same vast energy. As when we look at an iceberg, we see only a fraction of the vast portions that aren't readily available for view. Now, I hope, having come to this point in this particular book, you are beginning to glimpse that massive possibility below the surface of what most of us see when we do not hold the intention to see more.

To live in greatness is to keep sending out energetic messages to our inner world – by way of propelling energy to the far reaches of our inner Being, into every cell and fiber of every organ and tissue – or to our vast shared outer Being. As we learn to navigate these inner and outer worlds, we begin to see that doing one is the same as doing the other. As you come to fluidly move between your inner greatness and the greatness that surrounds you, just watch what happens in the months to come in your world. ❊

Chapter 75

Surrendering into Greatness

Greatness is my reality, and I am creating it and it is being created. It always has been and always will be.

It is being created, in fact, even as I sleep. In sleep, I breathe, and my heart goes on beating and all my organs, tissues and cells, my immune system and all other systems continue to serve their functions. We all have this greatness – that of a miraculous bio-ecology that supports our very lives.

When we sleep, we dream, and this is yet another miracle of greatness. When we are awake, we see, hear, smell and taste the world, and these too are qualities of greatness. The permutations are endless. If we lost even one of these capacities, we would soon realize just how great they are and how precious any aspect of greatness really is.

The beauty of greatness is that we get to design it as we go. Do you want to participate in the designing of your greatness of compassion? Of wisdom? Of gratitude? Energize any of these qualities in yourself or in others and to whatever extent you do that, that greatness will become your energetic reality.

As Susan McLeod said so eloquently in her Preface, it's not about changing – it's about choosing: choosing to reside in the treasure trove of our greatness, not just our own, but that of every person, every living being rather than sitting outside its door, in the rain, shivering and wishing we could go inside but thinking that the door is locked to us until we find that magical key.

There is no key. The door is open. Stand tall, take a breath and go inside. ❄

Epilogue

Lyrics to "Reset to Your Greatness"
(Words by Howard Glasser; music by John Frick)

I'm now a proponent
Of taking time to feel all the moments
Knowing what you want to do with these moments
Choosing to see the greatness of your moments
Breathe into greatness
Radiate your heart with greatness
Breathe it into every cell
And breathe out to the world as well
Reset to your heart's intention
Rededicate to this connection
Reset then to your greatness
Reset then to our greatness
Reset to your greatness
Reset to our greatness

Resources

Nurtured Heart Approach Support Information

Three websites are available to those who seek further information about the Nurtured Heart Approach: www.EnergyParenting.com, www.DifficultChild.com and www.NurturingGreatness.net.

EnergyParenting.com is the online learning center for the Nurtured Heart Approach. It is a members-only website where parents, educators, coaches and therapists gain quick acquisition of the approach techniques and then continually hone their expertise through innovative learning modules, discussion forums, tele-seminars as well as feature articles, products and services supporting the approach. Readers can join EnergyParenting.com at a special reduced rate by sending an e-mail to susan@EnergyParenting.com with the subject line: I want the "Friends of Howard Glasser" offer.

DifficultChild.com and NurturingGreatness.net both have research findings related to this work, information about coaching and therapy services, information about ongoing workshops and Advanced Trainings, and information about creating training events for your organization.

Books on the Nurtured Heart Approach

Those listed below are available in most libraries and bookstores and from online sources. They can also be ordered at the Nurtured Heart Approach websites, www.difficultchild.com or www.nurturinggreatness.net, or via a toll free call to 800-311-3132.

- *Transforming the Difficult Child: The Nurtured Heart Approach* (Revised 2008) by Howard Glasser and Jennifer Easley.
- *All Children Flourishing – Igniting the Greatness of Our Children* (2008) by Howard Glasser with Melissa Lynn Block.
- *Transforming the Difficult Child Workbook – An Interactive Guide to the Nurtured Heart Approach* (2008) by Howard Glasser, Joann Bowdidge and Lisa Bravo.
- *The Inner Wealth Initiative – The Nurtured Heart Approach for Educators* (2007) by Howard Glasser and Tom Grove with Melissa Lynn Block.

- *Transforming the Difficult Child: True Stories of Triumph* (2008) by Howard Glasser and Jennifer Easley.
- *101 Reasons to Avoid Ritalin Like the Plague Including One Great Reason Why It's Almost ALWAYS Unnecessary* (2005) by Howard Glasser with Melissa Lynn Block.

Audio-Visual Resources

Transforming the Difficult Child: The Nurtured Heart Approach training tapes are available on CD (audio only, 2.5 hours); on audiotape (audio only, 2.5 hours); on VHS (audio-visual, 2.5 hours); and on DVD (audio-visual, with a six-hour version and a four-hour version). These can be ordered via the websites and toll-free number listed above.

Heart Rhythm Meditation Support Information

There is a website supporting Heart Rhythm Meditation, www.appliedmeditation.org, which also gives information on The Institute for Applied Meditation and its programs. Puran and Susanna Bair can also be reached at 888-310-7881 or 520-299-2170. Their books are:
- *Energize Your Heart: In 4 Dimensions* (2007) by Puran and Susanna Bair.
- *Living From the Heart: Heart Rhythm Meditation* (1998) by Puran Bair.